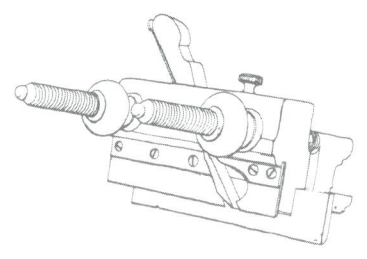

Instruments of Change

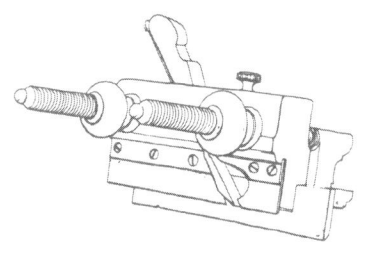

Instruments of Change

*New Hampshire hand tools
and their makers
1800 - 1900*

This catalogue of the exhibition held at the New Hampshire Historical Society December 20, 1984- May 30, 1985 was researched and written by James L. and Donna-Belle Garvin.

Published for the
NEW HAMPSHIRE HISTORICAL SOCIETY
by
PHOENIX PUBLISHING
Canaan, New Hampshire

The exhibition and this catalogue were funded in part by a grant from the National Endowment for the Humanities, a federal agency. Additional support was provided by the Early American Industries Association and the Elizabeth B. Carter Fund of the New Hampshire Charitable Fund.

Garvin, James L.
  New Hampshire hand tools and their makers, 1800-1900.

  Catalog of an exhibition held at the New Hampshire Historical Society, Dec. 20, 1984-May 30, 1985.
  Includes bibliographical references.
  1. Tools—New Hampshire—Exhibitions. 2. Tools—Collectors and collecting—New Hampshire. I. Garvin, Donna-Belle. II. New Hampshire Historical Society. III. Title.
  TJ1200.G33   1985   621.9'08'0974   85-21431
  ISBN 0-914659-16-2

Copyright 1985 by the New Hampshire Historical Society

All rights reserved. No part of this publication may be reproduced, stored in a retrieval system or transmitted in any form or by any means without the prior written permission of the publisher, except for brief quotations in a review.

Printed in the United States of America

Dedicated

to the memory of

Winthrop L. Carter

Acknowledgments

Inasmuch as the New Hampshire Historical Society owns only a modest collection of hand tools, this catalogue is a testimonial to the generosity of private lenders. Its content and emphasis also reflect the advice of friends who have guided the Society's halting efforts from the outset of the project. Chief among them are members of the advisory committee which was formed in 1980 to assist the staff in creating an exhibit and catalogue of New Hampshire hand tools:

William K. Ackroyd
The late Winthrop L. Carter
Fred W. Courser, Jr.
J. Lee Murray, Jr.
Charles S. Parsons
John Rexford
Kenneth D. Roberts

The list of those who have lent or donated objects for the exhibit is yet another testimonial to the generosity and camaraderie of tool collectors. The Society extends its deepest thanks to William K. Ackroyd, Wendall E. Badger, Russell A. Bigelow, Margaret Scott Carter, the Chemung County Historical Center, Janet Condon, Fred W. Courser, Jr., Richard Diehl, Neil English, Herman and Joseph M. Freedman, Gerald R. Hyde, Paul B. Kebabian, Wilfred E. Lahey, Malcolm G. MacGregor, Jr., Marshall E. Merrill, Norman F. Milne, Jr., Charles J. Mitchell, Paul W. Morgan, Robert P. Nugent, John F. Page, Doris H. Phillips, Emil S. Pollak, A. H. Reynolds, Kenneth D. Roberts, George F. and Charles H. Sawyer, William L. Warren, and several anonymous friends.

Many others provided help in countless ways: by giving advice, by sharing information or research, by offering tools or pictorial material for photography, by providing physical or clerical help, or by any number of kind acts without which this project would have faltered. They include J. P. Bittner, Prof. Homer O. Blair, David Boyle, Dr. Edward W. Colby, Fred W. Courser, Jr., Mildred M. Crandall, Richard Crane, Ann Davis, George A. Dodge III, Michael Dunbar, Roger Gibbs, the G. W. Griffin Company, Harriet Gross, Norman Harris, Eleanor Hart, Linda Hartman, Brenda Joziatis, Patricia Kienholz, Gerald E. Knight, Malcolm J. MacGregor, Jr., the Manchester Historic Association, Richard A. Martin, Robert Matthews, Allen Mayville, Sr., Donald Merchant, Nancy Merrill, Norman F. Milne, Jr., Frank R. Mooney, Mr. and Mrs. Harold B. Nelson, Leroy C. Noyes, Florence Ohlson, Eldon J. Owens, John F. Page, David S. Pinardi, David S. Proper, Dr. John P. Remensnyder, John Rexford, Dorothy Robinson, Gerhard R. Schade, Shaker Village, Inc., in Canterbury, Roger K. Smith, the Society for the Protection of New Hampshire Forests, Strawbery Banke, Inc., Leona B. Tyrrell, Colin Williams, Matt Willing, Roger S. Wood, and Howard Zea.

Two people deserve special thanks for their extraordinary labors in searching out obscure toolmakers or in locating additional information on craftsmen whose names were already known. Sandra Burt and David Ruell invested a tremendous amount of time, patience, and mental acuity in tracing much of the raw material that underlies the biographical list of toolmakers in this catalogue.

The staff of the New Hampshire Historical Society exercised great forbearance and contributed many hours of hard work, often on their own time, in assisting with the multitude of jobs required in completing the project. Douglas R. Copeley, Joan Desmarais, Wendy Burke, and Janet Condon deserve special thanks.

The catalogue owes much of its quality to two dedicated photographers who labored hard at difficult challenges: Bill Finney, who took most of the photographs reproduced here, and Ernest Gould.

Contents

Foreword ix

The Historical Perspective 1

The Tools 21

The Toolmakers 63

New Hampshire Toolmakers and Their Marks 65

List of Toolmakers by Town 96

List of Toolmakers by Product 104

Plates and Illustrations 112

A section of the exhibit installed at the New Hampshire Historical Society in Concord, New Hampshire.

Foreword

tion *Instruments of Change: New Hampshire Hand Tools and Their*
iire Historical Society between December 20, 1984, and
o the staff of the Society in 1980 by the late Winthrop L.
lea take form. This catalogue is dedicated to Win Carter, whose
hose wise counsel as a trustee, and whose generosities as a
cultural life of New Hampshire.
d in a northeastern state in the nineteenth century must confront
ed during the very decades when labor-saving machinery was
d tools. Nowhere is this more apparent than in New Hampshire
me and remains one of the most heavily industrialized states in
ilation. During the 1830s and 1840s, New Hampshire pioneered
working machinery and in the machine tool industry — in the

ew Hampshire reached their highest production during this
alization clearly stimulated both the trades that used hand tools
ater, in the twentieth century, would a new generation of
ility to supplant hand tools in most trades, rather than in merely

The complex relationships between mechanization and hand labor are beyond the scope of this study. Rather, this catalogue is intended to explore the eighteenth-century origins of hand tool manufacture in New Hampshire and to trace the nineteenth-century evolution of that manufacture, especially in relation to the state's dominant forest products industries. It is hoped that this study will reveal ways in which hand tool manufacturers responded to mechanization, both in their own business of making tools and in their need to find the increasingly specialized markets that would buy those tools.

Several tools in this catalogue give a hint of the inventiveness that suffused New England enterprise in the nineteenth century. Others show the beauty, fine craftsmanship, and choice materials that have long given hand tools a privileged status among collectors.

Finally, this catalogue offers the first available list of all known manufacturers of hand tools who worked in New Hampshire before 1900. This list which includes 1,000 names is certainly incomplete. Even so, the list demonstrates the astonishing scope of hand tool production in the state and, as a first offering, should assist researchers and collectors in those investigations which one day will render this present effort obsolete.

James L. Garvin
Curator
New Hampshire Historical Society

Concord, New Hampshire
May, 1985

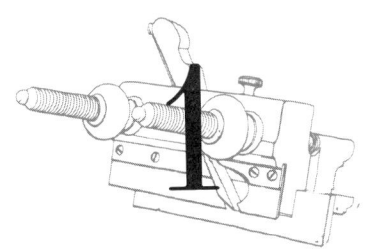

The Historical Perspective

Amoskeag Ax Company.   H. C. Reynolds. Agent.

This watercolor, which also appears on the cover, was painted circa 1875 by Henry Walker Herrick. By the period of this painting, Amoskeag Ax Company was producing 500 tools a day, using machinery patented by the company's agent, Henry C. Reynolds. Courtesy of Norman F. Milne, Jr.

THE MAN-MADE FABRIC of New Hampshire, as of any locale, was fashioned by tools, and many implements devised to transform that state's timberlands and granite ledges into useful form were themselves the product of local craftsmanship. Since the seventeenth century, New Hampshire has been nourished by a strong timber economy and has derived much of its economic vitality from the forests. For this reason, the majority of surviving New Hampshire-made hand tools were used in the felling, measuring, and working of timber and lumber.

In contrast to its popular image, however, the state has also long been heavily industrialized. New Hampshire's limited agricultural potential; its network of swift, small streams; and the native inventiveness of its people combined to encourage an economy that focused on the production of finished goods as well as food and raw materials. This industrialization worked to increase rather than diminish the production of hand tools. The growth of the state's industrial economy in the nineteenth century required the use of more hand tools than ever before, both within the factory and in the traditional crafts and trades. Much of this tool production, moreover, developed in response to the needs of local industries.

A naturally wooded environment that was settled by predominantly agricultural people, New Hampshire first called forth the use of the tools of the woodsman, the surveyor, the lumberman, the farmer, and the builder. Among the supplies listed at the settlements of Piscataqua in the summer of 1635 were "quantities of all sorts of smith's, cooper's, carpenter's and mason's tools," together with some of their products: pitch, tar, boards, and planks.[1] While the early settlers of New Hampshire drew much of their sustenance directly from the natural environment through fishing and trapping, their attention was also drawn immediately to the potential of a more complex extractive economy. Early settler Francis Small testified in 1685 that Captain John Mason, the proprietor of the Piscataqua grant, "sent into this Country Eight Danes to build Mills, to saw Timber, and tend them, and to make Potashes; and... the first Saw Mill and Corn Mill in New England was erected at Capt. Mason's Plantation at Newichewannock."[2] Although the presence of the "Eight Danes" has been hard for later researchers to document, the production of potash and pearlash from wood ashes long remained an important component of New Hampshire's forest economy.

More important were the water-powered sawmills erected by early settlers, by investors from Boston, and by the proprietors or inhabitants of nearly every well-watered inland New Hampshire township. The presence of such machines quickly established New Hampshire as one of the most heavily industrialized regions of colonial North America. From the seventeenth century onward, the production and use of hand tools developed in tandem with the increasing presence of powered machinery — machinery largely devoted to the exploitation of the forest wealth of the region. It

---

1. Nathaniel Adams, *Annals of Portsmouth* (Portsmouth, N.H.: by the author, 1825; reprinted Hampton, N.H.: Peter E. Randall, 1971), p. 393.
2. Ibid., p. 396.

is small wonder, then, that the majority of surviving New Hampshire hand tools, even as late as the nineteenth century, are those of the woodsman, the carpenter, and the joiner.

Recent research has documented the crucial role of the sawmill in New Hampshire's early history.[3] Owing to the strong opposition of guilds of hand sawyers, the water-powered sawmill was an unfamiliar device in England. In their determination to utilize such machines in New Hampshire, the early sponsors of settlement were forced to send "modells" (probably drawings) of sawmills to guide the housewrights and carpenters responsible for creating the little-known technology in the New World. In providing such "modells," English entrepreneurs may have turned to Scandinavian prototypes which were commonplace in the Baltic nations with which English shipbuilders and merchants had traded for years. In the spring of 1633/34, Captain John Mason sent three carpenters to the Piscataqua River with the task of building a sawmill and a stamping mill for grain. At about the same time, Sir Ferdinando Gorges erected a second sawmill nearby in present-day York, Maine. By the mid-1600s a vigorous milling industry developed from these halting beginnings. In 1655 the cartographer "I. S." produced an elaborate map of Piscataqua intended to show "how Englands strength doth lye / Unseen in *Rivers* of the new Plantations." This survey indicates no fewer than fifteen sawmills in operation upon the river system,[4] and by 1700 more than sixty sawmills had been built between Hampton, New Hampshire, and Casco, Maine.[5] Contemporary accounts place the number still higher; Jonathan Bridger, Surveyor-General of the King's Woods between 1705 and 1718, stated that his inquiries revealed at least seventy sawmills within a day's ride of Portsmouth in 1706.[6]

The output of New Hampshire's mills became prodigious during the eighteenth century. Only a portion of the early manufacture of forest products can be chronicled, since customs records list merely the surpluses which were exported from the colony, omitting the materials consumed in the ever expanding settlements at home. Moreover, because Massachusetts capitalists owned many of New Hampshire's mills and much of its land, quantities of forest products were shipped to Boston and were misleadingly represented as Massachusetts exports rather than as products of New Hampshire.[7]

Still, the recorded quantities of New Hampshire's exports, representing as they do only a portion of local production, indicate clearly that the economy of the province was solidly based upon its forests. In the year between the summers of 1718 and 1719, some 915,000 feet of pine boards; 55,000 feet of pine joists; 615,000 shingles; 11,000 clapboards; 314,000 pipe, hogshead, and barrel staves; and 6,000 hoops were exported.[8] In the five years between the autumns of 1770 and 1775, over 1,000 vessels left Piscataqua for the West Indies, southern Europe, and Africa. These ships carried nearly 74 million board feet of pine planks and boards, over 6 million staves and headings, 1.7 million hoops, almost 42 million shingles, and some 98,000 clapboards.[9] Well after the Revolution, in the two years from the fall of 1789 to the fall of 1791, New Hampshire exported over 18 million feet of pine boards, nearly 3 million staves and headings, over 86,000 hoops, 2.7 million shingles, and 21,000 clapboards.[10] Such production, documented over the better part of a century, graphically reveals the vigor with which New Hampshire people exploited their forests as they pushed back the frontiers of settlement.

These figures likewise suggest the industry with which the inhabitants of the region wielded their hand tools; the astonishing numbers of staves, headings, hoops, clapboards, and shingles sent forth from Piscataqua were fashioned by hand with the axe, the frow, and the drawknife rather than by the tireless sawmill. It is small wonder that Jeremy Belknap, the early historian of New Hampshire, noted in 1792 that the inhabitants of the state were "very dextrous in the

---

3. Richard M. Candee, "Merchant and Millwright: The Water Powered Sawmills of the Piscataqua," *Old-Time New England* 60 (April-June 1970):131-49, and "Wooden Buildings in Early Maine and New Hampshire: A Technological and Cultural History, 1600-1720" (Ph.D. diss., University of Pennsylvania, 1976), chap. 3.
4. Candee, "Merchant and Millwright," p. 142.
5. Candee, "Wooden Buildings in Early Maine and New Hampshire," p. 115; Candee, "Merchant and Millwright," pp. 146-49.
6. Joseph J. Malone, *Pine Trees and Politics: The Naval Stores and Forest Policy in Colonial New England, 1691-1775* (Seattle, Wash.: University of Washington Press, 1964), p. 57.
7. Ibid., p. 154; Candee, "Wooden Buildings in Early Maine and New Hampshire," pp. 150-54.
8. Malone, *Pine Trees and Politics*, p. 153; Samuel Justus McKinley, "The Economic History of Portsmouth, New Hampshire, From Its First Settlement to 1830" (thesis, Harvard University, 1931), p. 311.
9. "Port of Piscataqua, Colonial Customs Records, 1770-1775," copy, Portsmouth [N.H.] Athenaeum.
10. Jeremy Belknap, *Belknap's New Hampshire: An Account of the State in 1792* (facsimile edition, *The History of New Hampshire*, vol. 3), edited and with an introduction and notes by G. T. Lord (Hampton, N.H.: Peter E. Randall, 1973), p. 162.

use of edge tools, and in applying mechanical powers to the elevation and removal of heavy bodies."[11]

Given the nature of New Hampshire's economy from the first days of settlement, it is not surprising that surviving evidence of tools and their use in the province tends to arise from the trades of carpenter, joiner, and shipbuilder, especially in the seventeenth and early eighteenth centuries. While no tools from this early period have come to light, evidence of their use is ample in the documentary record. To some extent, this documentary record can be corroborated by surviving artifacts and buildings. From the few remaining New Hampshire buildings of the seventeenth century we can derive two major themes: the importance of (1) the eastern white pine as the major timber for framing and finish alike and (2) the water-powered sawmill as a means of preparing this timber for use.[12] Likewise, the few pieces of seventeenth-century joined furniture which can be linked to the Piscataqua region of New Hampshire combine oak, the favored wood for such furniture, with the more plebeian pine.[13]

Several joiners are known to have been at work at Piscataqua in the mid-1600s. One of these was Thomas Dennis, who was in Portsmouth between 1664 and 1668; Dennis would later marry and settle in Ipswich, Massachusetts, where his name is associated with an important group of joined chests and chairs.[14] Another was Edward Clarke, whose 1675 probate inventory includes chisels, gouges, hammers, a brace and bits, twenty planes, augers, and other tools; significantly, the inventory also lists "2 wainscot chairs unfinished" and "1 chest new."[15] Added to the seventeenth-century joiners of Piscataqua are some seventy-five carpenters known to have resided there before 1680.[16]

A study of the tools used by these and other early New Hampshire craftsmen is hampered both by the extremely low rate of survival of the buildings and furniture they fashioned and by scanty records. The situation changed markedly after 1700, however, when a number of craftsmen, some of them from England, arrived in New Hampshire bearing new ideas and the tools necessary to give form to these ideas.

We may see the first hints of new tools in the region in the years around 1700. For the first time, houses built at that period begin to display classical mouldings in the form of room cornices or applied bolection enframements around panels and fireplace openings. At the same time, the frames of houses, hitherto exposed to view and perhaps treated with decorative chamfers, begin to be clothed in casings; now, for the first time in local building, the work of the joiner begins to take precedence over the work of the carpenter. For the first time, too, the special tools of the joiner—bench planes for finishing boards and moulding tools for providing decorative contours—begin to play a predominant role.[17]

These initial hints of a revolution in local woodworking were quickly transformed to a full ascendancy of the new style in New Hampshire architecture and furniture. In the years around 1715, some fifteen joiners, carvers, or turners arrived in Boston from Great Britain.[18] Within a year or two, five new joiners appeared at Piscataqua, at least three of them drawn from the English newcomers who had recently appeared in Boston.[19]

These men, with their English training and tools, brought a fully classical style of joinery to New Hampshire. Chief among them was John Drew (c. 1675-c. 1738), who supervised the construction of the great brick Macpheadris-Warner House in Portsmouth in 1716, bringing to that job a knowledge of the prevailing styles in both Britain and Boston. Drew went on to train many apprentices in the new Georgian style, and his descendants trained many more; 100 years later many of the most ambitious buildings in southeastern New Hampshire owed their origins to a regional fraternity of builders who had sprung from this single immigrant.

Dwellings like the Macpheadris-Warner House established the Georgian style as the dominant mode of building in New Hampshire during the next eighty years. Such buildings reveal the full range of the new

11. Ibid., p. 196.
12. Abbott Lowell Cummings, *The Framed Houses of Massachusetts Bay 1625-1725* (Cambridge: Harvard University Press, 1979), pp. 47-50; Candee, "Merchant and Millwright," passim; Candee, "Wooden Buildings in Early Maine and New Hampshire," passim.
13. Jonathan L. Fairbanks and Robert F. Trent, *New England Begins: The Seventeenth Century*, 3 vols. (Boston: Museum of Fine Arts, 1982), 1:536-37.
14. Ibid., 3:514-19; Helen Park, "Thomas Dennis, Ipswich Joiner: A Re-examination," *Antiques* 78 (July 1960):40-44; Portsmouth, N.H., Town Records (microfilm, New Hampshire State Library), 1:126, 133, 141, 151, 259; 10:655.
15. New Hampshire Provincial Probate Records, 1:157-60.
16. Candee, "Wooden Buildings in Early Maine and New Hampshire," pp. 164-65.
17. James L. Garvin, "Academic Architecture and the Building Trades in the Piscataqua Region of New Hampshire and Maine, 1715-1815" (Ph.D. diss., Boston University, 1983), pp. 26-74.
18. *Boston Furniture of the Eighteenth Century*, Publications of the Colonial Society of Massachusetts 48 (1974): 270-302.
19. Garvin, "Academic Architecture," pp. 40, 72.

The Historical Perspective

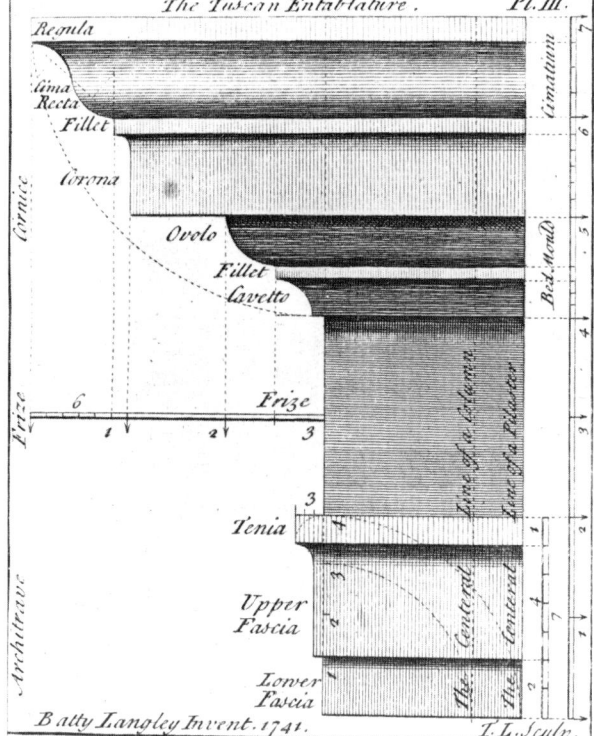

Plate III (1741), showing the mouldings and components of the Tuscan entablature from Batty and Thomas Langley's, *The Builder's Jewel: or, the Youth's Instructor and Workman's Remembrancer*, printed for R. Ware in London in 1754. The Langleys' books, popular among American workmen, illustrated details that derived from ancient Roman architecture.

New England joiners of the early 1700s took the concept of the moulding, little seen in house joinery of the 1600s, and embellished it to a degree hardly ever attempted in later years. The bolection is a boldly projecting moulding, usually combining a torus or half-round, a cavetto or cove, and several beads and fillets. The moulding stands in relief above the surface of the surrounding walls or woodwork, sometimes taking the place of a casing, sometimes providing a raised enframement for panels. John Drew, equipped with new tools and ideas, used the bolection moulding with good effect throughout the Macphreadris-Warner House. An unknown joiner of the same period surrounded the fireplace openings of the Lieutenant Governor John Wentworth House with bolection mouldings more than six inches in width. Drawing upon a common European understanding of the use of bolection-moulded panelling, Piscataqua joiners produced rooms of bold, three-dimensional articulation, relishing the play of light and shadow across the curves and planes of their walls.

During the first half of the eighteenth century, as the Georgian style became established and elaborated in coastal New Hampshire, craftsmen learned not only from the masters and journeymen with whom they worked but, to a limited extent, from books as well. English architectural books of the first half of the eighteenth century fell into two primary groups: those intended for wealthy estate builders or gentleman patrons of architecture and those intended for the craftsman. Few of the larger gentlemen's folios found their way to America before the Revolution, but a good number of the craftsmen's books have been recorded.[20] Among the most popular of these was Batty Langley's *The City and Country Builder's and Workman's Treasury of Designs*, first published in 1740. A 1756 edition of this work eventually found its way into the library of joiner Ebenezer Clifford of Kensington and Exeter. When carver William Lewis died in Portsmouth in 1764, his estate included one "Book Relating to the Carver Business"—possibly Abraham Swan's architectural folio *The British Architect* (1745) or perhaps a furniture carver's guide such as Thomas Chippendale's *The Gentleman and Cabinet-maker's Director* (1754) or Thomas Johnson's *One Hundred and Fifty New Designs* (1761). The grand mantelpiece of Governor Benning Wentworth's country estate at Little Harbor in Portsmouth was carved by local craftsmen and derives ultimately from a plate in William Kent's folio, *The Designs of Inigo Jones*

tools introduced by joiners in the early 1700s and used throughout the century. These tools produced new architectural features—including an array of mouldings so new to the English experience that they still bore the Greek or Latin names that originally described them. The stiles and rails of the newly fashionable panelling are embellished with quarter-round or ovolo mouldings; the panels have smooth-planed fields and feather-edged margins created by special planes; the casings or architraves of door and window openings are embellished with S-curved or ogee backband mouldings; the sliding window sashes, introduced into New Hampshire shortly after 1700, have ovolo-moulded muntins; the rooms are finished with a double-ogee crown moulding or with a full classical cornice; and, in the grander houses, the complex bolection moulding often appears around fireplace openings and even around doors.

The bolection moulding was the special hallmark of the early Georgian style. As if to proclaim the revolutionary change represented by the new style,

---

20. Helen Park, *A List of Architectural Books Available in America Before the Revolution* (Los Angeles: Hennessey & Ingalls, 1973).

Instruments of Change

(1727); its immediate source may have been Edward Hoppus's smaller and cheaper book of plates plagiarized from other volumes, *The Gentleman's and Builder's Repository* (c. 1737).

Such books were of importance, not only in guiding the hand of the carver who might be called upon to execute a Corinthian capital or an enriched moulding, but also in codifying more basic classical elements. All these books provided rules of proportion useful for designing doorways and mantelpieces. Still more fundamentally, such volumes illustrated the common classical mouldings with sufficient detail to guide a craftsman who needed to buy or make a moulding tool appropriate for a job, and they showed the proper method of combining mouldings into more complex architectural elements. These volumes thus served as touchstones to guide the craftsman in his selection of tools and to assure him that his use of those tools was in accord with internationally recognized canons of classical design.

In a period when New Hampshire's joinery was confined to tidewater areas, much elaborate craftsmanship was invested in ships. John Drew, who was a painter as well as a joiner, revealed that ship's work was often as elaborate as house joinery when he recalled that in 1722 he was hired by Captain Joseph Warren at Piscataqua to "Compleat the Cabbin with a Square State room, Sashes and Lockers [and] to make a hansom beaufait [cupboard] & raised Arched pannels" on Warren's ship. "I was painting of Capt. Warrens great Cabbin," Drew wrote, "and he asked me what Couler I designed to paint it with. I told him I should do all plain & of one Colour & he said that he would have the Mouldings done with vermillion, the sides or mergents with green & the Collums with blew."[21] One can well imagine the bold Baroque effect of such early craftsmanship.

Ship's work remained of great importance to coastal carpenters, joiners, carvers, painters, and smiths even as their inland counterparts were turning their attention to house construction and other needs of an agricultural economy in New Hampshire's newly settled interior. In coastal New Hampshire, where three or more generations of craftsmen had enjoyed a monopoly in their respective trades, a labor surplus was a real danger. Under such circumstances, coastal tradesmen maintained a jealous guard over their specialties. In 1765 a band of unidentified men entered the cabins of two ships being fitted out in Portsmouth "and cut and hack'd the Joyners Work in such a manner as entirely to ruin the same." The captains of these vessels had violated a local understanding by having their cabins finished by men from country towns, probably at a lower rate than was being charged in Portsmouth. A short time previously notices had appeared in Portsmouth "to Inform Those that have hitherto imploy'd Country Joyners, not to employ them any more, for... we Joyners belonging to Town are determined to make a bold Push."[22]

Until the mid-1770s, the New Hampshire joiner also made nearly all of the furniture fabricated within the province. Although a higher style of furniture became available in the vicinity of Portsmouth with the arrival of a few specialized cabinetmakers and upholsterers after the mid-century, the joiner remained the chief manufacturer of furniture in New Hampshire long after this period. This tradition had its beginnings in the seventeenth century and flourished in the eighteenth. In 1734, for example, John Drew filled the orders of a single mariner for two 3-foot maple tables, one 3½-foot maple table, a similar table of walnut, two "Curl'd maple Desks," and nineteen picture frames— the latter probably of the bolection-moulded profile fashionable at the time.[23] Like much of the furniture produced in coastal New Hampshire during the eighteenth and early nineteenth centuries, this consignment may have been intended for exportation to Newfoundland or the Caribbean.

In a New Hampshire which had yet to release a great proportion of its population into the hinterlands, exportation of the products of the craftsman remained an essential means of allowing coastal craftsmen to specialize in their proper trades and to dispose of the surplus of goods generated by that specialization. As was the case with sawn lumber, hoops and shooks for casks, clapboards, and shingles, New Hampshire craftsmen found distant markets ready to absorb any surplus generated at home. Boats and oars were among the products sought by Caribbean customers; between 1770 and 1775, some 346 moses boats (tenders for Caribbean merchant ships) were shipped from Piscataqua, mostly to the West Indies, together with 124,000 feet of oars.[24] New Hampshire's housewrights and carpenters also benefited from an opportunity to export their handwork, which

---

21. New Hampshire Provincial Superior Court Records, #6080.
22. *Boston Evening Post*, January 6, 1766.
23. New Hampshire Provincial Superior Court Records, #20717.
24. "Port of Piscataqua, Colonial Customs Records, 1770-1775."

evidently exceeded local demand even in an era when frontier expansion must have called forth tremendous building activity. In the five years immediately preceding the Revolution, 147 building frames left Piscataqua for the West Indies in twenty-eight separate shipments.[25] The demands of the Piscataqua export market reached a considerable distance from the coast. In an instance in 1772, one housewright from the inland town of Nottingham helped fill a contract for a building frame, plus doors and windows, to be shipped to the Caribbean island of Grenada.[26]

Equally impressive was the opportunity offered the furniture craftsman by distant markets. In the 1730s, for example, Portsmouth turner John Gains was making dozens of chairs for export in the ships of local merchants John Moffatt and William Pepperrell.[27] The Bristol-trained turner John Mills was sending out his own venture cargoes of chairs within ten years of his arrival in Portsmouth about 1725. By the eve of the Revolution, export of furniture from New Hampshire had reached impressive proportions. Between 1770 and 1775, some 2,800 chairs were shipped from Piscataqua. Joiners produced no fewer than 111 tables and 355 bureaus and desks for export.[28]

Such craft activity, initially confined to southeastern New Hampshire, covered much of the state by 1800. New Hampshire's population rose from an estimated 62,700 in 1770 to 183,858 in 1800.[29] This threefold increase in three decades required tremendous individual and collective enterprise, much of it embodied in the houses, public buildings, and furnishings which survive in New Hampshire from the decades before 1800.[30] Tools for the production of objects, as well as for clearing the land and tilling the soil, were essential in New Hampshire's expanding frontier economy throughout the 1700s. Surviving objects and the changed New Hampshire landscape bear mute testimony to the presence of vast numbers of hand tools during this period. Yet documentation of either tool importation or domestic manufacture is regrettably slight for the 1700s.

Most tools of complexity or technological sophistication had to be imported into New Hampshire during the 1700s. This was especially true of edge tools or other implements requiring the use of steel. New Hampshire's few eighteenth-century ironworks, beginning with the two "mills" built at Lamprey River in present-day Newmarket in 1719 and 1720, were simple bloomeries for the direct production of wrought iron from bog ore and never met local demand.[31] Much of the province's wrought iron, and virtually all its steel, had to be imported during the 1700s; many pieces of iron surviving from the eighteenth and early nineteenth centuries bear the trademarks of European manufacturers.[32] Such importation was advertised in 1763 by Noah Parker, a Portsmouth blacksmith and ironmonger, who informed his customers that he could supply "Bloomery Iron for Cart Wheels: Best Heart and Club German Steel, English dit[to]."[33] Other advertisements in the *New-Hampshire Gazette* in the 1760s and 1770s document the importation of cutlery, ironware of every sort, joiner's tools, bar and pig iron, and agricultural tools. One notice of 1763 advertises "A Compleat Chest of House Joyner's Tools, sufficient for the best of Workmen, as it consists of all Manner of the best Tools," just imported from London.[34]

Yet throughout the eighteenth century many craftsmen expected to fashion their own tools, or parts of their tools, even if some of their raw materials came from abroad. Edge tools could be forged, welded, and tempered by New Hampshire blacksmiths from the iron and steel being imported into the province. In 1768 Joseph Shillaber, a smith who moved from Salem, Massachusetts, to Portsmouth, advertised "Scythes, Axes, Hoes, and all sorts of edge Tools, at Wholesale or Retail, made in the best manner," presumably by Shillaber himself.[35]

Smiths were intimately allied with other craftsmen in the production of tools. Ebenezer Clifford, a young

---

25. Ibid.
26. *Journal of the Society of Architectural Historians* 23 (March 1964):43-44.
27. John Moffatt, Ledger 1 (1725-1740), New Hampshire Historical Society, pp. 46, 120; New Hampshire Provincial Superior Court Records, #12253; Misc. MSS., 17A-4, New Hampshire Historical Society.
28. "Port of Piscataqua, Colonial Customs Records, 1770-1775."
29. Belknap, *Belknap's New Hampshire*, pp. 175-76, 265; *Heads of Families, At the Second Census of the United States, taken in the Year 1800: New Hampshire* (Madison, Wis.: John Brooks Threlfall, 1973), p. 8.
30. Bryant F. Tolles, Jr., with Carolyn K. Tolles, *New Hampshire Architecture* (Concord, N.H.: New Hampshire Historical Society, 1979); Donna-Belle Garvin, James L. Garvin, and John F. Page, *Plain & Elegant, Rich & Common: Documented New Hampshire Furniture, 1750-1850* (Concord, N.H.: New Hampshire Historical Society, 1979).
31. Garvin, "Academic Architecture," pp. 12-13.
32. *Bulletin* of the Association for Preservation Technology 8:4 (1976):118-22.
33. *New-Hampshire Gazette*, July 1, 1763.
34. Ibid., September 23, 1763.
35. Ibid., July 15, 1768.

joiner and turner from Kensington, is recorded as having bought quantities of plane and plow irons; shaves; and carpenter's, joiner's, and turner's chisels from neighboring blacksmith Jeremiah Fellows, Jr., during the 1770s. In 1784, as he was preparing to do the joiner's work in the stairhall of Governor John Langdon's new house in Portsmouth, Clifford bought from Fellows two "Cornish irons" and a "Cornish bed mold Plain Iron," probably for shaping the large crown and bed mouldings used in Langdon's hallway. During the eighteen years that Fellows and Clifford remained neighbors, the blacksmith sold the joiner hammers, knives, pincers, augers, axes, hatchets, saws, screwdrivers, drills, bits, shears, frows, plane and plow irons, ferrules, and holdfasts, as well as a myriad of hardware items for architecture and cabinetwork. For local shoemakers and tanners, Fellows furnished flesh hooks, awls, shaves, and fleshing knives. For farmers, the blacksmith made or repaired shovels, hoes, scythes, and scythe "tackling," as well as making chains, sled runners, harrow teeth, plow plates, and iron tires for their equipment. Among Fellows's most frequent services for Clifford and others was the "stealing" of edge tools—welding fresh steel cutting edges to chisels, bits, axes, and plane irons that had been worn down by frequent sharpening.[36]

Whenever accounts survive, the same relationships between blacksmiths and other craftsmen are to be found. When the nineteen-year-old country-trained joiner Bradbury Johnson moved from Sanbornton to Exeter in 1785, he immediately began to purchase both regular and large plane irons from blacksmith Daniel Jones.[37] In Bedford the farmer and craftsman Matthew Patten (whose skills were too numerous to be described with the name of any single trade) often dealt with his local blacksmith, James Kennedy. Patten frequently bartered with neighbors for bars of wrought iron, Swedish steel, and German steel, which he later used to reduce the cost of newly made tools. In 1758, for example, Patten noted in his diary that "James Kennedy made me 3 small plain Irons the Steel was mine and the iron was his."[38] Being resourceful, Patten reduced his smith's bills still further. In 1756, when Kennedy performed several jobs for Patten, the diarist noted that the work was done "all of my Iron and all workt with my [char]Coal"; in 1785, when Patten hired another smith to forge an iron crank for a new grindstone, "I blowed for him and struck some."[39]

Though most trades were dependent upon blacksmiths for the metal parts of tools, woodworkers, at least, expected to make many components of their own tools. When William Houston of Bedford apprenticed himself to Major John Dunlap of Goffstown for two years in 1775, the master promised, not only to "Learn the Aforesaid William the Art or Mistry of a cabinett-maker and Joyner," but also to "help him to make the Wooden part of a set of tools fit for the trade" at the expiration of the term.[40] The process of making wooden parts for joiner's tools is clearly depicted in the diary of Dunlap's neighbor, Matthew Patten. In 1754 Patten made and sold a fore plane and a smoothing plane.[41] In 1767 Patten made several jointers, including " a Cooper joynter for Hugh Orr[;] he found the stick."[42] In 1769 Patten

workt at plane stocks along with and for joseph Kennedy until about the middle of the afternoon and we finished a plow and a Rabit and a large O:G: and he got a back O:G: with a beed from one of my own, which was New both Wood and Iron. . . .[43]

This description hints at the use of one of Patten's ogee planes as a "mother" plane for the production of an ogee for Kennedy, or at least indicates that the moulding profile of Patten's plane was copied on Kennedy's stock.

Patten's production of wooden parts for tools included handles as well. In 1764 he made a handle for a neighbor's hand saw.[44] In 1773 he "went and cut a Walnut tree. . . and split it in quarters"; two days later, "We hewed and Shaved 22 ax handles of the stick of Wallnut I cut."[45] This tendency to supply wooden handles or stocks for iron or steel parts was not unique to rural New Hampshire or even to North America. Charles F. Hummel notes that in the eighteenth and even the nineteenth centuries English tool catalogues illustrated only the iron and steel components of implements "without wooden handles or other parts. These elements would have been made and the parts

36. Account Book of Jeremiah Fellows, Jr., 1772-1826 (privately owned).
37. Rockingham County Superior Court Records, A-19851.
38. Matthew Patten, *The Diary of Matthew Patten of Bedford, New Hampshire* (Bedford: by the town, 1903), p. 48.
39. Ibid., pp. 24, 502.
40. Charles S. Parsons, *The Dunlaps & Their Furniture* (Manchester, N.H.: Currier Gallery of Art, 1970), p. 53.
41. Patten, *Diary*, pp. 5-6.
42. Ibid., p. 187.
43. Ibid., p. 233.
44. Ibid., p. 142.
45. Ibid., p. 299.

The Historical Perspective

Detail of stock certificate, c. 1805.

assembled by craftsmen outside the tool factory."[46]

Although it is clear that many tools were imported into New Hampshire and that many others were fashioned by local craftsmen for their own use as the need arose, it is also clear that a few craftsmen other than blacksmiths began during the eighteenth century to fabricate tools for sale to other craftsmen. Much of this work was probably done as a sideline rather than as a specialty, much as Patten hewed and shaved twenty-two axe handles when a choice piece of wood became available. Instances of one joiner selling tools to another can be found in Portsmouth as early as the 1720s. Between 1721 and 1723, for example, John Drew sold fellow joiner Samuel Waters a rabbet plane, two chisels, a plow and two plow irons, and three other planes; he also rented Waters the use of his panel-raising plane for seven weeks at six shillings a week.[47] Evidence appears in New Hampshire of similar small-scale transactions between joiners throughout the eighteenth century.

What appears to be the first specialized production of joiner's tools on a commercial scale in New Hampshire occurred, not in the long-settled seacoast region, but in the southwestern corner of the province. In the 1760s several members of the Briggs family came to Keene from Norton, Massachusetts, along with many other settlers from southern New England. Several eighteenth-century planes with the stamp "E:BRIGGS/IN·KEEN" have been located. The identity of the maker remains unclear, since Eliphalet Briggs (1713-1780) and his two sons, Captain Eliphalet, Jr. (1735-1776), and Elisha (c. 1738-1803), all bore the same first initial. The family were skilled woodworkers, Eliphalet III (1765-1827) and Eliphalet IV (1788-1853) being noted cabinetmakers.[48]

The use of the legend "IN·KEEN" to denote the origin of Briggs planes points to a localized tradition in southeastern Massachusetts; that tradition, in turn, explains the early appearance of commercially produced planes in southwestern New Hampshire. The earliest-known commercial planemaker in the English colonies was Francis Nicholson (1683-1753) of Wrentham, Massachusetts. Nicholson marked his planes with his name and the phrase, "LIVING*IN/WRENTHAM." Nicholson's son, John, adopted the same tradition, denoting his working locations as "IN/WRENTHAM" and "IN/CUMBERLAND [Rhode Island]." Francis Nicholson's freed black slave, Cesar Chelor, inherited and used his former master's "LIVING*IN/WRENTHAM" die. Others in towns surrounding Wrentham adopted the same tradition: S. Partridge and E. Taft "IN:MENDON"; I. Jones "LIVING IN/MEDWAY"; David Clark "IN/CUMBERLAND"; Joseph Fuller "IN/PROVIDENCE"; A. Hide "IN:NORWICH [Connecticut]"; and H. Wetherel "IN·NORTON," the birthplace of the Briggses of Keene. A number of other planemakers also worked in these and neighboring towns, including Simeon Presbrey, also from Norton. Thus, the area of southern Massachusetts, Rhode Island, and eastern Connecticut became a specialized region of early plane production in New England—a region where makers stamped their tools with their town's name as well as their own.[49]

This is the area from which the Briggs family and many of their neighbors migrated; Elisha Briggs was married in Wrentham, the center of planemaking in southern New England. Although the demand for bench planes and moulding tools would have been less in southwestern New Hampshire than in southern New England or coastal New Hampshire, it is not surprising that some of the craftsmen who moved to the Keene area carried on a tradition with which they had been familiar. Others in Keene apparently maintained the same tradition: one surviving tongue plane is marked "N.BRIGGS," very likely denoting Nathaniel Briggs (1744-1777), a cousin of the earlier Briggs settlers in Keene. Nathaniel Briggs arrived in Keene about 1773, and his estate included joiner's tools when he died at thirty-three from wounds received at the Battle of Bennington.[50] His brother, Rufus, remained in Massachusetts and married a Margaret Wetherel, probably a relative of Norton planemaker Henry Wetherel.[51]

If the Keene area was one of the first in New Hampshire where commercial planemaking was carried on, other parts of the state began to see such

---

46. Charles F. Hummel, "English Tools in America: The Evidence of the Dominys," *Winterthur Portfolio* 2 (1965):29.
47. New Hampshire Provincial Superior Court Records, #17354.
48. Garvin et al., *Plain & Elegant*, pp. 128-29, 142.
49. Emil Pollak and Martyl Pollak, *A Guide to American Wooden Planes and Their Makers* (Morristown, N.J.: The Astrigal Press, c. 1983), pp. 12-14, 66, 101-4, 122, 125-26, 129-30, 145, 164, 168, 178-79, 226-27, 235, 263-64, 278, 308.
50. Russell A. Bigelow, unpublished research notes; Edna Anne Hannibal and Claude W. Barlow, "Richard, William, and Hugh, Sons of John Briggs of Taunton, Massachusetts," *New England Historical and Genealogical Register* 125 (Oct. 1971):268; 126 (July 1972):211-13; 126 (Oct. 1972):277.
51. *Vital Records of Norton, Massachusetts, to the Year 1850* (Boston: New England Historic Genealogical Society, 1906), pp. 27, 332.

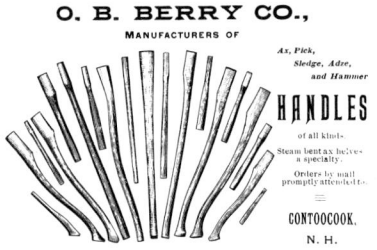

activity before the end of the century. The versatile Ebenezer Clifford (1746-1821) of Kensington, destined to become a builder/architect and inventor of local fame, was already a respected joiner and furniture-maker by the time he moved to Exeter in 1793. It appears that he was also a productive toolmaker. Several planes bearing his stamp have come to light. Clifford's accounts with Kensington blacksmith Jeremiah Fellows, Jr., between 1772 and 1794 show that the joiner made over 200 purchases of plane irons (many of them multiple purchases of an unspecified number of blades) during that period.[52] Since Clifford remained active beyond the age of sixty, he probably continued to make planes for his own use and for sale until well after 1800, especially since the new moulding profiles dictated by a change of fashion at the turn of the century would have increased the demand for such tools. When Clifford's last surviving daughter died in 1863, local reminiscence records that two wagonloads of planes and other tools were carted off for firewood.[53]

Not far from the towns of Kensington and Exeter, the village of Chester emerged as a planemaking center after 1814. In that year John Sleeper (1754-1834) came from Newburyport, Massachusetts, where he and his older brother had been woodworkers and planemakers. Although the local belief that Sleeper fashioned "the first joiner's moulding tools made in this country" is inaccurate, Sleeper's planes were distinctive and influential.[54]

In the Merrimack Valley of central New Hampshire, the town of Hopkinton emerged as a local center of plane manufacture. In 1816 and again in 1819, Joshua Morse, Jr. (1774-1826), a local joiner and cabinetmaker, advertised bench planes and moulding tools made with stocks of second-growth beech. One of Morse's innovations was his particular effort to solicit orders by mail. While few of his planes have come to light, Morse appears to have had a considerable influence. Joseph Milton (1789-1864) of Canaan, one of New Hampshire's more prolific mid-century planemakers, grew up near Hopkinton and may have been trained by Morse. Another Hopkinton resident, Deacon Isaac Long (1765-1840), was a joiner whose daughter married Morse's son; planes bearing the stamp "I LONG" exist, perhaps pointing to yet another Hopkinton maker.

Other planemakers followed the precedent of the Briggs family and made the Connecticut Valley of New Hampshire a region of long-lived plane manufacturing. Arad Simons (1754-1836), a native of Mansfield, Connecticut, came to Lebanon about 1785 and was another joiner who apparently made planes as a secondary trade.[55] Downing Amsden (working between 1807 and 1828), reared in both Henniker and Lebanon, may have learned the planemaker's trade from Simons. The wide range of Amsden's products and the variations in his die stamps suggest that he devoted more of his time to planemaking than did some of the earlier joiner/planemakers.[56]

Throughout the greater part of the eighteenth century, New Hampshire joiners and planemakers, like craftsmen elsewhere in North America, made or used moulding tools which produced a limited and prescribed range of contours. These mouldings were derived from Roman prototypes, as rediscovered and codified during the Renaissance by various Italian authors. During the early 1700s, such mouldings were being introduced into New Hampshire and the rest of colonial North America by immigrant craftsmen. At the same time, certain English authors were publishing a number of expensive and elaborate books to justify and confirm Renaissance principles of design and to encourage wealthy patrons to build according to these principles. In order to ensure that craftsmen would be capable of understanding and reproducing details required by these grand designs, other authors published a great number of builder's handbooks during the century. Many of these smaller, more practical volumes found their way to the American colonies; some found their way to New Hampshire. Joiners who derived their moulding profiles from such books, or from moulding tools based on such books, were assured of producing standard Roman profiles. These are the mouldings seen throughout New Hampshire and other colonies before the Revolution.

By the 1760s new refinements were being applied to Roman mouldings in England. In the architecture

52. Account Book of Jeremiah Fellows, Jr.
53. James L. Garvin, "Ebenezer Clifford, Architect and Inventor," *Old-Time New England* 65 (Winter-Spring 1965):22-37.
54. Pollak and Pollak, *Guide to American Wooden Planes*, pp. 261-62.
55. Mrs. Amos G. Draper, comp., "Pension Papers of New Hampshire Soldiers in the Revolutionary War," 64 vols. (typescript, New Hampshire Historical Society library), 1:77-82; Lebanon, N.H., Town Records (microfilm, New Hampshire State Library), 2:122.
56. Murray B. Brown, comp. "Some Descendants of Isaac Amsden of Cambridge, Massachusetts" (typescript, New Hampshire Historical Society library), pp. 25-26; Grafton County deed research by Herman Freedman; Pollak and Pollak, *Guide to American Wooden Planes*, p. 59.

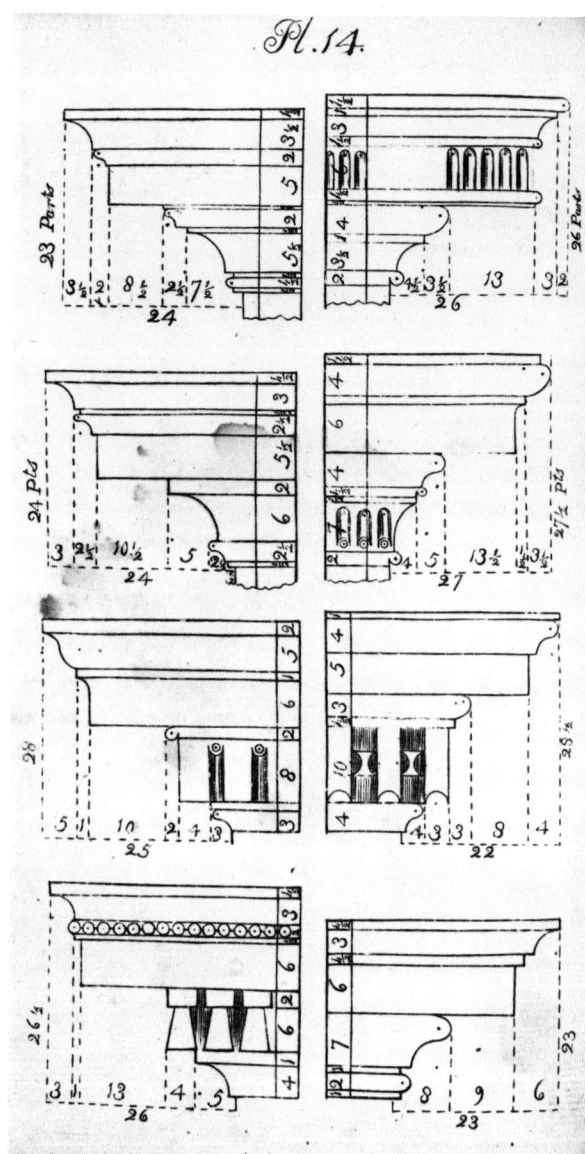

Plate 14, showing quirked mouldings used in cornices, from Asher Benjamin's, *The Country Builder's Assistant*, printed by Thomas Dickman, in Greenfield, Massachusetts in 1797. Benjamin based many of his details on the English books of William Pain. Pain, in turn, reflected the style of the fashionable architects Robert and James Adam.

and furniture designed under the influence of architects Robert and James Adam, mouldings became smaller and more delicate than previously. Craftsmen also began to embellish mouldings with quirks—small grooves that separate the moulded contour from the accompanying fillets or flat surfaces. The addition of quirks to mouldings greatly increases the subtlety of profile and enhances the play of light and shadow across the curved surfaces.

57. Asher Benjamin and Daniel Raynerd, *The American Builder's Companion...*, first edition (Boston: Etheridge and Bliss, 1806), pp. 26-27.

English authors of builder's handbooks began to illustrate quirked mouldings during the 1770s. William Pain showed such details in his *The Practical Builder* (1774), a book which was being used in Portsmouth in the Woodbury Langdon House as early as 1786. That book and Pain's *The Practical House Carpenter* appeared in Boston editions in 1794 and 1796 and immediately had an effect on moulding profiles throughout New England. Asher Benjamin of Massachusetts, the first American to publish an original work on architecture, took his inspiration from Pain's English volumes and illustrated quirked mouldings in his influential 1797 book, *The Country Builder's Assistant*. So intrigued was Benjamin with such mouldings that he altered the subtitle of the second edition of his book (1798) to focus attention on "the best methods for striking regular and quirked mouldings."

As moulding fashions changed, new tools were needed to cut the new profiles. Benjamin's references to the "striking" of mouldings in all his books represented his attempt to help the American joiner to lay out and fashion the tools needed to produce unfamiliar contours. Joiners responded quickly; the Peirce Mansion in Portsmouth (1799) and most ambitious houses built after it in coastal New Hampshire reveal delicate quirked mouldings cut by the new tools.

The quirked moulding imparted new grace and delicacy to American buildings and furniture of the late 1700s and early 1800s. But a far more profound change was destined to occur in American joinery, and hence in American joiner's tools, shortly after 1800. In 1806 Benjamin published a second book which would have an even greater influence on American architectural design and woodwork than had *The Country Builder's Assistant*. In *The American Builder's Companion*, Benjamin took a fresh look at the character and purpose of mouldings in general, and especially at the use of mouldings for exterior cornices. He again called attention to the effect of the quirked moulding, noting that "their quirks ought to be large, and as many as the cornice will admit of, as the principal beauty of plain cornices [without carved or enriched mouldings] depends upon the shadows of their quirks."[57]

But in *The American Builder's Companion* Benjamin moved away from the simple quirked moulding and recommended a completely different profile, the Grecian moulding. Whereas Roman mouldings like those used in North America throughout the eighteenth century had been based upon combinations

Instruments of Change

of segments of a circle, the Grecian moulding had soft and subtle curves based upon conic sections. Such mouldings had been discovered on ancient Greek buildings during the mid-1700s by architects like Julien David LeRoy of France and James Stuart and Nicholas Revett of England. The British architects Robert and James Adam adopted and recommended Grecian mouldings in their commissions for wealthy clients, writing in 1774:

The mouldings in the remaining structures of ancient Rome are considerably less curvelineal than those of the ancient monuments of Greece. We have always given a preference to the latter, and have even thought it advisable to bend them still more in many cases, particularly in interior finishings, where objects are near, and ought to be softened to the eye.[58]

The contours recommended by the Adam brothers were published in a form accessible to the workman by the English writer Peter Nicholson in *The Principles of Architecture* (1795-1798). Benjamin duplicated one of Nicholson's plates showing the profiles of Grecian mouldings in the second edition (1811) of *The American Builder's Companion* and copied verbatim Nicholson's explanation of the Grecian moulding:

If mouldings are only composed of parts of a circle, and straight lines, they are called Roman; because the Romans, in their buildings, seldom, or never, employed any other curve for mouldings, than that of a circle; but if a moulding is made of a part of an ellipsis, or a parabola, or an hyperbole, the mouldings are then in the Grecian taste; hence it appears, that mouldings of the Grecian taste, are of a much greater variety than those of the Roman....[59]

Benjamin went a step beyond Nicholson, recommending Grecian mouldings of extreme projection and shallow depth. Regarding cornices, especially those elevated well above the viewer's eye, Benjamin wrote that

it is easy to conceive that the size and effect of a cornice... does not so much depend upon its height as it does upon its projection; because cornices are always elevated a considerable distance above the eye, and, of course, the apparent size depends principally upon the projection.[60]

Benjamin accompanied this statement with a diagram which compared the effect of a high cornice copied from one of Batty Langley's books with that of a shallow "modern" cornice of equal horizontal projec-

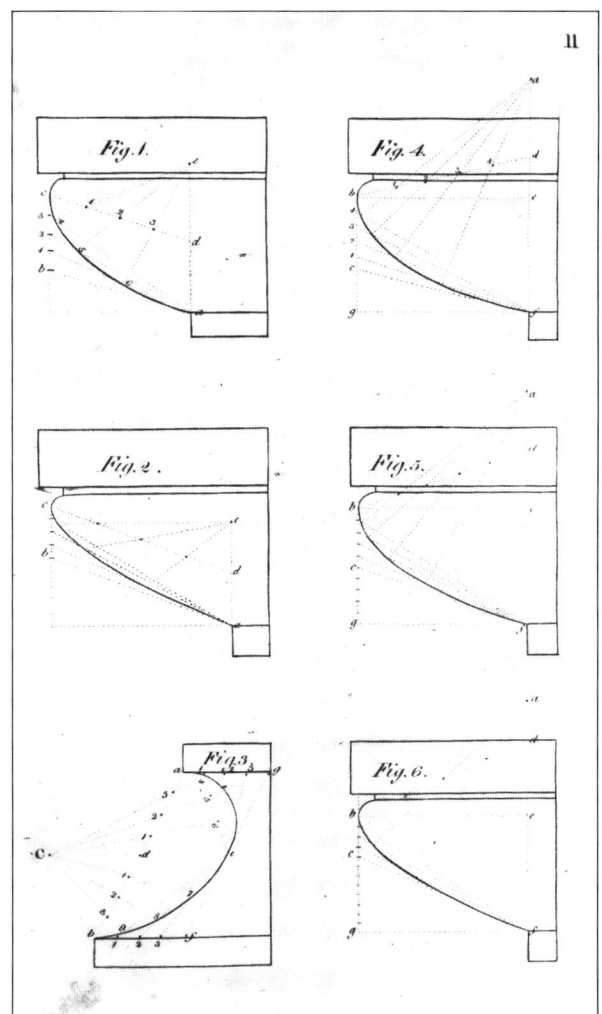

Plate 11, showing Grecian ovolo mouldings, from Asher Benjamin's, *The American Builder's Companion*, printed by Samuel Etheridge in Charlestown, Massachusetts in 1811. Plates like this, showing how to reproduce complex and beautiful Grecian mouldings, helped American joiners and planemakers fashion a new generation of tools.

tion but only two-thirds the height. Benjamin's diagram illustrated the fact that, when both are viewed at an upward angle of 45° or 50°, the shallow cornice makes nearly as great a visual effect as the other while not dominating the building's wall surface as much. Although Benjamin initially recommended cornices of strong projection and shallow height in the interest of

58. Robert and James Adam, *The Works in Architecture of Robert and James Adam...* (London: T. Becket, 1773-1774), vol. 2, book 1:7, quoted in Arthur T. Bolton, *The Architecture of Robert and James Adam, 1758-1792*, 2 vols. (London: Country Life, 1922), 1:84; and in Martin Eli Weil, "Interior Details in Eighteenth Century Architectural Books," *Bulletin* of the Association for Preservation Technology 10:4 (1978):53.
59. Asher Benjamin, *The American Builder's Companion...*, second edition (Charlestown, Mass.: Samuel Etheridge, Jr., 1811), p. 20.
60. Benjamin and Raynerd, *The American Builder's Companion*, p. vii.

economy, his several plates illustrating such cornices both for interior and exterior use proved the beauty and fitness of such details for the emerging Federal style.

Benjamin's mouldings, combining shallow height, bold projection, quirks, and Grecian profiles, were different from anything previously published in America. One of Benjamin's most far-reaching contributions to American architecture was his transformation of the native joiner's conception of the importance of the moulding. The singular beauty and subtlety of the American Federal style of architecture was largely due to the sensitive application of highly refined Grecian moulding contours to buildings.

The American Builder's Companion had an immediate impact in New Hampshire. By 1807 details and moulding profiles from the book were being used on St. John's Episcopal Church in Portsmouth, the first brick church in the state, and on ambitious mansions like that of James Rundlet of Portsmouth. Ebenezer Clifford was the chief joiner on Rundlet's house. Like every other craftsman who wished to work in the new style, Clifford was compelled to equip himself with new moulding tools different from those he had used, for example, on John Langdon's house twenty years earlier. The necessity to retire a great proportion of one's old moulding tools and to replace them with others for working Grecian profiles must have impressed itself forcibly on every joiner, especially on those who, like Clifford, doubled as planemakers. For such men, the importance of Benjamin's illustrations of simple, mechanical methods of laying out the complex curves of ellipses, parabolas, and hyperbolas was very clear: these geometrical illustrations were the means by which joiners or planemakers fashioned the tools needed to execute the new mouldings.

Between 1810 and 1820 Grecian mouldings became universal in New England joinery. As early New England planemakers (most of them joiners whose toolmaking occupied only part of their time) were supplanted by a younger generation of toolmaking specialists, the contours of Grecian mouldings were the accepted standard for ogees, ovolos, and scotias in the myriad combinations in which these profiles were used in architecture. After 1830, too, the Federal style of architecture began to be supplanted by the Greek Revival, where at last the contours of Grecian mouldings matched the overall style of American buildings. Grecian mouldings used in conjunction with the Greek Revival style tended to be heavier and flatter than those used earlier with the Federal style, but the principles of their layout were similar.

Probably as a result of this rapid evolution of moulding styles, the period after 1840 saw the development of specialized planemaking businesses. One of the most prominent of New Hampshire's professional planemakers was Cyrus Warren (1804-1888) of Hudson and Nashua. Trained as a carpenter in Windsor, Vermont, where he would have seen several buildings constructed by Asher Benjamin, Warren first came to Nashua in 1824 to work for the Nashua Manufacturing Company at a time when Benjamin was employed as agent for that textile firm. Learning the craft of planemaking after 1829 in Lowell, Massachusetts, Warren moved to Hudson about 1836 to practice his specialty. His influence on his co-workers (some of whom were family members) was considerable, and his planes were among the most beautifully made of any produced in New Hampshire. By 1850 Warren was employing four men, consuming 4,000 feet of beech timber and 1,200 pounds of boxwood each year, and annually producing 150 sets of bench planes and 1,000 sets of moulding planes.[61]

The life of David Page Sanborn (1810-1871), who carried on the Connecticut Valley tradition of planemaking in the town of Littleton, illustrates a somewhat similar history of specialization. Beginning his work before 1840 (perhaps taught by his father-in-law, James Dow, whose name appears on planes), Sanborn moved briefly to Worcester, Massachusetts, where he may have refined his skills. When he returned to Littleton about 1850, Sanborn was one of the most polished planemakers ever to work in New Hampshire. His production of an average of 240 planes a year, made by himself and one or two employees, appears to have continued for the next two decades.[62]

Also active as a planemaker by the 1840s was Philip Sargent (1790-1858) of Concord. Beginning his career as a joiner in the neighboring town of Bow, Sargent came to Concord in 1827. Moving away from his original trade, Sargent was listed specifically as a planemaker after 1844. Sargent appears to have responded to Concord's specialization in coach and wagon manufacture, producing a proportionately greater number of carriagemaker's planes than did other New Hampshire toolmakers.

---

61. United States Census, New Hampshire, 1850. Products of Industry.
62. United States Census, New Hampshire, 1850, 1860, 1870.

These specialized craftsmen filled a need in a state with an economy still based strongly upon forest products. In 1850 New Hampshire had over 500 water-powered sawmills. These mills produced over 100 million board feet of pine and hemlock boards and planks, nearly 30 million shingles, and 4 million to 5 million clapboards each year.[63] Although many of these mills retained "upright" or reciprocating saws similar to those introduced more than two centuries earlier, many also had circular saws by 1850. The introduction of the water-powered turbine throughout New Hampshire during the mid-1800s made the transmission of power to such saws a relatively simple process and readily produced the speed of rotation needed for the effective operation of the circular saw.[64] Such saws were especially useful in the mechanical production of shingles and clapboards, eliminating the handwork that had formerly been necessary to fashion these products; many small mills, in fact, specialized in the production of shingles alone.

New Hampshire inventors made their share of contributions to the technological revolution being introduced by powered machinery. In 1831 Josiah Fay of Hollis developed machinery with rotary cutters that fashioned tenons; in 1835 and 1836 Ira Gay of Dunstable (Nashua) patented machines for planing, mortising, and tenoning doors, window sashes, and blinds; during the 1830s Henry Mellish of Walpole, George Page of Keene, and Jonathan Page of Henniker all developed a variety of machines for mortising and tenoning; during the same period, Cyrus McGregory of Newport responded to the needs of New Hampshire's many coopers and shook mill operators by developing devices for sawing and jointing staves; and in 1837 Samuel Whitney of Dunstable patented a machine for planing boards. The results of such creativity were soon felt across the state.

By far the most noteworthy of New Hampshire's contributions to the mechanization of joinery sprang from the creativity of George Page of Keene. A prolific inventor of drill stocks, mortising chisels, and mortising machines, Page manufactured a screw gimlet invented by Gideon Newcomb of Roxbury, New Hampshire, and was involved in many other local enterprises. About 1834 Page formed a partnership with fellow inventor Jerub Amber Fay (1808-1854) and with Edward Joslin (1810-1901) for the manufacture of woodworking machinery. Eventually incorporated under the name of J. A. Fay and Company, this firm is recognized as having introduced the first powered mortising, tenoning, and moulding machines manufactured in the United States. In 1847 the company established branches in Worcester, Massachusetts; Norwich, Connecticut; and Cincinnati, and in 1848 it began to produce the first successful moulding machine built for general use. Growing swiftly, the company abandoned its New Hampshire shops in 1862, but the legacy of New Hampshire's pioneering enterprise lived on as the J. A. Fay Company of Cincinnati became the largest manufacturer of woodworking machinery in the world.[65]

By 1850 New Hampshire contained some forty shops specializing in the production of doors, sashes, and blinds, or in the mechanical planing of lumber. Although exact figures were not kept, it is clear that in 1850 more than 26,000 doors and 10,000 pairs of blinds were being manufactured in such shops and that others possessed machines used for shaping window muntins, architectural mouldings, and picture frames. A number of these specialized shops were located in urban areas and were powered by steam rather than by water.

Although mechanization was making inroads in the wood products industries, it is clear that technological innovation was encouraging the production of many kinds of hand tools rather than rendering them obsolete. Hudson, Nashua, and Nashville, for example, were at once centers of millwork shops and of hand plane production, and the manufacture of hand planes increased throughout New Hampshire even as powered woodworking machinery was being developed and introduced in the state.

Despite the fact that steam- or water-powered rotary planers were rendering bench planes far less necessary for the large-scale dressing of rough lumber, there was still a place for such planes in any good craftsman's shop or chest. And despite the fact that machines were beginning to produce mouldings in quantity, it is clear that hand moulding tools were still

63. United States Census, New Hampshire, 1850. Products of Industry.
64. James Emerson, *Treatise Relative to the Testing of Water-Wheels and Machinery, with Various Other Matters Pertaining to Hydraulics*, second edition (Springfield, Mass.: by the author, 1878).
65. J. H. Englund, "An Outline of the Development of Wood Moulding Machinery," *Bulletin* of the Association for Preservation Technology 10:4 (1978):20-46; S. G. Griffin, *A History of the Town of Keene* (Keene, N.H., 1904; reprinted Bowie, Md.: Heritage Books, Inc., 1980), pp. 452, 617-18; obituary of J. A. Fay, *New Hampshire Sentinel* (Keene, N.H.), May 5, 1854; obituary of Edward Joslin, *Cheshire Republican* (Keene, N.H.), November 22, 1901.

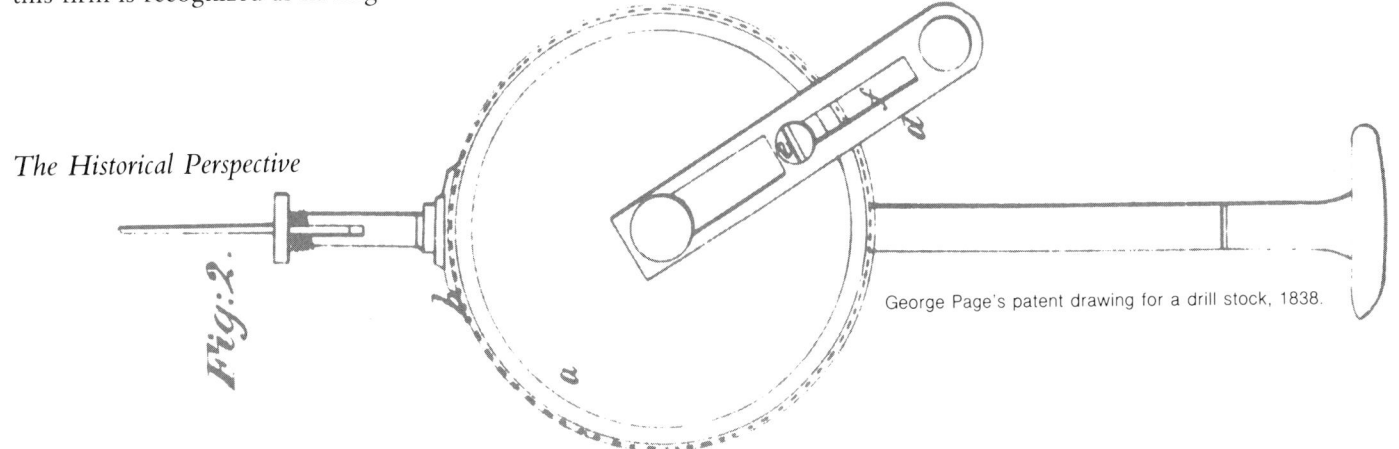

George Page's patent drawing for a drill stock, 1838.

in widespread use, even for the production of the many yards of standardized door and window casings or baseboards required in the average dwelling, and even in the fashioning of some mouldings utilized in semimechanized door and sash factories.

In fact, the makers of hand tools were themselves quick to utilize power-driven machinery in their work. In 1850 Cyrus Warren of Hudson had a four-man shop equipped with a water-powered planer, four circular saws, an upright saw, a power press, a turning lathe, a boring lathe, and emery wheels.[66] David Page Sanborn of Littleton was also using waterpower in 1850; by 1860 his shop included a planer, two circular saws, and a lathe. The benefits of such progressive manufacturing become clear when we see that in 1850 Warren was able to produce $2,200 worth of products from his mechanized shop, while Concord planemaker Philip Sargent, who used only handpower, had an annual output worth only $500.

Increasingly, though, machinery did begin to supplant handwork in the manufacture of components for buildings and furniture. By 1870 the number of planing mills in New Hampshire had increased to about ninety; the number of mechanized door, sash, and blind shops was more than twenty-five; and the number of turning mills had reached forty-five.[67] The state was becoming more and more industrialized. Out of a work force of 120,000 in 1870, 46,500 were engaged in manufacturing—virtually equal to the number working in agriculture. The state's hundreds of small streams were increasingly harnessed for small-scale industry, just as the Merrimack and other major river systems were channeled into textile manufacture. In 1870 New Hampshire had 640 water-powered lumber, shingle, clapboard, and stave mills, in addition to turning mills and door, sash, and blind factories. In that year, waterwheels and turbines supplied a total of 70,000 horsepower for manufacturing, while steam, a growing source of power, contributed over 7,000 horsepower. By 1874 lumber mills had increased to 762 and were annually producing 305 million board feet of boards and dimension timber, 6.5 million clapboards, and nearly 70 million shingles.[68]

Mechanization increasingly tended to moderate the demand for tools like moulding planes, whose products were slowly supplanted by machine-made elements. Yet the production of other hand tools flourished with the introduction of new industries. This was especially true of edge tools, which had formerly been imported or produced in specialized centers in Massachusetts or elsewhere. By 1850 such tools at last began to be produced in New Hampshire in quantities sufficient both for local demand and for sale to distant points. Edge tools seem to have been among those categories of implements that found an increasing market as industrialization brought an expansion of construction. The long persistence in New Hampshire of the mortised and tenoned building frame maintained a demand for slicks and mortising chisels, while the fitting and joining of interior woodwork, even when the mouldings were prepared at the mill, required the traditional set of joiner's chisels. And New Hampshire's forest-based economy maintained a steady demand for axes and adzes of all types.

The invigorating effects of industrialization can be seen in the history of the Underhill Edge Tool Company of Nashua. A family business which began with Chester blacksmith Josiah Underhill (1758-1822), the company was in the hands of grandson George Washington Underhill (1815-1882) by 1850. In that year, Underhill employed seven men in a water-powered shop equipped with four forges. The shop consumed fifteen tons of wrought iron and four tons of steel and annually produced chisels and hatchets worth $10,000.[69] Under the impetus of a growing economy, the firm grew in ten years to employ forty men. By 1880, after absorbing the rival Amoskeag Ax Company of Manchester, the Underhill Company was employing ninety men and producing $80,000 worth of axes, hatchets, chisels, and pickaxes each year.

Much the same growth is seen in competing edge tool firms. By 1860 the Blodgett Edge Tool Company of Manchester employed forty-five men and annually used 200 tons of wrought iron and 100 tons of steel. By 1870 Blodgett had been reorganized into the Amoskeag Ax Company and employed fifty men. The shop was powered by two waterwheels generating 400 horsepower and driving fourteen triphammers, one rolling machine, ten power grindstones, and four polishing machines.[70] Before being bought out by the Underhill firm, Amoskeag Ax Company was annually

---

66. United States Census, New Hampshire, 1850. Products of Industry.
67. United States Census, New Hampshire, 1870; Alonzo J. Fogg, comp., *The Statistics and Gazetteer of New-Hampshire* (Concord, N.H.: by the author, 1874), pp. 500-501.
68. Ibid., p. 407.
69. United States Census, New Hampshire, 1850. Products of Industry.
70. Ibid., 1860, 1870.

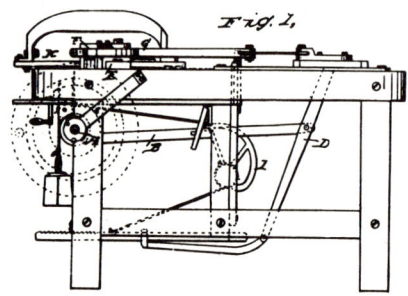

Richard Walker's patent drawing for a file cutting machine, 1847.

Instruments of Change

Engraving of the Blodgett Edge Tool Manufacturing Company, published in 1858. Predecessor of the Amoskeag Ax Company, the Blodgett Edge Tool Company employed 45 men and made 300 tools each day.

producing 800 broad axes, 90,000 chopping axes, 26,000 hatchets, 1,600 adzes, and 32,000 other edge tools.

Such statistics make it clear that mechanized industry was being applied energetically to the manufacture of hand tools after the mid-nineteenth century. The increasingly complex technology of hand tool production inspired a number of New Hampshire inventors to patent machines for toolmaking. In 1847, for example, Richard Walker of Portsmouth patented a machine which not only cut files but cut both faces of a flat file simultaneously, obviating the traditional laborious process of hand-hammering each groove with a special chisel.[71] Between 1858 and 1867 George and Henry C. Reynolds of Manchester obtained three patents for machines to shape the iron and steel components of axe heads and to smooth the surface of the welded head, thus reducing the tremendous amount of labor formerly invested in hand forging and finishing.[72] Responding to a widespread need, Alfred S. Philbrook of Claremont developed a device in 1865 to imprint the characteristic compound curve upon scythe snaths, doing away with the old process of shaving, smoothing, bending, and finishing by hand.[73]

New Hampshire inventors were still more resourceful in developing improvements to hand tools themselves. Approximately 100 patents relating to hand tools were granted to New Hampshire residents between 1820 and 1870. These included many different forms of leather splitting and cutting tools, a number of scythe components, a variety of saw sets adapted to hand and circular saws, and other inventions inspired by the trade specialties that developed in several regions of New Hampshire during the 1800s.

Much of New Hampshire's tool production did, in

71. United States Patent #5149 (June 12, 1847).
72. United States Patents #20,957 (July 20, 1858), #49,156 (August 1, 1865), #67,584 (August 6, 1867).
73. United States Patent #50,272.

The Historical Perspective

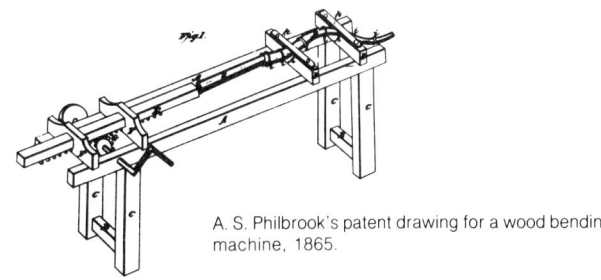

A. S. Philbrook's patent drawing for a wood bending machine, 1865.

Right: This wood engraving used in an 1872 Concord advertisement illustrates the pre-industrial method of cutting files. Using a triangular chisel, a special hammer, and skill, strength, and speed, a good working man could cut from sixty to eighty grooves a minute.

Far right: Engraving of Gage, Warner, and Whitney's Machine Shop in Nashua, published in 1865. John H. Gage, the founder of this business, is said to have built "the first establishment in the United States devoted exclusively to the manufacture of machinists' tools."

fact, reflect local craft economies within the state. The Connecticut Valley of New Hampshire, for example, inherited a tradition of auger and bit manufacture from settlers who came from the state of Connecticut; one small town, Chesterfield, boasted ten auger makers during the nineteenth century. Portsmouth, with its maritime economy and its several cordage manufactories, dominated the blockmaking craft in New Hampshire with some forty specialists in this trade. The southern part of the state was an area of extensive shoe manufacture. Rockingham and Strafford counties had forty-three shoeshops in 1870, employing over 4,300 people. High concentrations of shoe production were to be found in the Farmington-Rochester-Dover and Manchester vicinities, with a vast additional production just south of the border in Haverhill, Massachusetts. It is therefore not surprising that the invention and manufacture of leatherworking tools, and especially of shoe knives and chamfering tools, was concentrated in towns near Farmington, Manchester, and Haverhill. A similar specialization can be seen in the vicinity of Hollis and Milford. The extensive oak forests of these and neighboring towns made this district an early center of coopering, and local demand in turn made the manufacture of cooper's tools a specialty of the region.

Since New Hampshire people always engaged in agriculture in addition to whatever manufacturing or handcraft specialties they might develop, it is not surprising that agricultural tools should have been manufactured almost everywhere in the state. It is possible, however, to discern a distinct specialization both in agricultural edge tools and in the wooden handles for such tools in the western part of the state. The towns of the Connecticut River Valley and of the Lake Sunapee area were particularly productive of scythes, shovels, hoes, and pitchforks. One of the earliest water-powered scythe shops in New England

Instruments of Change

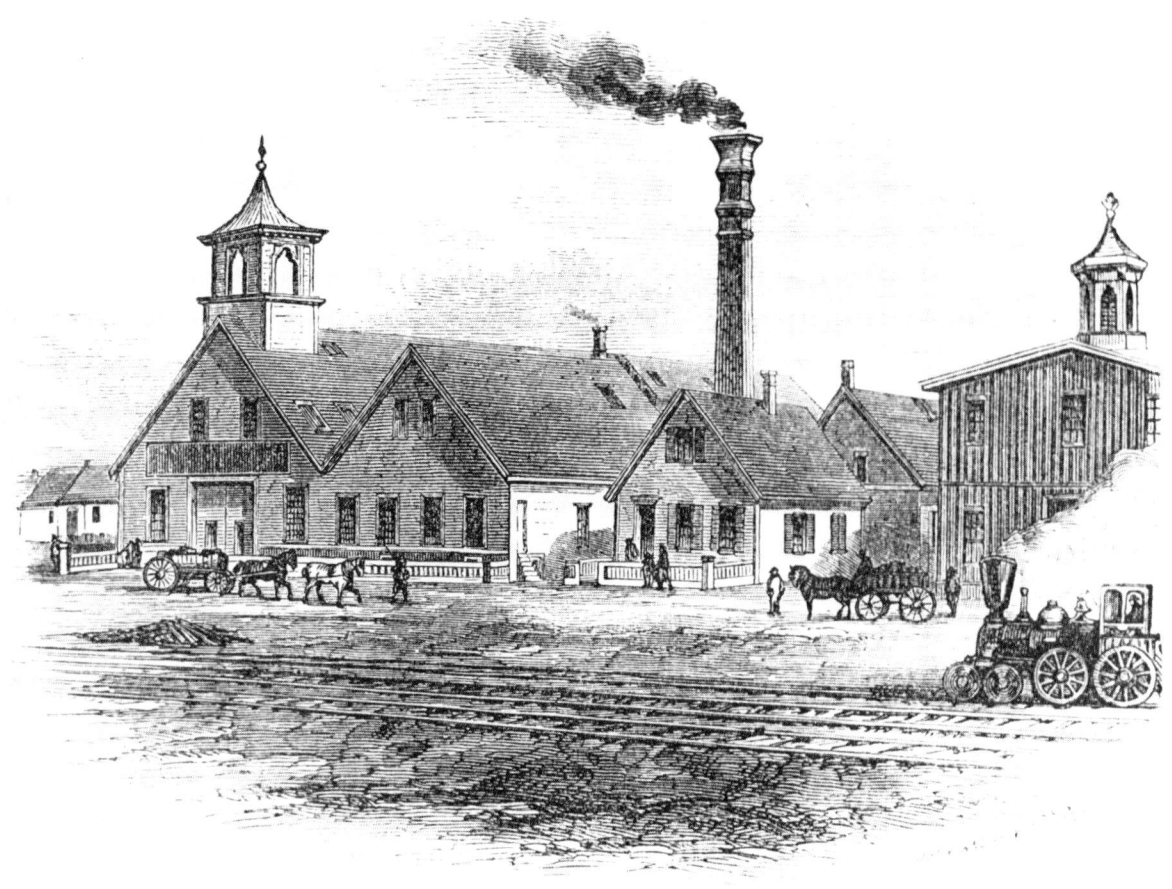

was established in Newport in 1787, and that town remained productive in this manufacture throughout the nineteenth century. The village of Scytheville in New London became prominent in this specialized trade, producing 10,000 dozen scythes, 1,000 dozen hay knives, and 5,000 dozen axes in 1880—more than the scythe production of the entire state ten years earlier. Although the most enterprising agricultural tool manufacturers of the Connecticut Valley found an international market for their products, the original impetus for their productivity was doubtless the fertility of the region itself—a region that has always held New Hampshire's most prosperous agricultural townships.[74]

Lesser specialties also developed where certain trades called attention to a potential market for unusual tools. The manufacture of lumber rules and calipers, for example, centered on Littleton, on the Groton-Bristol-Plymouth region and, farther south, on an area southwest of Concord. Each of these centers of rule production was within a district of high activity in lumber manufacturing at the end of the nineteenth century. Similar, but much smaller, was the response of cutlery manufacturers to the requirements of the orchard and nursery businesses that flourished in southern New Hampshire. It is hardly surprising that a specialized production of pruning and grafting knives should have developed in Nashua and nearby Pelham, since these communities are located near the center of a rich apple-growing district.

Throughout the nineteenth century, New Hampshire people applied their enterprise to whatever resources the state could offer. Recognizing early that

74. Scytheville-Elkins Sesquicentennial Committee, *Reflections in a Millpond: Stories of Scytheville-Elkins, 1835-1985* (New London, N.H.: by the committee, 1984), p. 26; Fogg, comp., *Statistics and Gazetteer of New-Hampshire*, pp. 403-5.

The Historical Perspective

much of New Hampshire's land offered little inducement to agriculture, the people of the state turned to handcrafts and manufactures. Alonzo J. Fogg, one of New Hampshire's energetic promoters in the post-Civil War era, was probably voicing the sentiments of most New Hampshire people when he expressed satisfaction with the demands and opportunities proffered by the state's geography:

It is a noted fact that the more diversified is any country with mountains, hills, valleys, plains, lakes and rivers, the more diversified are the people who live there in their occupations of life. . . . The employments of the people of New Hampshire are as varied as the surface of the country in which they live . . . . The greater the variety of labor in any country, the more rapid the accumulation of wealth and the more general the diffusion of it among the people.[75]

The people of New Hampshire accepted this philosophy. Following the Civil War, local enterprise made the state one of the most heavily industrialized regions in the nation in relation to the size of the population—a status which New Hampshire continues to hold to this day. New Hampshire became an early center for industrial manufactures, and even for the production of the machinery that powered such manufactures; the shop of John H. Gage in Nashua, established in 1838, is credited with being the first in the nation devoted exclusively to machine tool production.[76] Yet despite the impressive scale of its mechanized production, much of the state's wealth and activity continued to be the product of the skilled hand. The hand often wielded a New Hampshire-made tool and frequently used that tool to make other tools. As the following pages show, New Hampshire's contribution to the legacy of hand tool production is one of utility and beauty.

---

75. Fogg, comp., *Statistics and Gazetteer of New-Hampshire*, p. 402.
76. J. Leander Bishop, *A History of American Manufactures from 1608 to 1860...*, 2 vols. (Philadelphia: Edward Young & Co., 1864), 2:777-78.

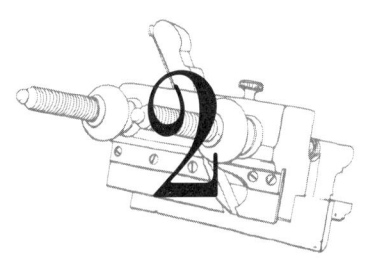

The Tools

Plow by Cyrus Warren of Hudson and Nashua.
(Ref. Plate 9)

1. HALVING PLANE
by E. Briggs of Keene.

Marks: "E·BRIGGS" in irregular outline, "IN·KEEN" in rectangle, "II" in square, on fore end of plane.

One of New Hampshire's earliest professional planemakers, E. Briggs remains something of a mystery. Three members of the Briggs family, each potentially the maker of this plane and others with the same mark, came to Keene from Norton, Massachusetts, in the 1760s. Elisha Briggs (c. 1738-1803) was married in 1758 in the planemaking center of Wrentham, Massachusetts, where he may have served an apprenticeship. Less is known about his father, Eliphalet (1713-1780), and brother, Eliphalet, Jr. (1735-1776), who also moved to Keene.

Materials: Birch.
Dimensions: L. 9¾ in. (24.8 cm.)
W. ⅞ in. (2.1 cm.)
H. 5⅜ in. (13.5 cm.)
Courtesy of Paul B. Kebabian.

2. MOULDING TOOL
by John Hill of Portsmouth.

Marks: "I+HILL/PORTSM NH/1792" in pricked dots on flat side of stock.

This small plane is probably typical of many made by joiners for their own use on special jobs. The plane produces an ogee curve but not one commonly found in complex architectural mouldings. The maker was probably John Hill, a joiner who in 1803 became an incorporating member of the Associated Mechanics and Manufacturers of New Hampshire.

Materials: Birch.
Dimensions: L. 5¾ in. (14.5 cm.)
W. 2 in. (4.9 cm.)
H. 6 in. (15.1 cm.)
Courtesy of Margaret Scott Carter.

The Tools

3. SASH PLANE
by Ebenezer Clifford (1746-1821) of Kensington and Exeter.

Marks: "E. CLIFFORD" in rectangle on fore end of plane.

A joiner, turner, cabinetmaker, and builder/architect, Clifford was one of New Hampshire's most enterprising and intelligent craftsmen during the late 1700s and early 1800s. At least two books from his architectural library survive. Standing buildings finished in part by his hand include the Governor John Langdon Mansion (1783-86) and the James Rundlet House (1807-8) in Portsmouth and the First Parish Meeting House (1798) in Exeter. Clifford was one of the earliest professional planemakers in the seacoast region of New Hampshire.

Materials: Birch.
Dimensions: L. 12¾ in. (32.4 cm.)
W. 2 in. (5.0 cm.)
H. 5⅞ in. (14.8 cm.)
Courtesy of Herman and Joseph M. Freedman.

4. MOULDING TOOL
by John Sleeper (1754-1834) of Newburyport, Massachusetts, and Chester.

Marks: "I.SLEEPER" in rectangle on fore end; owners' marks, "N. TASKER," "C. G. HOLMES" on fore end.

This quirked ogee moulding tool probably belonged to Nathaniel Tasker (1784-1868), a carpenter and joiner from Northwood. The moulding it produced was a standard contour in New Hampshire from the 1790s. The fence on the flat side of the stock is attached by screws and is probably a replacement.

Materials: Beech, boxwood (single boxed).
Dimensions: L. 9¾ in. (24.7 cm.)
W. 1⅞ in. (4.7 cm.)
H. 6¼ in. (15.8 cm.)
Courtesy of Malcolm G. MacGregor, Jr.

5. PANEL RAISING PLANE
by John Sleeper (1754-1834) of Newburyport, Massachusetts, and Chester.

Marks: "I.SLEEPER" in rectangle on fore end; "WELDON" on skewed iron.

While the assertion in Benjamin Chase's 1869 History of Old Chester *that Sleeper fashioned "the first joiner's tools made in this country" is inaccurate, Sleeper was nevertheless an important early maker of a variety of joiner's tools both before and after he came to Chester in 1814. Hallmarks of his work, especially the distinctive type of wedge he used with narrow plane irons, appear to have been copied by other planemakers who worked north of the Merrimack River.*

Materials: Beech, lignum vitae or rosewood (striking button).
Dimensions: L. 13⅜ in. (33.9 cm.)
W. 2½ in. (6.2 cm.)
H. 6⅛ in. (15.5 cm.)
Courtesy of Malcolm G. MacGregor, Jr.

Instruments of Change

6. MOULDING TOOL
by Arad Simons (1754-1836) of Lebanon.

Marks: "ARAD:SIMONS" in rectangle on fore end.

Simons was one of the many natives of Connecticut who settled in the Connecticut Valley of New Hampshire, arriving about the end of the Revolution. Trained in Connecticut as a joiner, and practicing that trade in Lebanon, Simons also carried on the Connecticut River tradition of planemaking. This plane produces a quarter-round or ovolo of ½-inch radius, and a fillet.

Materials: Birch.
Dimensions: L. 10⅛ in. (25.5 cm.)
W. 1⅜ in. (3.3 cm.)
H. 6¼ in. (15.8 cm.)
Courtesy of Emil S. Pollak.

7. PANEL RAISING PLANE
by Downing Amsden (working between 1807 and 1828) of Lebanon.

Marks: "D.AMSDEN" in serrated rectangle, "LEBANON" in serrated rectangle, "NH" in serrated rectangle, on fore end.

Perhaps learning his trade from Arad Simons, Amsden worked primarily in Lebanon, N.H., but died in Norwich, Vermont. His known products range from moulding tools for elegant cavettos and Grecian ogees with beads, through plows, rabbets, hollows, and rounds. This plane has features in common with late raising planes manufactured after the Civil War, including the scoring iron placed ahead of its 3¼-inch-wide skewed primary iron.

Materials: Beech.
Dimensions: L. 21⅞ in. (55.5 cm.)
W. 4⅛ in. (10.3 cm.)
H. 7¾ in. (19.8 cm.)
Courtesy of Emil S. Pollak.

8. MOULDING TOOL
by Joshua Morse, Jr. (1774-1826) of Hopkinton.

Marks: "J.MORSE" in serrated rectangle on fore end; owners' marks, "H. Robinson," "A.D.S." on fore end.

Like Ebenezer Clifford, Morse was a joiner who developed into one of the state's early professional planemakers. In 1816 and again in 1819, Morse advertised bench planes and moulding tools made of second-growth beech. Making use of newspapers and the mails to widen his market, Morse also appears to have influenced the work of one or more later planemakers from the Hopkinton area. This plane produces a ⅜-inch quirked edge bead.

Materials: Beech.
Dimensions: L. 9⅜ in. (23.9 cm.)
W. 1 in. (2.5 cm.)
H. 5⅞ in. (15.0 cm.)
Courtesy of Emil S. Pollak.

The Tools

The Warrens

CYRUS WARREN (1804-1888) of Hudson and Nashua was probably the most influential as well as the most productive of New Hampshire's many planemakers. Born in Hardwick, Massachusetts, and trained as a carpenter in Windsor, Vermont, Warren first came to New Hampshire in 1824, apparently to work on construction for the Nashua Manufacturing Company. In 1829 he returned to Massachusetts where he learned the craft of planemaking in Lowell. In 1836 or 1837 Warren erected his own plane shop in Hudson, New Hampshire, the home of his wife's family. While in Hudson, Warren apparently transmitted his skills not only to his younger brother William (1818-1861) and to his son George Henry Warren (1829-1900) but also to Hudson native Dana Sargent (1818-1884), who later worked in both Nashua and Manchester. The prominent planemaker Addison Heald (1817-1895) of Milford also seems to have learned his trade from the Warrens. In 1857 Cyrus Warren moved to Nashua, where he continued plane manufacturing until his health forced him to retire about 1875. Since Cyrus Warren's younger brother, William, died in his forties and his son, George H., transferred early in life to another trade, Cyrus Warren was the most prolific member of the important planemaking family which he founded.

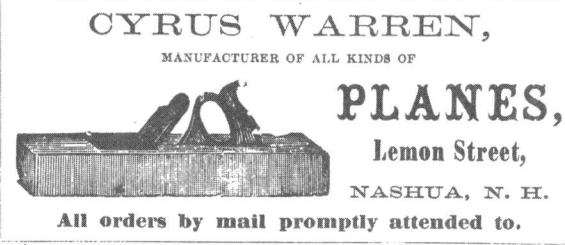

9-12. FOUR PLOWS
by Cyrus Warren (1804-1888) of Hudson and Nashua.

The four plows which follow represent the height of Warren's virtuosity as a toolmaker. With their varying combinations of native and exotic woods, their crisply moulded arms and fences, and their carefully fitted brass hardware, these are among the most impressive joiner's tools ever made in New Hampshire. Warren manufactured many variations of the plow, including some with closed totes and others, less expensive, with sliding rather than screw arms. Less costly examples are made wholly of beech, and some have wooden rather than brass thumbscrews.

9.
Marks: "C.WARREN" in serrated rectangle, "NASHUA" in serrated rectangle on fore end; owner's mark, "J.P.NOURSE" on fore end.

Materials: Rosewood, boxwood.
Dimensions: L. 9⅜ in. (23.6 cm.)
　　　　　　　W. 10⅝ in. (26.8 cm.)
　　　　　　　H. 6¾ in. (17.0 cm.)
Courtesy of Margaret Scott Carter.

Instruments of Change

10.
Marks: "C.WARREN" in serrated rectangle, "NASHUA" in serrated rectangle on fore end; owner's marks, "G.KNOWLES," once on fore end, once on breech end; ["PROV. TO]OL CO CAST STEEL" on iron.

Materials: Rosewood, boxwood.
Dimensions: L. 9½ in. (24.0 cm.)
W. 10⅞ in. (27.7 cm.)
H. 6⅜ in. (16.2 cm.)

Courtesy of William K. Ackroyd.

11.
Marks: "C.WARREN" in serrated rectangle, "NASHUA" in serrated rectangle on fore end; owner's marks, "J.FOSS" three times in triangular arrangement.

Materials: Rosewood.
Dimensions: L. 9⅜ in. (23.7 cm.)
W. 10¾ in. (27.2 cm.)
H. 7⅞ in. (20.0 cm.)

Courtesy of Margaret Scott Carter.

The Tools

12.
Marks: "C.WARREN" in serrated rectangle, "NASHUA" in serrated rectangle on fore end; "PROV. TOOL CO CAST STEEL" on iron.

Materials: Beech, boxwood (arms).
Dimensions: L. 9 3/8 in. (23.7 cm.)
                W. 10 3/4 in. (27.2 cm.)
                H. 7 3/4 in. (19.5 cm.)
Courtesy of William K. Ackroyd.

Instruments of Change

13. MOULDING TOOL
by Cyrus Warren (1804-1888) of Hudson and Nashua.

Marks: "C.WARREN" in serrated rectangle, "NASHUA" in serrated rectangle on fore end; "JAMES CAM" in serrated rectangle on iron.

This large tool fashions a cavetto and ovolo moulding about 4½ inches wide. Such a combination is often found as a bed moulding in exterior cornices throughout the nineteenth century. Among other large Warren moulding tools to survive is a beech plane for fashioning a convex interior door or window casing 5¾ inches in width. Such tools show that the handmade architectural moulding survived many years after the invention of machine stickers which used rotary cutters to shape wood.

Materials: Beech.
Dimensions: L. 14⅞ in. (37.7 cm.)
W. 12 in. (30.3 cm.)
H. 7⅛ in. (18.2 cm.)
Courtesy of Margaret Scott Carter.

14. MOULDING TOOL
by Cyrus Warren (1804-1888) of Hudson and Nashua.

Marks: "C.WARREN" in serrated rectangle, "NASHUA" in serrated rectangle on fore end; "⅝" on breech end above boxing; owner's mark, "A.P.K." on fore end.

The serpentine double ogee produced by this plane is often seen as a moulding applied around door panels. This tool, and a graduated set of Grecian ogees which survive in the same collection and bear the same owner's stamp, probably belonged to Artemus Parkman Kelsey (1813-1895), a Nashua door and sash maker. Kelsey's ownership of such planes (all typical door panel mouldings) suggests the continued use of handwork in mechanized shops of the mid-to-late nineteenth century.

Materials: Beech, boxwood.
Dimensions: L. 9⅝ in. (24.4 cm.)
W. 2½ in. (6.2 cm.)
H. 5¼ in. (13.4 cm.)
Courtesy of William K. Ackroyd.

The Tools

15. MOVING FILLETSTER
by Cyrus Warren (1804-1888) of Hudson and Nashua.

Marks: "C.WARREN" in serrated rectangle, "NASHUA" in serrated rectangle on fore end; owner's marks, "B.B.PUTNAM" stamped twice on fore end with different dies.

This is one of several known examples of moving filletsters by Warren. This tool almost certainly belonged to Barnes Bigelow Putnam (1825-1899), a prominent Nashua carpenter. An active craftsman throughout his life, Putnam met his death in a fall from the rafters of his son's barn.

Materials: Beech, boxwood.
Dimensions: L. 9¼ in. (23.5 cm.)
W. 3 in. (7.5 cm.) (fence closed)
H. 5⅝ in. (14.2 cm.)
Courtesy of Margaret Scott Carter.

16. SMOOTHING PLANE
by William Warren (1818-1861) of Hudson.

Marks: "W.WARREN" in rectangle, "NASHUA N.H" in serrated rectangle, "BAILEY'S PATENT/AUG. 31, 1858/JUNE 22, 1858" on fore end; owners' marks, "ALL" on fore end, "H.H. CLEVELAND/BOSTON" on breech end; "PATENT/AUG. 31-58" on plane iron cap; "MOULSON BROTHERS/ WARRANTED/CAST STEEL" on cutter of double iron.

This plane incorporates the lever plane iron cap and the lateral adjusting lever which were patented in 1858 by Leonard Bailey (1825-1905). A native of Hollis, N.H., Bailey was noted for his many ingenious tool improvements and became a leading plane manufacturer in Massachusetts and Connecticut. Warren's use of Bailey's patents on an old-fashioned wooden smoothing plane stock represents an attempt to incorporate convenient new features without making the transition to the cast-iron planes which Bailey himself was developing.

Materials: Beech.
Dimensions: L. 8 in. (20.2 cm.)
W. 2½ in. (6.4 cm.)
H. 4½ in. (11.5 cm.)
Courtesy of William K. Ackroyd.

Instruments of Change

18. JOINTER
by George Henry Warren (1829-1900) of Hudson.

Marks: "G.H.WARREN" in serrated rectangle, "NASHUA" in serrated rectangle on fore end; "HUMPHREY[SVILLE MFG. CO.]/WARRANTED/CAST STEEL" on double iron.

This bench plane probably dates from before 1857, when George H. Warren gave up toolmaking to become a tailor. The various members of the Warren family continued to make bench planes well after the introduction of machine jointers and planers, filling a need that clearly did not end even after the advent of powered machinery in mills and large woodworking shops.

Materials: Beech.
Dimensions: L. 28 in. (71.2 cm.)
W. 3½ in. (8.8 cm.)
H. 7⅜ in. (18.6 cm.)
Courtesy of Margaret Scott Carter.

17. SMOOTHING PLANE
by William Warren (1818-1861) of Hudson.

Marks: "W.WARREN" in rectangle, "NASHUA" in serrated rectangle on fore end; "PROVIDENCE/ TOOL CO./WARRANTED/ EXTRA/CAST STEEL" on double iron.

This coffin-shaped plane is fashioned from a large piece of boxwood. Vermont native William Warren, the younger brother of Cyrus, died at age forty-three, and comparatively few of his tools survive. Although evidence suggests that William Warren worked only in the small town of Hudson, all his known planes are marked with the name of the adjacent city, "NASHUA." Other members of the planemaking family seem to have followed the same practice, probably for easy recognition of their locale.

Materials: Boxwood.
Dimensions: L. 7¾ in. (19.6 cm.)
W. 2⅞ in. (7.4 cm.)
H. 5⅝ in. (14.1 cm.)
Courtesy of Margaret Scott Carter.

The Tools

The Healds

ADDISON HEALD (1817-1895), a native of Nelson, New Hampshire, best known for his long career as a Milford plane manufacturer, was originally trained in Keene in the allied woodworking trade of cabinetmaking. He later prepared for the ministry at New Hampton Academical and Theological Institution and spent two years in Ohio, where he was involved in a school for escaped slaves. Between 1852 and 1860 Heald's father-in-law was acting Congregational minister of Hudson, New Hampshire, living across the street from planemaker William Warren. During part of this time, Heald lived in Hudson with his father-in-law and is said to have "frequently supplied the pulpit." The influence of the Warren brothers seems to have revived Heald's interest in specialized woodworking, for by 1856 "A. Heald" of "Heald & Co." was listed in Nashua as a "manufacturer of tools." After further experience as a planemaker both in the partnership of Warren & Heald in Nashua and alone in Hudson, Heald moved to Milford in 1868 and set up a plane shop in the steam-powered furniture factory of his brother David. In 1873 Addison Heald went into partnership with his son Daniel Milton Heald (1852-1929), who in 1878 was granted a patent for an "improvement in bench-planes." The partnership of Addison Heald & Son specialized in bench planes and cooper's tools but also produced toy planes, room mouldings, and picture frames. After the father's death in 1895, Daniel Milton Heald continued the manufacture of planes and cooper's tools under the old firm name until 1906. Thereafter, Daniel Milton Heald worked in the family furniture factory and specialized in picture frames.

19. MOULDING TOOL
by Addison Heald (1817-1895) and Daniel Milton Heald (1852-1929) of Milford.

Marks: "A.HEALD & SON" in serrated rectangle, "MILFORD.N.H." in serrated rectangle, on fore end; "1" impressed, "INCH" in serrated rectangle, on breech end.

Many planes marked "A.HEALD & SON" are fitted with the characteristic wedge seen on this ogee moulding tool. The wedge was not patented, but the fact that it evidently never appears on tools marked by Addison Heald alone suggests that the son, Daniel Milton Heald, invented the device. The wooden wedge is pivoted on a steel pin, and tightening the knurled steel screw at the top of the wedge causes the toe of the wedge to press the plane iron against its bed. Some examples of the device, presumably early, use a wooden rather than a steel screw.

Materials: Beech.
Dimensions: L. 9⅝ in. (24.2 cm.)
W. 1⅞ in. (4.8 cm.)
H. 5 in. (12.5 cm.)
Courtesy of William K. Ackroyd.

Instruments of Change

20. RAZEE SMOOTHING PLANE
by Addison Heald (1817-1895) of Milford.

Marks: "ADDISON HEALD" in curved serrated banner, "MILFORD.N.H." in serrated rectangle, on fore end; owner's mark, "J.W.CHRISTY" on fore end.

Although marked by Addison Heald alone, this plane incorporates the plane iron cap which was patented by the son, Daniel Milton Heald (1852-1929), in 1878. Elegant in its simplicity, this patented device apparently evolved from Daniel Milton Heald's earlier pivoted wooden wedge and tightening screw. In the fully developed invention, the cast-iron plane iron cap is pivoted on a steel pin. A steel screw penetrates a slide in the cap and holds the double plane iron. A second screw permits the vertical adjustment of the slide, moving the plane iron in or out of the mouth of the plane.

Materials: Beech.
Dimensions: L. 9⅝ in. (24.8 cm.)
W. 2⅝ in. (6.5 cm.)
H. 4⅞ in. (12.4 cm.)

Courtesy of William K. Ackroyd.

21. MITER PLANE
by Addison Heald (1817-1895) and Daniel Milton Heald (1852-1929) of Milford.

Marks: "A.HEALD & SON" in serrated rectangle, "MILFORD.N.H." in serrated rectangle on fore end; "BUCK BROTHERS/WARRANTED/ [CAST STEEL]" on double iron.

This plane has narrow proportions and an iron set at an angle of about 40° to facilitate cutting the end grain of miters on picture and looking-glass frames. The tool is also unusual in being fashioned from ebony. Despite the hardness of the wood, the plane has sustained wear on its sole and damage from being struck to loosen the wedge.

Materials: Ebony, rosewood (wedge and striking button).
Dimensions: L. 9 in. (22.9 cm.)
W. 2¼ in. (5.6 cm.)
H. 4½ in. (11.3 cm.)

Courtesy of Fred W. Courser, Jr.

22. SMOOTHING PLANE
by Addison Heald (1817-1895) of Milford.

Marks: "ADDISON HEALD" in curved serrated banner above star with rays, "MILFORD.N.H." in serrated rectangle under star, on fore end; "BUCK BROTHERS/ WARRANTED/CAST STEEL" on double iron.

This attractive and little-used plane may represent Heald's work soon after he moved to Milford in 1868. It is one of several planes marked either by Addison Heald alone or with his son which are fashioned from exotic woods. Possibly Heald found such woods available in his brother David's furniture factory, where the planemaker reestablished his business after moving from Hudson.

Materials: Rosewood.
Dimensions: L. 7⅝ in. (19.2 cm.)
W. 2⅝ in. (6.6 cm.)
H. 5⅜ in. (13.5 cm.)

Courtesy of Margaret Scott Carter.

The Tools

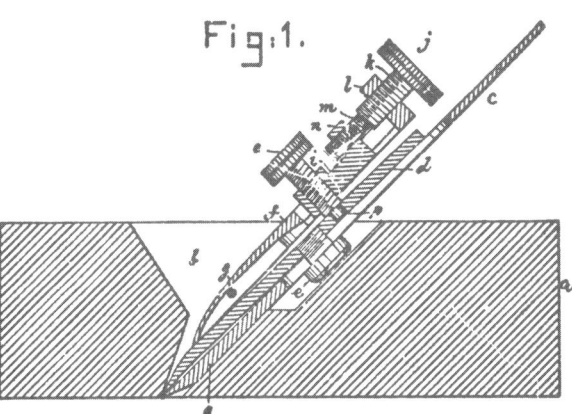

D. M. Heald's patent drawing for a bench plane, 1878.

The Sanborns

*D*ESCENDED *from skilled woodworkers on both sides of his family, Littleton planemaker David Page Sanborn (1810-1871) was a native of Sanbornton. At the age of fifteen he moved with his family to Littleton, where in 1831 he married a daughter of the local builder James Dow (1792-1876), and where he was manufacturing planes as early as 1840. By the late 1840s Sanborn was in partnership with his brother-in-law, Franklin J. Gouch, manufacturing planes in Worcester, Massachusetts. In 1849 or 1850 Sanborn returned to Littleton where he made planes until his death in 1871. At times he supplemented the plane business with the manufacture of churns, washing machines, and other woodwork. In 1866 Sanborn was in partnership with his son, Francis Davidson Sanborn (1834-1880), and by 1869 one or both of the Sanborns were associated with their in-law Minot Weeks (1841-1873) in the Littleton planemaking partnership of Sanborn & Weeks. After David P. Sanborn's death in 1871 and Minot Weeks's death in 1873, the younger Sanborn continued to make all kinds of woodenware, including rules and tool handles, but no longer advertised planes.*

23. MOULDING TOOL
by David Page Sanborn (1810-1871) of Littleton.

Marks: "D.P.SANBORN/ LITTLETON" in impressed letters on fore end; owner's mark, "W. E. BADGER" impressed on fore end.

This large tool, with its two staggered single irons, produces a 3½-inch-wide ogee moulding of the type often used in cabinetwork during the mid-nineteenth century. Sanborn may have substituted two irons for a single wide cutter for ease of sharpening, or to allow the outer edges of the mouths to be cut close to the sides of the stock without weakening the tool. A surviving letter from Sanborn to a potential customer tells that the planemaker fashioned his tools from "timber seasoned 8 years."

Materials: Beech.
Dimensions: L. 16⅛ in. (40.9 cm.)
W. 4⅜ in. (11.0 cm.)
H. 7¼ in. (18.3 cm.)

Courtesy of Wendall E. Badger.

24. MOULDING TOOL
by David Page Sanborn (1810-1871) of Littleton.

Marks: "D.P.SANBORN" in impressed letters, "N.H" in oval with tails, on fore end; owner's marks, "C.Q.GILMAN" in impressed letters stamped diagonally twice on fore end; "PROVIDENCE/TOOL CO." stamped on one single iron; and "PHILIP LAW" in serrated semicircle enclosing a crown on the second single iron.

If passed over a six-inch board from alternate ends, this large tool would produce a complex, delicate, and symmetrical door or window casing of the type popular in the mid-nineteenth century. The survival of many similar casing planes by various makers attests the continued importance of the handmade moulding well after the introduction of machine stickers.

Materials: Beech.
Dimensions: L. 14⅞ in. (37.8 cm.)
W. 5⅛ in. (13.1 cm.)
H. 6⅞ in. (17.5 cm.)

Courtesy of Margaret Scott Carter.

25. PLOW
by David Page Sanborn (1810-1871) of Littleton.

Marks: "D.P.SANBORN/ LITTLETON" in impressed letters on fore end; owner's mark, "W. E. BADGER" in impressed letters on fore end.

Sanborn's tools are second to those of no other New Hampshire maker in design and workmanship. This beautiful tool, though fashioned of native beech rather than an exotic wood, has refined and delicate mouldings and turnings. Coupled with its workmanlike quality of construction, these features place the tool among the finest ever made in New Hampshire.

Materials: Beech, boxwood (arms, nuts, boxing on fence).
Dimensions: L. 9⅜ in. (23.7 cm.)
              W. 10½ in. (26.7 cm.)
              H. 7⅛ in. (18.0 cm.)
Courtesy of Wendall E. Badger.

26. MOULDING TOOL
by David Page Sanborn (1810-1871) of Littleton.

Marks: "D.P.SANBORN/ LITTLETON" in impressed letters, "N.H" in oval with tails, on fore end; owners' marks, "J.K.KELSEY" and "W. E. BADGER" on fore end; "WM. ASH & CO." on iron.

This tool produces a two-inch-wide double torus and cavetto moulding which might have served as picture frame stock or as an architectural backband to enframe an interior door or window casing. The persistence of hand tools for fashioning such complex mouldings points out the incomplete dominance of the machine moulder during the late nineteenth century.

Materials: Beech.
Dimensions: L. 9½ in. (24.2 cm.)
              W. 3 in. (7.5 cm.)
              H. 6 in. (15.3 cm.)
Courtesy of Wendall E. Badger.

The Miltons

JOSEPH MILTON (1789-1864) and his son Matthew Harvey Milton (1819-1905) worked as cabinetmakers and planemakers in Canaan, New Hampshire, a small town surprisingly active in the nineteenth century in the production of hammers and awls as well as planes. As Joseph Milton was born in Henniker and married a native of neighboring Hopkinton, he was probably influenced, if not actually trained, by Hopkinton joiner/cabinetmaker Joshua Morse, Jr. (1774-1826), one of the first woodworkers in the state to advertise his emphasis on planemaking. Joseph Milton moved to Canaan by 1818 but named his son, born the following year, after a prominent Hopkinton citizen, Matthew Harvey. Joseph Milton may have continued planemaking until his death in 1864, but Matthew followed the trade he learned from his father only until 1854. After that time, he became a merchant, operating businesses at various times in Canaan and Lowell, Massachusetts.

27. JOINTER
by Joseph Milton (1789-1864) and Matthew Harvey Milton (1819-1905) of Canaan.

Marks: "M.H.MILTON" in serrated rectangle, "CANAAN, N.H." in serrated rectangle, "J.MILTON" in serrated rectangle on fore end; "BUCK BROTHERS/WARRANTED/CAST STEEL" in serrated semicircle on iron.

Because M. H. Milton stamped this plane, yet retired from toolmaking to become a merchant in 1854, the tool must date before that time. Other known jointers stamped only by Joseph, M. H. Milton's father, retain the eighteenth-century characteristic of very wide chamfering and may reflect Joseph's presumed training in Hopkinton, a planemaking center in the early nineteenth century. In 1850, when father and son apparently were working together, M. H. Milton appears to have run the business and to have produced about 250 planes, worth $500, each year.

Materials: Beech.
Dimensions: L. 30 in. (76.2 cm.)
W. 3½ in. (8.9 cm.)
H. 7⅞ in. (19.9 cm.)
New Hampshire Historical Society, gift of Kenneth D. Roberts.

28. PLOW
by Joseph Milton (1789-1864) of Canaan.

Marks: "J.MILTON" in serrated rectangle on fore end.

This sliding-arm plow is unusual in having a brass skate or keel—perhaps a replacement, since other known examples by Joseph Milton have the usual steel skate. Though carefully made, this form of plow is one of the least expensive variations commonly manufactured, having wooden thumbscrews to hold the depth stop and the unthreaded arms.

Materials: Beech.
Dimensions: L. 9⅞ in. (25.1 cm.)
W. 9⅛ in. (23.0 cm.)
H. 6¾ in. (17.0 cm.)
Courtesy of Fred W. Courser, Jr.

29. FIXED PLOW
by Philip Sargent (1790-1858) of Concord.

Marks: "P.SARGENT" in serrated rectangle, "CONCORD" in serrated rectangle, "N.H." in serrated rectangle, on fore end; "J.L.F." in serrated rectangle on fore end.

Similar to a grooving plane but equipped with a scoring iron set into the skate ahead of the $3/16$-inch blade, this tool bears the inititals of John L. French (1824-1891). French worked as a coach body-maker for the Concord carriage manufactories of J. Stephens Abbot and the Abbot-Downing Company from 1850 until his death. A similar plow in another collection has the initials of Charles H. Adams, another Concord coach builder who died in 1892 and whose career, like French's, spanned forty years. Since toolmaker Sargent died in 1858, both carriage builders must have bought these tools within the first years of their employment in Concord.

Materials: Beech.
Dimensions: L. 12 in. (30.4 cm.)
W. 1 3/8 in. (3.3 cm.)
H. 6 1/4 in. (15.8 cm.)

Courtesy of an anonymous lender.

30. COACHMAKER'S T RABBET COMPASS PLANE
by Philip Sargent (1790-1858) of Concord.

Marks: "P.SARGENT" in serrated rectangle on fore end; owner's mark, "C.P.V." in impressed letters on fore end; "W.ASH & CO." on iron.

A specialized form used (with both straight and curved soles) by carriagemakers, this plane illustrates Sargent's custom toolmaking for the many Concord craftsmen who worked in the coachbuilding trades. The owner's initials on this plane almost certainly denote Charles P. Virgin (1824-1910), who worked as a carriagemaker at J. Stephens Abbot's shop and at the Abbot-Downing Company from about 1853 until about 1900.

Materials: Beech.
Dimensions: L. 7 in. (17.8 cm.)
W. 1 3/8 in. (3.4 cm.)
H. 5 1/2 in. (13.7 cm.)

Courtesy of an anonymous lender.

Philip Sargent

PHILIP SARGENT (1790-1858), the leading planemaker of the state capital, is now identified as a joiner who came to Concord about 1827 from neighboring Bow, where he was born and married. Beginning in 1827 Sargent served his adopted town for many years as surveyor of lumber, an office frequently assigned to joiners and other skilled woodworkers. After 1844 Sargent was listed in directories specifically as a "plane maker," but he had probably sold tools to some extent before deciding to concentrate on their manufacture. In comparison with the state's other major planemakers, Sargent seems to have produced a relatively high percentage of the specialized planes used by carriagemakers, probably reflecting Concord's growing reputation as a coachmaking center. Unlike his counterparts in other New Hampshire towns, Sargent was not able to establish a family toolmaking business because his two children had died just before his move to Concord.

31. PLOW
by Philip Sargent (1790-1858) of Concord.

Marks: "P.SARGENT" in serrated rectangle, "CONCORD" in serrated rectangle, "N.H." in serrated rectangle, on fore end; owner's mark, "J.HODGE." in impressed letters on fore end.

Though not an expensive model, this sliding-arm plow is trimmed with brass and has a finely moulded fence. It probably belonged to Jeremiah Hodge (1830-1917), a Concord carpenter who moved to Manchester in 1853 and became the city's largest door, sash, and blind manufacturer. About 1865 Hodge became the first to introduce machine moulders to Manchester, and later advertised himself as the proprietor of the "only block corner and fancy panelling machine in the city." His machines were eventually capable of cutting some 2,000 different moulding profiles.

Materials: Beech.
Dimensions: L. 11⅛ in. (28.1 cm.)
W. 10 in. (25.4 cm.)
H. 7⅛ in. (17.9 cm.)
Courtesy of William K. Ackroyd.

Instruments of Change

32. MOULDING TOOL
by Philip Sargent (1790-1858) of Concord.

Marks: "P.SARGENT" in serrated rectangle, "CONCORD" in serrated rectangle, "N.H." in serrated rectangle, on fore end.

This tool makes a beautiful quirked ogee and bead, popular for backband mouldings around door and window casings through the early nineteenth century. Given its early profile, this tool may date from the first years of Sargent's career. Although he maintained only a small shop with no mechanical power, Sargent remained a progressive planemaker throughout his life. Just before his death, Sargent made and marked at least one beech jack plane which utilized a cam-action plane iron cap patented in 1857 by William Stoddard of Lowell, Massachusetts.

Materials: Beech.
Dimensions: L. 9½ in. (24.2 cm.)
             W. 2¼ in. (5.7 cm.)
             H. 5⅜ in. (13.6 cm.)
Courtesy of Kenneth D. Roberts.

33. RAZEE JACK PLANE
by Elias Rugg (1803-1882) of Keene.

Marks: "E.RUGG" in rectangle on fore end; "DWIGHTS FRENCH & CO." on iron.

Many have speculated whether razee planes (planes with the top of the stock dropped at the breech end) were used uniquely by shipbuilders, or by any carpenter according to his preference. Since this plane was made in a corner of New Hampshire some seventy-five miles from the sea, it may have been intended for use by inland woodworkers. The maker, Elias Rugg, probably served a close-knit circle of local customers. Since Rugg is commonly listed as a "pattern maker," his production of planes may have been a sideline. There was a strong connection between the precise and sometimes sculptural woodworking required of patternmakers and planemakers alike; Cyrus Warren, one of New Hampshire's leading planemakers, was described in his son's obituary in 1900 as a "well-known pattern maker."

Materials: Beech.
Dimensions: L. 16¼ in. (41.1 cm.)
             W. 2¾ in. (6.8 cm.)
             H. 5¼ in. (13.4 cm.)
Courtesy of Margaret Scott Carter.

34. SMOOTHING PLANE
by Daniel Durgin (1792-1847) of Dover.

Marks: "D.DURGIN★" in serrated rectangle, "DOVER, N.H" in serrated rectangle, on fore end; "W.GREAVES/& SONS" in conforming serrated outline, "WARRANTED/CAST STEEL" in conforming serrated outline, on cutter; "SHEAF WORKS" in cartouche on cap iron of double iron.

This well-formed tool is one of several surviving bench planes made by Durgin. The son of a carpenter, Durgin moved from the country town of New Durham to Dover in 1824 and worked as a house carpenter until dying suddenly in the summer of 1847. His production of planes is likely to have been occasional and limited in quantity, but his workmanship was excellent.

Materials: Beech.
Dimensions: L. 8 in. (20.2 cm.)
             W. 2¾ in. (7.0 cm.)
             H. 4⅞ in. (12.3 cm.)
Courtesy of Malcolm G. MacGregor, Jr.

The Tools

35.
¼-inch side bead.
Marks: "D.SARGENT." in serrated rectangle, "NASHUA" in serrated rectangle, "NH" in plain rectangle, on fore end; owners' marks, "W.W.H.," "J.DOW," "W.D.J." in serrated rectangle, "W. E. BADGER," on fore end; "W.W.H.," "¼" on breech end.

Materials: Beech, boxwood (single boxed).
Dimensions: L. 9⅝ in. (24.3 cm.)
W. 1 in. (2.6 cm.)
H. 5⅞ in. (15.0 cm.)
Courtesy of Wendall E. Badger.

36.
¾-inch side bead.
Marks: "D.SARGENT." in serrated rectangle, "MANCHESTER." in serrated rectangle, "NH" in plain rectangle, on fore end; owners' marks, "S.FELLOWS" in serrated rectangle, "W. E. BADGER," on fore end; "¾" on breech end.

Materials: Beech, boxwood (double boxed).
Dimensions: L. 9½ in. (24.1 cm.)
W. 1¾ in. (4.3 cm.)
H. 5⅞ in. (14.8 cm.)
Courtesy of Fred W. Courser, Jr.

35-36. TWO MOULDING TOOLS
by Dana Sargent (1818-1884) of Hudson, Nashua, and Manchester.

These two tools illustrate the complex entrepreneurial career of planemaker and merchant Dana Sargent. A native of Nottingham West (Hudson), Sargent "learned the trade of making carpenters' planes" in his youth and "followed that occupation for some time in his native place." It is likely that Sargent was trained by Cyrus Warren, with whom he later lived upon returning from a career in the hardware business in Manchester and Lawrence, Massachusetts. During his early Hudson years, Sargent apparently marked his planes "NASHUA," as did the Warrens. The tool directly above, marked "MANCHESTER," represents the eight-year period during the 1840s when Sargent engaged in the hardware business in Manchester, evidently continuing to manufacture planes or to employ others to do so under his name. The tool apparently belonged to Stillman Fellows, who worked as a joiner and carpenter in Manchester during the 1840s and early 1850s. Returning to Nashua about 1860, Sargent became a leading merchant and, in 1871, the mayor of the city.

Instruments of Change

37. Smoothing plane.
Marks: "EAYRS & CO." in serrated banner, "MAKER'S" in serrated rectangle, "NASHUA.NH" in serrated rectangle, on fore end; owners' marks, "L.E.BEEDE" over earlier owner's mark, on fore end; "A.D.GREENE/CAST STEEL/ WARRANTED" on double iron.

Materials: Rosewood.
Dimensions: L. 7¾ in. (19.6 cm.)
               W. 2¾ in. (6.8 cm.)
               H. 5 in. (12.7 cm.)

Courtesy of Margaret Scott Carter.

38. Toothing plane.
Marks: "EAYRS & CO." in serrated banner, "MAKER'S" in serrated rectangle, "NASHUA.NH" in serrated rectangle, on fore end; "BUCK BROTHERS/ WARRANTED/CAST STEEL" on iron.

Materials: Rosewood.
Dimensions: L. 7½ in. (19.0 cm.)
               W. 2⅝ in. (6.5 cm.)
               H. 7¾ in. (19.5 cm.)

Courtesy of William K. Ackroyd.

37-38. TWO BENCH PLANES by Eayrs & Company (at work c. 1850), Nashua.

Beautifully fashioned from choice exotic woods, these tools represent the somewhat enigmatic partnership of John and James Eayrs of Nashua. Listed in the 1850 census as John Eayrs & Company, the firm combined the manufacture of emery with sawmilling. Consuming 100 tons of emery stone and employing five men to manufacture $12,000 worth of fine emery, the company also had a water-powered saw and produced 100,000 board feet of lumber in 1850. The firm's production of planes and moulding tools, while evidently a sideline, must have been considerable; a number of bench planes of various sizes, and some moulding tools (mostly of beech), survive in private collections.

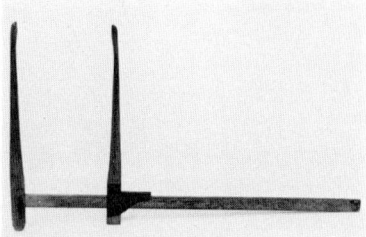

39. LOG CALIPERS
by Gustavus B. Sanborn (1848-1902) of Bristol.

Marks: "Manufactured by/G. B. SANBORN/BRISTOL, N.H." on sliding arm.

Sanborn advertised that his log calipers had tally holes for pegs used to keep running totals of the volume of logs as they were measured, "without making a mark or figure." Sanborn sold calipers which were calibrated in various ways according to the needs of users and which utilized various long-established tables for calculating the marketable volume of a round sawlog of any diameter. By measuring the diameter of logs with the caliper arms and reading the line on the blade which corresponds to the length of the log, the user can calculate the cubic feet available after squaring the log or, with different calipers, the contents of the log in fractions of a cord (128 cubic feet). The calipers illustrated here measure the volume, in cubic feet, of logs varying in length from 15 to 31 feet.

Materials: Birch.
Dimensions: L. 36 in. (91.2 cm.)
             W. 19⅞ in. (50.3 cm.)
             H. ¾ in. (1.8 cm.)
Courtesy of William K. Ackroyd.

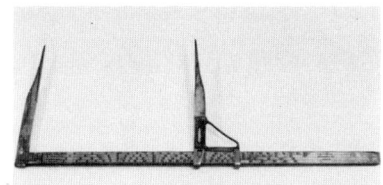

40. LOG CALIPERS
by L. B. Sargent of Plymouth.

Marks: "L. B. SARGENT/PLYMOUTH N.H./MAKER," "N.H. CALIPER/3/4 INCH BARK/ALLOWANCE/No. 203," on blade; "NEW HAMPSHIRE/DEPARTMENT OF AGRICULTURE/TESTED/AND/SEALED/N.H. 53" on reverse of blade.

The Plymouth-Bristol-Groton region of New Hampshire was one of several centers of log caliper and board rule production during the late nineteenth century. Sargent's "New Hampshire Calipers," calibrated in this instance to measure the number of marketable cubic feet contained in logs from eight to twenty feet long, share a type of brass casting with calipers made by the Greenleafs in Littleton. A single foundry probably served as a common source for hardware used by several caliper makers.

Materials: Maple.
Dimensions: L. 48 in. (121.9 cm.)
             W. 19⅝ in. (49.9 cm.)
             H. 1⅛ in. (2.9 cm.)
Courtesy of Margaret Scott Carter.

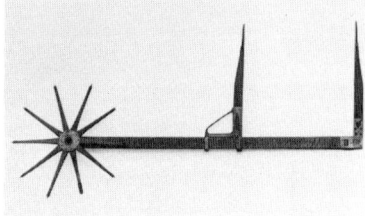

41. LOG CALIPERS
by William Gardner Greenleaf (1834-1916) of Littleton.

Marks: "WM. GREENLEAF/LITTLETON/N.H./MAKER" on blade.

William G. Greenleaf spent most of his career as a woodworker, carriagemaker, and wheelwright, retiring about 1903. According to his obituary, he spent his retirement "occupied at his home in the manufacture of calipers," but presumably he had mastered the trade earlier and engaged in it part-time. The calipers illustrated here measure the usable volume in cubic feet for logs ranging in length from twelve to thirty-eight feet. Many calipers, like this one, have weighted wheels for the rapid measurement of log lengths without a tape or stick. In this case, one revolution of the wheel measures five feet; each spoke marks off six inches. Many collectors believe that such wheels were added to calipers for convenience after their manufacture.

Materials: Maple.
Dimensions: L. 56½ in. (143.3 cm.)
             W. 28⅛ in. (71.6 cm.)
             H. 3 in. (7.7 cm.)

New Hampshire Historical Society, gift of Janet Condon in memory of Lee Vincent.

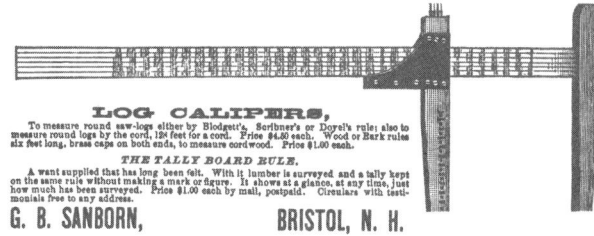

Instruments of Change

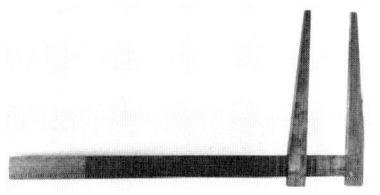

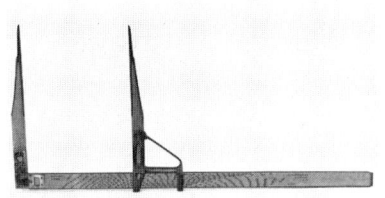

42. LOG CALIPERS
by Florence M. Greenleaf (b. 1882) of Littleton (later of Belmont, Massachusetts, and Jacksonville, Alabama).

Marks: "F. M. GREENLEAF/ LITTLETON/N.H./MAKER" on blade.

Florence Greenleaf was one of New Hampshire's few identified woman toolmakers. Evidently taught to make calipers by her father, "Flossie" Greenleaf occasionally marked the wooden blades of calipers on which the brass fittings bore the name of William. Florence Greenleaf was a violinist both in Littleton and, later, in Belmont, where she lived until 1921 while playing professionally with the Boston Symphony Orchestra. Wherever she traveled, Greenleaf used her skill as a maker of calipers; some are marked in Belmont, and others in Jacksonville, Alabama, where she was living until 1926.

Materials: Maple.
Dimensions: L. 42¼ in. (107.0 cm.)
             W. 18½ in. (46.9 cm.)
             H. 1⅛ in. (2.7 cm.)

Courtesy of William K. Ackroyd.

43. LOG CALIPERS
by W. A. Wheeler of Littleton.

Marks: "MADE BY/W. A. WHEELER/LITTLETON, N.H." star in circular impression, on opposite sides of brass slide; "N.H." on blade.

Like the calipers of Gustavus B. Sanborn, these Wheeler calipers have tally pegs and holes (on the reverse of the side seen in the photograph) for keeping a total of log volumes measured in hundreds or thousands of cubic feet. These calipers calculate the marketable volume of logs in cubic feet and are calibrated for logs ranging from twelve to thirty-one feet in length.

Materials: Birch.
Dimensions: L. 38 in. (96.4 cm.)
             W. 23⅛ in. (58.8 cm.)
             H. ⅞ in. (2.2 cm.)

New Hampshire Historical Society, purchase.

44. LOG CALIPERS
by Humphrey Machine Company of Keene.

Marks: "Improved Calliper Scale of Cord or Cubic Measure/ MANUFACTURED BY/John Humphrey & Co., Keene, N.H."; "J. HUMPHREY/KEENE. [N.H.]" on paper labels on each face of fixed arm.

John Humphrey & Company was a partnership, from about 1868 to about 1872, of John Humphrey and Lewis Herrick of Keene. By 1874 the firm had been renamed the Humphrey Machine Company and was manufacturing water turbines, pumps, machine tools, shafting and pulleys, woodworking machinery, and log calipers. The company used its engineering skill to devise calipers which, according to an 1882 brochure, were "based on correct mathematical principle and [were] thoroughly proven by actual tests by practical lumbermen during nearly forty years of use." These calipers computed the volume of logs in board feet or cords, or both (on opposite sides of the blade). The board measure scales were designed "to show the number of square feet of one inch square edge and parallel sided boards which . . . should be produced from ordinary straight and merchantable logs of different diameters and lengths," while the cord scales showed contents of a log in hundredths of a cord.

Materials: Birch.
Dimensions: L. 48⅛ in. (122.1 cm.)
             W. 23⅛ in. (58.9 cm.)
             H. 1⅛ in. (2.8 cm.)

Courtesy of Kenneth D. Roberts; brochure (1882) of Humphrey Machine Company courtesy of Paul B. Kebabian.

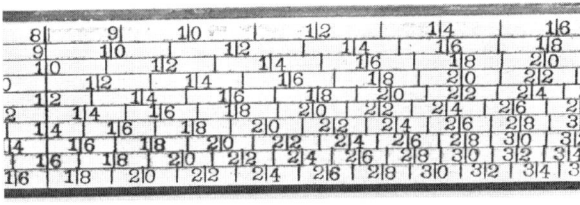

Detail of calibration of a Greenleaf log caliper.

The Haseltons

NEW HAMPSHIRE's most prolific makers of rules and gauges in the late 1800s were Rufus B. Haselton (1828-1879) and his son Hermon R. Haselton (1856-1939). Rufus Haselton is said to have begun the production of maple yardsticks, wine gauges, calipers, and framing squares in Groton in 1847. A few years later, according to tradition, Haselton went to California, prospected successfully for gold, returned to Groton, went to California a second time, and returned permanently to New Hampshire. Perhaps encouraged by the sight of the large trees that were being harvested in the West as well as by the expansion of lumbering in the mountains of New England, Haselton commenced the production of board rules in lengths ranging from two to six feet, and of log calipers. At some point in his career, Haselton had dies cut for his name and for his eagle trademark. These dies were later used without change by the son, Hermon, who began to manufacture rules and gauges in Contoocook Village, in the town of Hopkinton, about 1880. Both father and son made many specialized measuring devices ranging from ordinary rulers and yardsticks to glazier's and saddler's rules, and including outing sticks, wantage rods, and wine gauges for use in cooperage. All Haselton rules were "Warranted Correct." Many are finished in an attractive orange color which is said to have been attained by a secret formula that was lost forever at the death of Hermon R. Haselton in 1939.

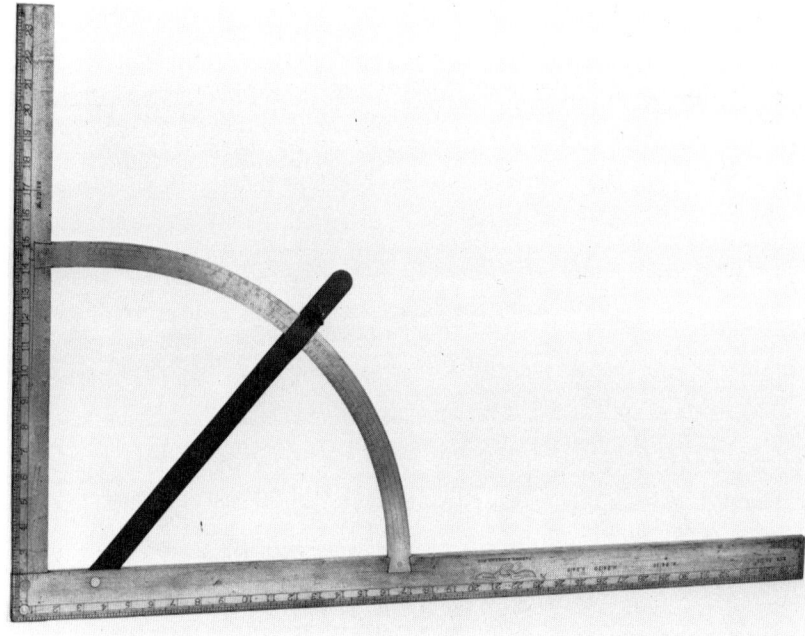

45. FRAMING SQUARE
by Rufus B. Haselton (1828-1879) of Groton (later of Contoocook).

Marks: "R.B.HASELTON/MAKER/GROTON.N.H." within eagle outline, "PATENT.APPLIED.FOR." in impressed letters, on blade.

The practice of framing buildings with sawn two-inch-thick scantlings rather than with hewn timber became increasingly prevalent during the nineteenth century. Old methods of calculating the length and cuts of framing members by graphic means, using carpenter's dividers and scribes, gradually gave way to the use of framing squares similar to those still manufactured today. Improvements in the square accumulated during the century, culminating in instruments with which a carpenter could carry out complicated calculations and solve elaborate framing problems. This square, designed by Rufus B. Haselton, makes use of an iron bevel and a brass quadrant to guide the layout of the complex cuts required where rafter ends intersect other members. Such cuts became increasingly difficult as new architectural styles during the latter half of the century introduced dormers, towers, and complex intersecting roof planes. While there is no record of Haselton's having secured a patent for this sophisticated square, its invention demonstrates a powerful mathematical mind.

Materials: Maple.
Dimensions: L. 36 in. (91.5 cm.)
W. 24 in. (61.0 cm.)
H. 3/8 in. (1.0 cm.)

New Hampshire Historical Society, purchase.

46. WANTAGE ROD
by Thomas Salter Bowles (1785-1851) of Portsmouth.

Marks: "Made by.Thomas S. Bowles.Portsmouth.NH."

This rule computes the wantage or empty portion of a partly filled cask and is graduated for barrels, hogsheads, pipes, puncheons, and tierces. Such rules were essential in an age when all liquid commodities were stored and shipped in casks. The maker was a native of Portsmouth who began work as a mathematical instrument maker about 1806 and moved to Portland, Maine, by 1825. Bowles not only fashioned surveying compasses, navigating instruments, and telescopes but also advertised "Callipers, Guaging Rods, Board Rules, Want Sticks, &c."

Materials: Cherry.
Dimensions: L. 15⅝ in. (39.8 cm.)
W. ⅝ in. (1.5 cm.)
H. ⅝ in. (1.5 cm.)

New Hampshire Historical Society, James Cowan Sawyer Collection, gift of George F. and Charles H. Sawyer.

47. WANTAGE ROD
by Rufus B. Haselton (1828-1879) of Groton (later of Contoocook).

Marks: "R.B.HASELTON/MAKER/GROTON.N.H."

Graduated for barrels, tierces, and hogsheads, this rule is exceptional in being made of brass; it may have been intended as a standard for the rulemaker's use in laying out wooden duplicates for sale. Hermon Haselton, who took over the business after his father's death, advertised that he manufactured wine gauges, and some of these, made of wood, are privately owned. These measuring devices for liquids, like those for measuring solids and for calculating joints in carpentry, demonstrate the tremendous versatility and mathematical sophistication required of a rule manufacturer.

Materials: Brass.
Dimensions: L. 23⅝ in. (59.9 cm.)
W. 4⅛ in. (10.3 cm.)
H. 1¼ in. (3.3 cm.)

Courtesy of Fred W. Courser, Jr.

48. GAUGING ROD
by Thomas Rowell Hoyt (1811-1898) of Goffstown.

Marks: "T.R.HOYT." in impressed letters around perimeter of scribed semicircle, "1865" in impressed numerals within scribed semicircle; paper label with title "HOYT'S IMPROVED, CORRECT GAUGING ROD, FOR MEASURING CASKS AND LIQUORS./Very useful for Traders in taking account of Stock," with instructions for use (see below).

Thomas R. Hoyt possessed an inquiring mind which led him to combine mathematical instrument making with civil engineering, farming, and the composition of poetry. A paper label attached to this gauging rod tells how this and similar rules were used:

"TO FIND WHAT A CASK WILL HOLD. — Put the brass end of the rod into the bung-hole, and run the rod down obliquely or slanting to the bottom of one head at the chime, the side marked A up; then look where the bung-hole cuts the rod and there is the answer in gallons. Every Farmer who has a Cider Mill should have one of these rods.

"TO MEASURE LIQUOR IN A CASK PARTLY FULL. — You have measured your cask and find it will hold 40 gallons [for example], then run the brass end of the rod straight down the bung-hole to the bottom of the cask; as far up on the 40 gallons [scale] as where the liquor cuts the rod is the answer in gallons. So of the rest of the numbers: 16, 32, 46, 120 and 150 gallons."

Materials: Cherry, brass.
Dimensions: L. 46¾ in. (118.9 cm.)
W. ⅞ in. (2.1 cm.)
H. ¾ in. (2.0 cm.)

Courtesy of Paul B. Kebabian.

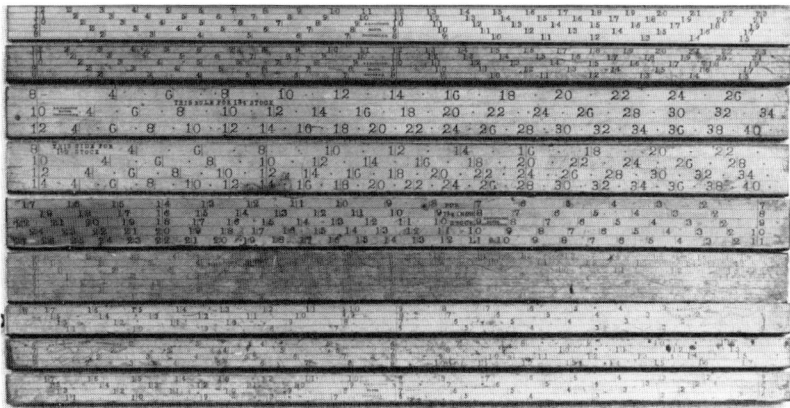

49. LUMBER RULES
by Rufus B. Haselton (1828-1879) and/or Hermon R. Haselton (1856-1939) of Groton and Contoocook.

Marks: "R.B.HASELTON./MAKER./GROTON.N.H." or "R.B.HASELTON./MAKER./CONTOOCOOK.N.H."

The Haseltons appear to have begun to work in Contoocook in the mid-1870s. Because Rufus Haselton died in 1879, most of the rules bearing the Contoocook mark are assumed to be the work of Hermon, who continued to use his father's old die throughout his career. This selection of lumber rules, held against the ends of boards in either the right or left hand, calculate the number of board feet in lumber of various lengths and thicknesses. Top to bottom:

Materials: Maple.
1. RUFUS B. HASELTON or HERMON R. HASELTON, Contoocook, maple right-hand 24-inch rule for board lengths from 8 to 19 feet.
2. RUFUS B. HASELTON, Groton, maple right-hand 24-inch rule for board lengths from 8 to 21 feet.
3. RUFUS B. HASELTON or HERMON R. HASELTON, Contoocook, maple right-hand 24-inch rule for 1¾-inch-thick boards in lengths from 8 to 18 feet.
4. RUFUS B. HASELTON or HERMON R. HASELTON, Contoocook, maple right-hand 24-inch rule for 1½-inch-thick boards in lengths from 8 to 14 feet.
5. RUFUS B. HASELTON or HERMON R. HASELTON, Contoocook, maple left-hand 24-inch rule for 1¼-inch-thick boards in lengths from 7 to 16 feet.
6. RUFUS B. HASELTON or HERMON R. HASELTON, Contoocook, maple right-hand 24-inch rule for board lengths from 3 to 20 feet.
7. RUFUS B. HASELTON or HERMON R. HASELTON, Contoocook, maple left-hand 24-inch rule for board lengths from 6 to 20 feet, with eagle trademark.
8. RUFUS B. HASELTON or HERMON R. HASELTON, Contoocook, maple right-hand 24-inch rule for board lengths from 6 to 20 feet, with eagle trademark.
9. RUFUS B. HASELTON, Groton, maple left-hand 24-inch rule for board lengths from 6 to 20 feet.

Courtesy of Fred W. Courser, Jr.

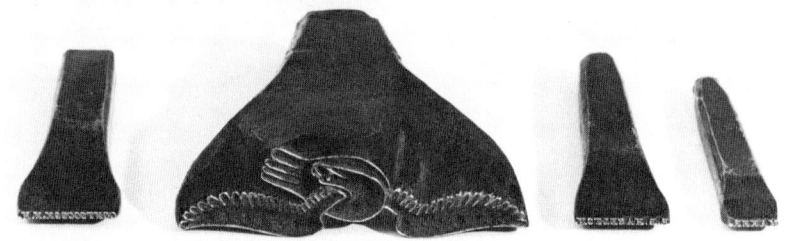

50. DIES
used by Rufus B. Haselton (1828-1879) and by Hermon R. Haselton (1856-1939) of Groton and Contoocook.

Marks: "A.GROVER./LOWELL, MASS."

These dies bear the words "R.B.HASELTON.," "MAKER.," and "CONTOOCOOK.N.H.," and provide the eagle outline which always served on larger products as the Haselton trademark. Other dies in the same set calibrate rules in eighths and sixteenths of an inch; one of these bears the owner's mark, "R.B.H." The stamp bearing the word "GROTON." has not been located, nor have the arabic numeral dies of various sizes used by the Haseltons. In the same collection is a claw hammer with octagonal face and owner's initials "RH." This is thought to have been used to strike the dies.

Materials: Steel.

Courtesy of Fred W. Courser, Jr.

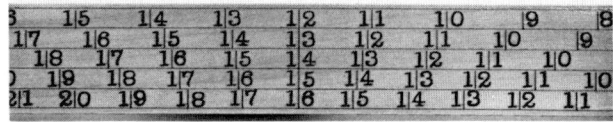

Detail of calibration on a Haselton lumber rule.

Instruments of Change

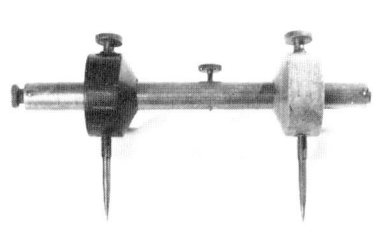

51. GAUGE AND DIVIDERS
by George Kenny of Nashua.

Marks: "KENNY'S U.S.STN'D," "PAT'D JAN. 4, 1870." on boxwood slide.

Kenny was a prominent Nashua carriage manufacturer who had worked previously at the same trade in Milford. He held several patents related to vehicles, including one for a carriage hub. The function Kenny claimed for this beautifully machined gauge in his patent application was "to produce a combined divider and gauge for carpenters' and others' use, which shall possess the advantages of the ordinary gauge, the splitting gauge, and a dividing gauge, for making mortises and other purposes."

Materials: Brass, boxwood, rosewood, steel.
Dimensions: L. 9½ in. (23.9 cm.)
W. 2⅛ in. (5.4 cm.)
H. 4⅞ in. (12.4 cm.)

Courtesy of Kenneth D. Roberts.

52. COOPER'S ADZE
probably by Benjamin Smith (c. 1736-1821) or Ballard Smith (1774-1863) of Nashua.

Marks: "·SMIT[H·]/CAST STE[EL]"

Nashua's prominence as a center of edge tool production derives from traditions begun in the early nineteenth century. Eleazer F. Ingalls, working near the site later occupied by the Underhill Edge Tool Company, specialized in edge tools from about 1810 to about 1822. The Smiths of Dunstable (Nashua) were also among the earliest New Hampshire blacksmiths to sell edge tools beyond their immediate vicinity. As early as 1766, Matthew Patten of Bedford noted in his diary that he "got 2 axes from Smith in Dunstable," and the Dunlap family of joiners, also from Bedford, purchased axes and drawknives from Smith of Dunstable in the early 1800s. By 1823 Dunstable supported four triphammer shops that collectively manufactured 1,500 dozen hoes each year, as well as scythes and axes. This adze is not stamped with the name of a town, but has a history of having been made in Hollis, a town adjacent to Nashua and once part of old Dunstable. Its mark, "CAST STEEL," recalls George Washington Underhill's assertion that his family made no use of this metal until about 1820. As stated in Benjamin Chase's History of Old Chester, *"It was first supposed to be incapable of standing, excepting laid on iron, and there was great secrecy about welding it. When it first came into use, it was not of assorted sizes, but about an inch square.... When blister steel was used, and in the early days of cast-steel, German steel was used for small tools."*

Materials: Steel, wrought iron, hickory handle.
Dimensions: L. 17 in. (43.2 cm.)
W. 2⅞ in. (7.2 cm.)
H. 9½ in. (24.0 cm.)

Courtesy of Fred W. Courser, Jr.

53. SOCKET FRAMING CHISEL
by William W. Leighton (1815-1885) of Manchester.

Marks: "LEIGHTON./MA[NCH]ESTER CAS[T] S[T]EE[L]"; owner's marks "RNH," "R.C.DOW" stamped twice (once covering "RNH").

William Leighton was one of those restless nineteenth-century mechanics who constantly sought new challenges. Born in Eliot, Maine, and trained in Boston by Samuel Graham Underhill, Leighton spent much of his life associated with the Underhills and their enterprises. He also maintained his own edge tool business at various periods. This chisel may date from the 1850s, when Leighton worked without partners in Manchester; other tools bear an "AUBURN" mark which denotes the nine years from 1856 to 1865 when the toolmaker had a four-man shop in that town. From 1850 to 1856, when he maintained his own Manchester business, Leighton produced some 4,800 axes each year. This chisel bears the owner's stamp of Robert C. Dow, a carpenter who worked in Manchester during the 1870s and 1880s.

Materials: Steel, wrought iron, hickory.
L. 15¾ in. (39.9 cm.)
W. 1⅛ in. (2.9 cm.)
H. 1½ in. (3.6 cm.)

Courtesy of an anonymous lender.

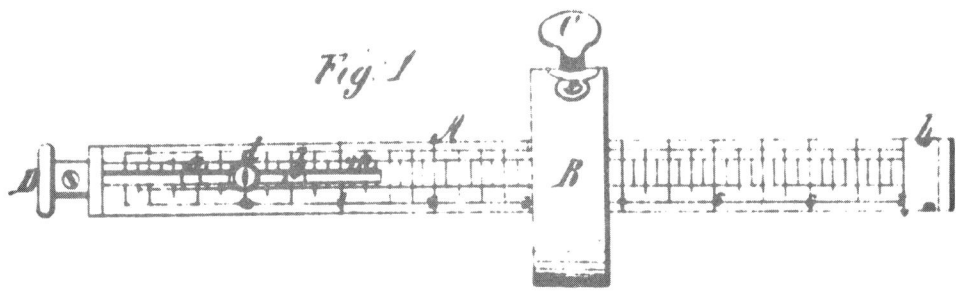

George Kenny's patent drawing for gauge and dividers, 1870.

The Underhills

THROUGHOUT the nineteenth century, the Underhill family was undoubtedly New Hampshire's leading manufacturer of axes, chisels, and related edge tools. At least eight members representing three generations of this family worked individually and in various partnerships and firms in Chester, Auburn, Manchester, Derry, and Nashua. The first Underhill known to have made edge tools was Josiah (1758-1822), a Chester blacksmith. During the 1820s, two of his sons gained experience in tool manufacture by working in Boston, where all four of the grandsons in the family business also spent part of their careers. In New Hampshire the Underhills were eventually involved with their in-laws, the Browns, and with a former employee, William W. Leighton, in a series of toolmaking enterprises centered either in Manchester or that part of Chester which was incorporated in 1845 as Auburn. In 1852 George Washington Underhill (1815-1882), a member of the third generation, established the Underhill Edge Tool Company in Nashua, where he had directed a smaller operation since 1839. After absorbing the Amoskeag Ax Company of Manchester (the firm's major New Hampshire competitor) in 1879, the Underhill Company maintained a large export trade with South America and Australia, but was itself purchased in 1890 by the American Axe and Tool Company, a national conglomerate known as the "Axe Trust." During its century of leadership, the Underhill toolmaking family took advantage of a series of technological advances both in power source and in furnace design.

54. SLICK
by Underhill, Brown & Leighton (at work 1849), Auburn.

Marks: "[U]NDER[HILL]/ [B]ROWN &/[L]EIGHTO[N]/ [CA]ST-STE[EL]," with first line inverted.

Though short-lived, this partnership continued a long tradition of edge tool manufacture in Auburn. William W. Leighton, the only partner in the firm to be identified with certainty, left Auburn in 1850 to establish his own axe business in Manchester, but the Underhill and Brown partnership continued in Auburn and in that year employed eight men to produce 1,200 axes, 1,200 hatchets, 2,400 chisels, and 650 shears. Owing to lack of rail transportation in Auburn, however, all manufacturers of edge tools had moved elsewhere by 1865. This slick, an unusually large and well-crafted example weighing nearly six pounds, is a specialized form of paring chisel meant to be pushed rather than struck. It was used by housewrights or carpenters and by shipwrights.

Materials: Steel, wrought iron, brass (ferrule), hickory.
Dimensions: L. 30⅞ in. (78.3 cm.)
W. 4 in. (10.0 cm.)
H. 2 in. (5.0 cm.)

Courtesy of Margaret Scott Carter.

55. SHIP CARPENTER'S LIP ADZE
by Underhill Edge Tool Company (at work 1852-1890), Nashua.

Marks: "UNDERHILL/EDGE TOOL C[O];" "HARTWELL [?]" in oval on handle.

This ship carpenter's adze, with a spur head for driving spikes or treenails into planking, is one of the many specialty items manufactured by the Underhill Company. The 1859 catalogue of the Underhill Edge Tool Company lists not only felling and hewing axes but also butcher's, cooper's, mason's, ice harvester's, and miner's implements. Underhill Edge Tool Company grew from the enterprise of George Washington Underhill (1815-1882), who learned his trade in the Chester shop of his father, Jesse Johnson Underhill (1784-1860), and then worked for his older brother Samuel Graham Underhill in Boston. Underhill's modest beginnings in Nashua are shown by his recollection that he carried the products of two days' labor to the railroad station in a wheelbarrow.

Materials: Steel, wrought iron, hickory (handle is apparently a replacement).
Dimensions: L. 30 in. (76.3 cm.)
W. 5 in. (12.5 cm.)
H. 10⅜ in. (26.2 cm.)

Courtesy of an anonymous lender.

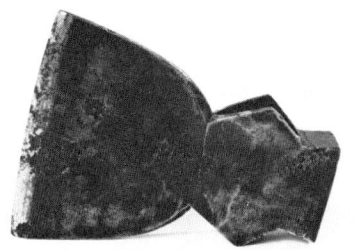

56-57. TWO HATCHETS
by the Underhill Edge Tool Company (at work 1852-1890), Nashua.

56. LEFT:
    Broad hatchet.
Marks: "UNDERHILL/EDGE TOOL CO"; "3" [pounds]

Materials: Steel, wrought iron.
Dimensions: L. 7¼ in. (18.3 cm.)
        W. 5½ in. (13.7 cm.)
        H. 1⅛ in. (2.9 cm.)

57. RIGHT:
    Claw hatchet.
Marks: "UNDERHILL/EDGE TOOL CO"

Materials: Steel, wrought iron.
Dimensions: L. 5¾ in. (14.5 cm.)
        W. 3½ in. (8.9 cm.)
        H. 1 in. (2.5 cm.)

These two hatchets represent a fraction of the varied production of New Hampshire's largest edge tool manufacturer. George Washington Underhill, the founder of the firm, recalled that when he established his business in Nashua in 1839 his daily production was nine felling axes or five broad axes. Eleven years later Underhill was employing seven men and making chisels and hatchets worth $10,000 a year. The enterprise became a stock company in 1852 and by 1865 was employing sixty men and producing 300 chopping axes and about 160 broad axes and other tools each day. The firm became still larger after buying out the Amoskeag Ax Company in 1879, employing ninety men ten hours a day and manufacturing $80,000 worth of edge tools each year.

Courtesy of an anonymous lender.

58. BROAD AXE
by Amoskeag Ax Company (at work 1862-1879), Manchester.

Marks: "AMOSKEAG AX CO"

With extreme flare and breadth of bit, this pattern of axe was called the "Pittsburg or Western" style by the Underhill Edge Tool Company (Amoskeag's major competitor in New Hampshire), and the "Pennsylvania" pattern by other American axe makers. The Amoskeag Ax Company was especially adept at producing a wide range of such specialized tools for varied markets. In 1870 fifty-five Amoskeag workmen, using fourteen triphammers, were producing 500 tools a day or 135,000 each year. Many Amoskeag axe patterns were produced with machinery for shaping and shaving axe heads patented by the company's inventive agent, Henry C. Reynolds (1829-1877); Reynolds also held patents on various axe and hatchet designs. The Amoskeag Ax Company had evolved from the earlier Blodgett Edge Tool Company (working from 1853 to 1862). It was absorbed in its turn by the Underhill Edge Tool Company in 1879.

Materials: Steel, wrought iron, hickory.
Dimensions: L. 35½ in. (90.1 cm.)
        W. 9⅛ in. (23.0 cm.)
        H. 1⅜ in. (3.5 cm.)

Courtesy of William K. Ackroyd.

59. BROAD AXE
by George D. Neville (1812-1892) of New Boston.

Marks: "G.D.NEVILLE/NEW-BOSTON"

This axe represents the work of one of New Hampshire's many small nineteenth-century edge tool factories. George D. Neville was a blacksmith who was "known far and wide for the axes he manufactured." He also made knives and shaves in a water-powered shop, employing two men. His annual product between 1850 and 1860 averaged 60 dozen knives, 20 dozen shaves, and 50 dozen axes.

Materials: Steel, wrought iron, hickory.
Dimensions: L. 24½ in. (62.3 cm.)
        W. 7⅝ in. (19.3 cm.)
        H. ⅞ in. (2.2 cm.)

Courtesy of Fred W. Courser, Jr.

H. C. Reynolds' patent drawing for an axe-making machine, 1867.

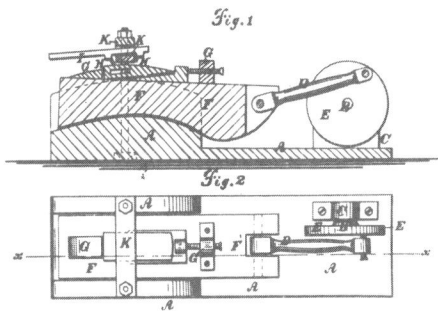

The Tools

60. FELLING AXE
by the New London Scythe Company (at work 1871-1888), New London.

Marks: "NEW LONDON SCYTHE C[O]/81/NEW LONDON N[H]"

In 1881 the New London Scythe Company built a "new axe shop" which permitted production to increase even beyond the 5,000 dozen axes manufactured the year before. A visitor described the scene at the completion of the new shop: "As one approaches the village in work hours he is saluted by an "Anvil Chorus," which is rhythmical if not musical.... Axes are made with the steel inlaid, or an overcoat. Here, as in the manufacture of scythes, skilled workmen are employed in the various stages of the work, from the crude bar iron and steel to the beautifully polished, painted, stenciled and finely tempered implement, the joy of the woodman, the bête noir of the farmer's son."

Materials: Steel, wrought iron (polished and bronzed on cheeks).
Dimensions: L. 7½ in. (19.1 cm.)
W. 4⅜ in. (11.0 cm.)
H. 1 in. (2.6 cm.)
Courtesy of Doris H. Phillips.

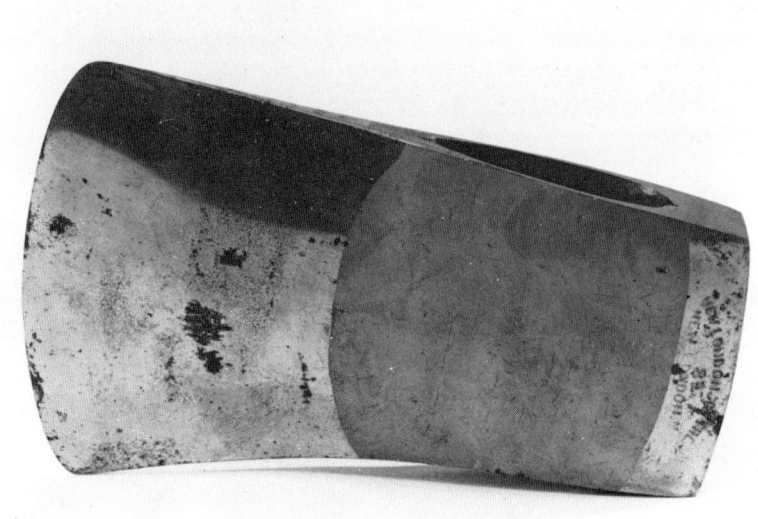

61. BROAD AXE
by William F. George (1818-1865) of Pittsfield.

Marks: "GEORGE/PITTSFIELD, N.H."; owner's mark, "J.LE[AVITT]" (?) in serrated rectangle.

Like other small edge tool makers, William F. George attained a strong local reputation for general work and specialized tools. Marked examples of his tools include axes and chisels. George died from injuries received from lightning while serving as a farrier in the Civil War.

Materials: Steel, wrought iron.
Dimensions: L. 10½ in. (26.7 cm.)
W. 7⅜ in. (18.7 cm.)
H. 1⅛ in. (2.7 cm.)
Courtesy of Neil English.

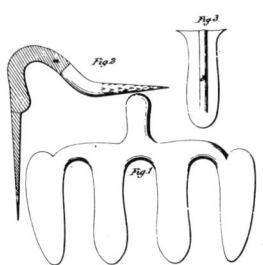

J. Willson's patent drawing for a pronged hoe, 1827.

Instruments of Change

62. SCYTHE

by Phillips, Messer & Colby (at work 1835-1842), New London.

Marks: "PHILLIPS, MESSER & COLBY/NEW LONDON.N.H."

This tool survives from an unusually early period, most scythes of its era having been worn out or cracked from metal fatigue. The original partnership of Joseph Phillips, Richard Messer, and Anthony Colby began production of scythes in 1835, relying on the skill of Phillips, who had been apprenticed in Fitchburg, Massachusetts, "to learn the Art, Trade, or Mystery of Scythemaking," and of Messer, a scythemaker from New London. In its early years the firm annually produced 1,500 dozen scythes. These were "painted blue, unsharpened, packed in straw, and disposed of to the traders and farmers throughout the neighboring towns and counties." The partnership evolved into Phillips, Messer, Colby & Company in 1842 and became the New London Scythe Company in 1871.

Materials: Steel, wrought iron.
Dimensions: L. 24⅛ in. (61.2 cm.)
W. 6¼ in. (15.7 cm.)
H. ⅝ in. (1.5 cm.)

Courtesy of Doris H. Phillips.

63. BUSH SCYTHE

by the New London Scythe Company (at work 1871-1888), New London.

Marks: "[NE]W LONDON SCYTHE [CO.]/CAST STEEL"

Phillips, Messer, Colby & Company was reorganized as the New London Scythe Company in 1871. By 1880 the firm was consuming 200 tons of iron and 50 tons of steel a year and was producing 120,000 scythes, 12,000 hay knives, and 60,000 axes. These were shipped by rail to wholesale dealers in most large American cities, and to Sweden and Scotland. The company maintained two forge shops with fourteen triphammers, a grinding shop, a polishing shop (all with waterpower), and many outbuildings. The grinding shop contained 12 three-ton grindstones, each a foot thick and seven feet in diameter; on the average, one of these was worn out from use each week. The final stage in production, seen in this pristine example, was "the painting and bronzing, to suit the different customers . . . one customer requiring the patriotic red, white, and blue stripes; one, this color; another, that."

Materials: Steel, wrought iron (bronzed and painted with red and black stripes).
Dimensions: L. 20⅞ in. (53.0 cm.)
W. 4⅝ in. (11.6 cm.)
H. ½ in. (1.3 cm.)

Courtesy of Doris H. Phillips.

64. SCYTHE

by the Sibley Scythe Company (at work 1873-1929), Newport.

Marks: "[SIB]LEY SCYTHE CO/NEWPORT NH"

Newport was one of the first New Hampshire towns where scythemaking was carried on as an industry, having a water-powered scythe shop before 1787. Ezra T. Sibley (1817-1909), trained as a scythemaker in Massachusetts, came to Newport in 1845 to carry on the local tradition, eventually founding the Sibley Scythe Company with his son in 1873. At about this period, Sibley employed fourteen men and produced some 30,000 scythes annually, consuming 44,000 pounds of steel and iron. Sibley scythes enjoyed an international reputation, being shipped to Germany and India, and used in quantities to clear marshes during construction of the Panama Canal. When he retired in 1891, Sibley was the oldest manufacturer of scythes in the United States.

Materials: Steel, wrought iron.
Dimensions: L. 38¾ in. (98.3 cm.)
W. 5¼ in. (13.4 cm.)
H. ½ in. (1.2 cm.)

Courtesy of an anonymous lender.

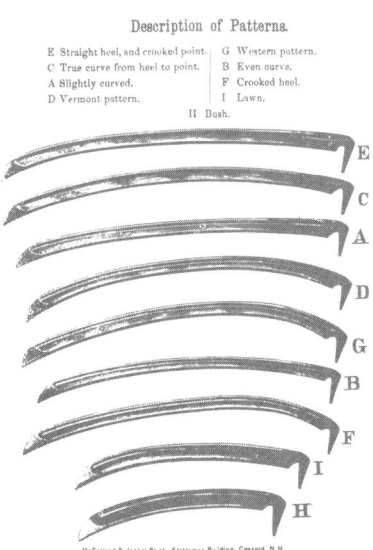

Cooper's Tools

THE MANUFACTURE of cooper's tools centered near the barrel-making towns of Hollis, Brookline, and Milford. According to the 1879 town history of Hollis:

The great abundance and good quality of its oak and chestnut timber, early in the present century, led many of the citizens of the town to engage in the manufacture of barrels and other casks for the Boston market, very many of the farmers having a *cooper's shop* near the farm house. This business for many years was carried on to such an extent that it was sometimes said by their neighbors of other towns, "that all the Hollis folks were coopers, except their minister, and that he hooped his own cider barrels!"

In the mid-1800s Hollis alone had sixteen barrel factories, as well as smaller shops where "the farmer and his sons worked during the winters and stormy weather," making kegs, mackerel kits (fish tubs), apple barrels, and firkins. The major market for these articles was Boston; from there, many were shipped to the West Indies and other distant points. Other New Hampshire towns, particularly in the Richmond area, also made great numbers of casks which were shipped to the Boston market in large racks and wagons. The invention of machinery for the shaping of softwood staves and heads after 1846 encouraged the production of pine and chestnut casks for dry commodities. Many shook mills began to produce cask parts, which were assembled elsewhere. Yet, even with the partial mechanization of coopering, many hand tools continued to be required and made in New Hampshire.

65-66. TWO COOPER'S HOWELS AND CROZES
by Addison Heald (1817-1895) and Daniel Milton Heald (1852-1929) of Milford.

These combination tools shape the concave depression called the "howel" below the chime of a cask and form the groove that receives the head. Such light, dual-purpose tools are said to have been favored by coopers who specialized in making apple barrels. It is no accident that many of New Hampshire's coopering tools came from Milford and its vicinity, since this was the center of the state's cask-making trade in the nineteenth century. Milford is also near a prime apple-growing area, so its production of "dry" barrels for fruit must have been extensive. These two tools illustrate the evolution of Daniel Milton Heald's characteristic pivoted plane iron cap and its adaptation to tools other than carpenter's bench planes. The blade on the upper howel is held by a pivoted wedge with a wooden tightening screw. The blade on the other is held by the fully developed cap patented by Daniel M. Heald in 1878, having a vertically moving slide to permit a delicate adjustment of the blade's depth.

65.
Marks: "A.HEALD & SON" in serrated rectangle, "MILFORD, N.H" in serrated rectangle.

Materials: Birch, beech (pivoted wedge).
Dimensions: L. 12⅞ in. (32.7 cm.)
W. 8⅛ in. (20.6 cm.)
H. 5⅛ in. (13.1 cm.)

Courtesy of William K. Ackroyd.

66.
Marks: "A.HEALD & SON" in serrated rectangle, "MILFORD, N.H" in serrated rectangle, "L.&I.J.WHITE" in impressed letters on iron.

Materials: Maple, beech (handle).
Dimensions: L. 12½ in. (31.9 cm.)
W. 7¾ in. (19.6 cm.)
H. 5⅛ in. (13.0 cm.)

Courtesy of Fred W. Courser, Jr.

67. COOPER'S LONG JOINTER

by Addison Heald (1817-1895) and Daniel Milton Heald (1859-1929) of Milford

Marks: "A. HEALD & SON" in serrated rectangle, "MILFORD NH" in serrated rectangle, stamped twice on each end of plane; "BUCK BROTHERS" in serrated semicircle, "WARRANTED/CAST STEEL" in serrated rectangle, on each iron.

This tool reflects yet another adaptation of Daniel Milton Heald's patented plane iron cap. As in George W. Manning's jointer, each pair of mouths is fitted for one single iron and one double iron. The pins on which the caps for these two irons are pivoted pass through the stock at different heights. In order to change the irons from one pair of mouths to the other, the pins must be drawn to free the caps. To make this job easier, the plane is made in two halves held together by dowels which can be driven out to split the tool and provide better access to the pivot pins.

Materials: Cherry.
Dimensions: L. 46⅞ in. (119.0 cm.)
             W. 5⅞ in. (15.0 cm.)
             H. 4⅞ in. (12.4 cm.)
Courtesy of Fred W. Courser, Jr.

68. COOPER'S LONG JOINTER

by George W. Manning (at work 1880-1886), Hollis.

Marks: "MADE BY/ G.W.MANNING," in impressed letters, stamped twice; "BUCK BROTHERS/WARRANTED/CAST STEEL" in serrated semicircle on each iron.

Although dating from the late 1800s, this tool reflects a form unchanged from early in the century. Made of a single piece of cherry, the jointer has two pairs of mouths, each pair fitted for one single iron and one double iron. The single iron was generally used in jointing the headings of casks, while the double iron was used on the staves. In use, cooper's jointers were secured in an inclined position with the mouths upward, and the staves of casks were passed over the blades to secure a smooth, unbroken curve for a tight fit when assembled. The jointer's body has an undulating curve which provides a concavity, corresponding to the shape of the stave, at each pair of mouths.

Materials: Cherry, lignum vitae (insert at mouth).
Dimensions: L. 48¼ in. (122.4 cm.)
             W. 4¾ in. (12.0 cm.)
             H. 4⅜ in. (11.0 cm.)
Courtesy of Emil S. Pollak.

69. COOPER'S LEVELING PLANE

by George W. Manning (at work 1880-1886), Hollis.

Marks: "MADE BY/ G.W.MANNING," in impressed letters; "BUCK BROTHERS/ WARRANTED/CAST STEEL" in serrated semicircle on iron.

This tool levels the chime of a cask to ensure an even groove when the howel and croze are used to form a seat for the head. This example has several unusual features. Its cherry fence, held with brass thumb screws and fittings, makes the tool easier to control than the usual flat-soled cooper's curved sun plane. The tool utilizes a cast-iron plane iron cap which pivots on pins set into brass receptacles. This appears to be a variation on Daniel Milton Heald's patented cap, but it lacks Heald's depth-adjusting screw.

Materials: Cherry, brass, cast iron.
Dimensions: L. 12⅜ in. (31.5 cm.)
             W. 6⅜ in. (16.0 cm.)
             H. 4 in. (10.0 cm.)
Courtesy of Emil S. Pollak.

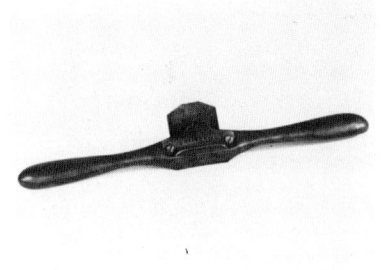

70. COOPER'S DOWNRIGHT
by Addison Heald (1817-1895) and Daniel Milton Heald (1859-1929) of Milford.

Marks: "A.HEALD & SON/ MILFORD N.H."cast into plane iron cap.

This is a cast-iron version of the tool (traditionally made of wood) used by coopers to smooth the outside of a completed cask. The sole and iron of the tool are made slightly concave to fit the curve of the staves. This example displays yet another use of the characteristic knurled steel screw which often appears in pivoted wooden plane iron wedges made by the Healds. In this case, the screw passes through a cast-iron cap and secures the single iron of the tool.

Materials: Cast iron, steel.
Dimensions: L. 17½ in. (44.4 cm.)
             W. 2½ in. (6.3 cm.)
             H. 1⅝ in. (4.1 cm.)
Courtesy of Fred W. Courser, Jr.

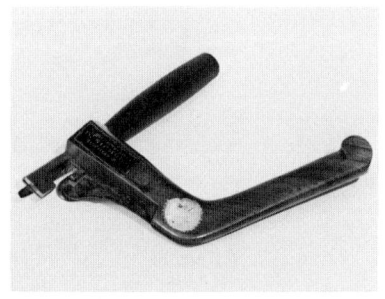

71. LEATHER CHAMFERING TOOL
by Daniel Nichols (1811-1885) of Hampstead.

Marks: "MANUFACTURED BY/ D. NICHOLS./HAMPSTEAD, N.H." on paper label.

Towns like Hampstead, near the shoe center of Haverhill, Massachusetts, were productive in the invention and manufacture of leatherworking tools. Daniel Nichols was one of several New Hampshire machinists who manufactured specialized products for a local market. This chamfering tool was patented in 1858 by William Johnson (1832-1906), Nichols's neighbor and the inventor of several comparable devices. This pattern of sole shave must have been popular, since many survive—some with ordinary shoe knives inserted in their blade holders and some with a short steel cutter.

Materials: Cherry, brass, steel.
Dimensions: L. 5¼ in. (13.4 cm.)
             W. 6⅛ in. (15.5 cm.)
             H. 1¼ in. (3.1 cm.)
Courtesy of Margaret Scott Carter.

72. LEATHER CHAMFERING TOOL
by William Johnson (1832-1906) of Hampstead.

Marks: "W^M JOHNSON/ HAMPSTEAD/N.H.," "PATENTED/ APRIL.12.1859"

Machinist and inventor William Johnson obtained three patents for shoe sole chamfering tools. His inventiveness was inspired partly by circumstance (Hampstead being near the shoe city of Haverhill, Massachusetts) and partly by example. Captain William Johnson, a neighbor but no relation, invented a machine for splitting the palm leaves used in the hats which were widely made in New Hampshire during the nineteenth century.

Materials: Brass, steel, birch handle.
Dimensions: L. 6 in. (15.0 cm.)
             W. 1¾ in. (4.3 cm.)
             H. 1½ in. (3.7 cm.)
Courtesy of William K. Ackroyd.

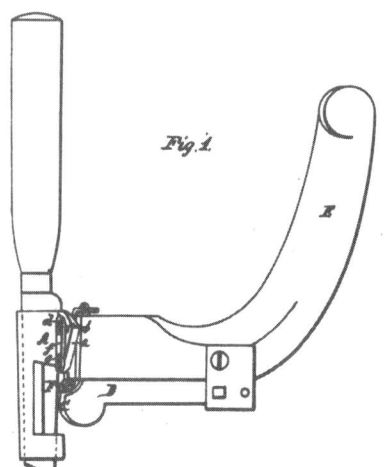

W. Johnson's patent drawing for a shoe shave, 1858.

Instruments of Change

73. LEATHER SPLITTING MACHINE
by John Winslow Chase (1813-1877) of North Weare.

Marks: "J.W.CHASE," "WEARE.N.H."

From 1846 until his death, John Winslow Chase carried on the manufacture of edge tools, specializing in the production of skiving machines—bench tools used to shave leather to a uniform thickness. In 1859 and 1864 Chase received patents for improvements in such devices. By 1870 he was employing two or three men year-round in his water-powered shop and was completing over 700 machines each year. Although shoe production in the Manchester-Weare area did not compare with that near Dover, Rochester, and Farmington, the shops near Chase's home produced 130,000 pairs of shoes in 1870 and provided a constant demand for boot and leather tools.

Materials: Steel, brass.
Dimensions: L. 5¼ in (13.1 cm.)
             W. 10⅝ in. (27.0 cm.)
             H. 3⅞ in. (9.7 cm.)

Courtesy of Paul W. Morgan.

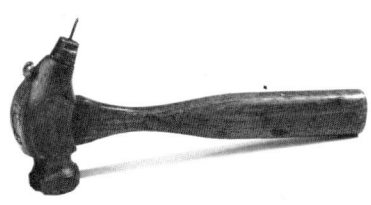

74. LASTING HAMMER
by Jethro W. Warner (1847-1875) of Dover.

Marks: "J.W.W[AR]NER/ DOV[ER] N.H.," "PAT'D OCT.19.186[9]"

A young Dover shoemaker, Jethro Warner patented this versatile hammer in 1869. The head of the hammer is provided with a chuck for an awl, and the handle of the tool originally had a "spacing wheel," evidently a roulette, set into its end. Although New Hampshire had an extensive shoe industry in the late nineteenth century, there was no single city which predominated as Lynn did in Massachusetts. Dover's shoe production at the time Warner invented this hammer was 1,150,000 pairs, while that of nearby Farmington was 1,300,000. The largest single shoeshop in New Hampshire at the time was said to have been that of E. G. and E. Wallace in the neighboring town of Rochester, so Warner's invention would have found a ready market within Strafford County.

Materials: Steel, hickory handle.
Dimensions: L. 8¾ in. (22.0 cm.)
             W. 1⅛ in. (2.9 cm.)
             H. 3⅜ in. (8.6 cm.)

Courtesy of Fred W. Courser, Jr.

75. SAW SET
by Francis Herrick Aiken (1843-1876) of Franklin.

Marks: "H. AIKEN['S]/PATENT.,"
"F.H. AIKEN, MAKER/FRANKLIN N.H"

The Aiken family of Franklin were among New Hampshire's most prolific inventors and machinists. Herrick Aiken (1797-1866), a native of Peterborough, was awarded several medals for his inventions, which included a spiral brush, leather splitting and edging machines, improvements in screw cutting machinery, wrenches, pliers, and the devices shown here. Aiken was the engineer who devised the principles that eventually led to construction of the famous cog railway to the summit of Mount Washington. This saw set, patented in 1836 while the inventor was living in Dracut, Massachusetts, was one of Herrick Aiken's most widely adopted devices. After the inventor's death in 1866, the set was manufactured by his son, Francis Herrick Aiken of Franklin, and after Francis's death in 1876, by the son's widow, Harriet A. Aiken. Others copied the invention, and the set was still being manufactured as late as 1931. Unlike the hand sets patented by Rust and Brooks in Somersworth, the Aiken set is a bench tool struck with a hammer.

Materials: Steel.
Dimensions: L. 3¾ in. (9.4 cm.)
             W. 1½ in. (3.9 cm.)
             H. 2¾ in. (7.0 cm.)

Courtesy of an anonymous lender.

The Tools

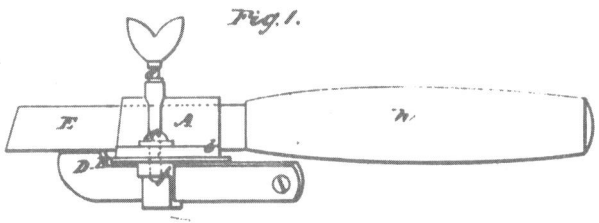

W. Johnson's patent drawing for a shoemaker's tool, 1859.

76. SAW SET
patented posthumously for Lebbeus Brooks (1819-1858) of Somersworth.

Marks: None.

New Hampshire was prolific in the invention and manufacture of saw sets, nine patents being issued to residents of the state between 1850 and 1900. This set is the second invented by Lebbeus Brooks, who died before patent papers were secured by his widow. Devised for great leverage and strongly made without a pivot pin to wear down, the set was intended for use on mill saws. A partner with Henry O. Rust in the Great Falls Saw Set Company, Brooks was enterprising and inventive, dying too soon to reveal his full potential. In 1854 Brooks invented a spirit level with an adjustable bubble which indicated the angle of an incline, and in 1856 he patented both a machine for sawing marble and his first saw set, for hand saws. Brooks held copyrights on several tables for calculating interest and, at his death, was about to patent a straw cutter and a spring bed, as well as an improved decimal interest table.

Materials: Steel.
Dimensions: L. 10⅞ in. (27.6 cm.)
W. 1⅜ in. (3.5 cm.)
H. 4¼ in. (10.7 cm.)

Courtesy of Paul W. Morgan.

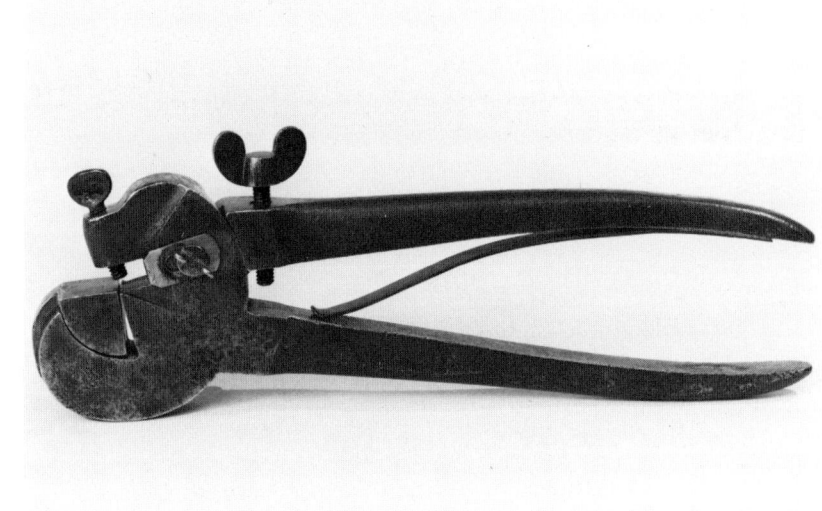

77. SAW SET
by William Orne Rust (1822-1885) of Somersworth.

Marks: "W.O.RUST'S/PATENT/ AUG. 22.1854," "Manuf'd by/W. O. RUST/Great Falls N.H."

Rust's patent for this device in 1854 was the first for a saw set in New Hampshire. Joining the inventive Lebbeus Brooks to form the Great Falls Saw Set Company, Rust helped to make Somersworth (Great Falls) a center of saw set invention and manufacture. The manufacturing firm evidently failed following Brooks's death in 1858. Refusing to declare bankruptcy, Rust was still laboring to pay old debts when he died in 1885 with the reputation of a local eccentric whose obituary described his workshop in Berwick, Maine, as "a veritable museum of mechanical curiosities."

Materials: Cast iron, brass, steel.
Dimensions: L. 8¾ in. (22.2 cm.)
W. 1⅞ in. (4.9 cm.)
H. 3⅜ in. (8.7 cm.)

Courtesy of an anonymous lender.

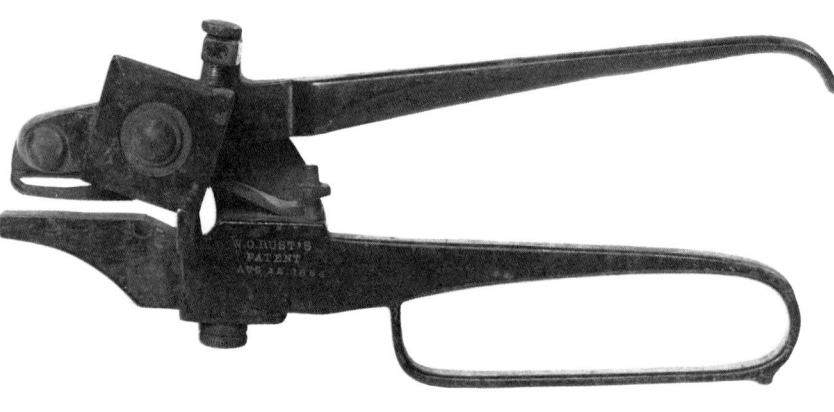

Gage, Porter & Company's saw works, Fisherville (Penacook), circa 1870.

78. CABINETMAKER'S BAR CLAMP

by Wendell Phillips Tarbell (born 1854) of Milford.

Marks: "W.P.TARBELL" in serrated rectangle, "MILFORD NH" in serrated rectangle, "PAT JULY 17 88" in serrated rectangle.

Characterized by a double screw mechanism which permits fine and rapid adjustment of the jaws, this clamp is based on an 1888 invention of Wendell Phillips Tarbell. Originally applied to common handscrew clamps, Tarbell's patent is here adapted to the longer bar clamp. The larger thread, turned by the long grip, is used for rough adjustment of the clamp. A smaller threaded rod, hidden within the larger one, is extended by turning the ribbed wooden nut and permits fine adjustment or additional tightening of the clamp. Tarbell may have made this clamp as well as inventing it, for in 1891 he was known as a "clamp and screw manufacturer." By 1895 Tarbell was employed in the Milford furniture factory of French and Heald, where Daniel Milton Heald made picture frames after 1907.

Materials: Birch.
Dimensions: L. 57⅝ in. (146.4 cm.)
W. 1⅝ in. (4.2 cm.)
H. 5¾ in. (14.6 cm.)
Courtesy of William K. Ackroyd.

79. BUSH HAMMER

by Luther M. Nutting and Henry W. Hayden (at work 1888-1908), Concord.

Marks: "NUTTING & HAYDEN./MANFR'S./CONCORD N.H./N^{O}. 2526/ PAT. OCT. 8 89." on side plates.

The bush hammer, a series of steel leaves bolted together and used for dressing stone, was a specialty of the Concord granite tool manufacturers Nutting & Hayden. An 1890 advertisement noted that "it will readily be believed that the tools used in working so hard and intractable a material as granite, must be skillfully made of the best material if they are to do good service, and as the productions of Messrs. Nutting & Hayden are in active and increasing demand among granite cutters, the natural presumption is that they are equal to the best in both these important respects.... A specialty is made of manufacturing bush hammers, and both a wholesale and retail business is done, employment being given to from six to eight assistants, and all orders being promptly filled at the lowest market rates." It appears that each hammer was given an individual serial number.

Materials: Steel, hickory handle.
Dimensions: L. 7¼ in. (18.5 cm.)
W. 2¼ in. (5.5 cm.)
H. 15¾ in. (40.0 cm.)
Courtesy of Fred W. Courser, Jr.

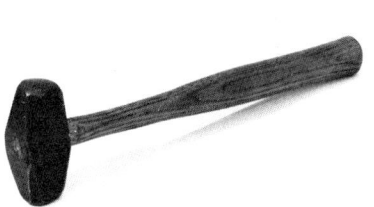

80. STONE HAMMER

by Luther M. Nutting and Henry W. Hayden (at work 1888-1908), Concord.

Marks: "NUTTING & HAYDEN/ CONCORD, N.H." on bottom of head.

Stimulated by the many granite quarries near Concord, Nutting & Hayden forged every kind of hand tool used in granite quarrying and shaping. One of the most basic of these implements was the double-faced hammer used to strike hand drills in splitting granite. Nutting & Hayden hammers are often found with an impressed star or crescent moon in addition to the company name; the meaning of these symbols is not known, though they could denote grades of quality.

Materials: Steel, hickory (handle is a replacement).
Dimensions: L. 3⅞ in. (9.6 cm.)
W. 1¾ in. (4.2 cm.)
H. 14⅞ in. (37.7 cm.)
Courtesy of Fred W. Courser, Jr.

81. TONGS
by Luther M. Nutting and Henry W. Hayden (at work 1888-1908), Concord.

Marks: "NUTTING & HAYDEN/ CONCORD, N.H." on inside of handle near rivet.

Few New Hampshire manufacturers made tools for blacksmiths, most smiths preferring to fashion their own implements until the twentieth century. Several special-purpose tongs by Nutting & Hayden have been reported, however, suggesting that this company produced at least a limited line of smith's tools in their small forge shop in Concord. This pair of tongs appears to be intended to grip the eye of an axe during forging of the poll or the bit.

Materials: Wrought iron.
Dimensions: L. 26⅛ in. (66.2 cm.)
W. 3¾ in. (9.6 cm.) closed.
H. 1⅞ in. (4.6 cm.)
Courtesy of Fred W. Courser, Jr.

82. MARKING GAUGE
by David Page Sanborn (1810-1871) of Littleton.

Marks: "D.P.SANBORN/ LITTLETON" in impressed letters on sliding head.

Though a simple tool made of native beech, this gauge shows Sanborn's usual fine workmanship. Sanborn appears to have extended his production beyond planemaking. He is listed in the 1855-1857 New-Hampshire Annual Registers as an edge tool maker, presumably fashioning handles for blades made by others. This gauge suggests that he fashioned other simple carpenter's tools as well.

Materials: Beech.
Dimensions: L. 6⅝ in. (16.7 cm.)
W. 2¼ in. (5.5 cm.)
H. 2¼ in. (5.6 cm.)
Courtesy of Wendall E. Badger.

Instruments of Change

83. AWLS AND TOOLS
by Francis Herrick Aiken (1843-1876) of Franklin.

Marks: "AWLS AND TOOLS PATENTED APRIL 10 18[5]8/ SOLE MANUF'R F. H. AIKEN FRANKLIN, N.H." in impressed letters on wooden handle, "H.AIKEN,/PATENT" on collar of chuck.

Like the Aiken Saw Set, this versatile awl and tool handle was invented by Herrick Aiken (1797-1866) and manufactured in Franklin by his son, Francis Herrick Aiken, and by his son's widow, Harriet A. Aiken. Like the saw set, too, the handle was widely copied despite its having been patented in 1858. The hollow handle contains twenty interchangeable tools, mostly brad awls of various sizes, small chisels and gouges, a screwdriver, and even a tiny saw. Herrick Aiken sued the copiers of his tool handles and received compensation. Publishing a broadside to warn others against such infringement, Aiken claimed superior quality for his tools and asserted that "every inventor has a reputation to sustain, which prompts him to make articles of the best quality, whereas the sole object of the base imitator is immediate gain."

Materials: Steel, birch handle.
Dimensions: L. 4⅜ in. (11.2 cm.)
W. 1¼ in. (3.2 cm.)
H. 1¼ in. (3.2 cm.)
Courtesy of Paul W. Morgan.

84. CARPENTER'S CLAW HAMMER
attributed to Phineas Eastman (1772-1858) of Canaan.

Marks: None.

The town of Canaan developed a specialty in the manufacture of carpenter's hammers during the early nineteenth century, and this specialization led to a patented improvement in hammer and hatchet design. Carpenter's hammer manufacture before the mid-century was plagued with the dual difficulties of insecure attachment for the wooden handle and weakness of the handle where it passed through the eye. In 1839 Phineas Eastman patented this hammer, which provided a strong reinforcing collar at the point of greatest weakness. The cone-shaped socket is threaded at its upper end and screws securely about halfway through the hammer head. The wooden handle projects through the socket and is wedged firmly at the top of the eye, which is flared slightly to prevent the socket from becoming unscrewed or the handle from pulling out.

Materials: Steel.
Dimensions: L. 4 in. (10.0 cm.)
W. 1⅜ in. (3.4 cm.)
H. 2¾ in. (7.0 cm.)
Courtesy of Fred W. Courser, Jr.

The Tools

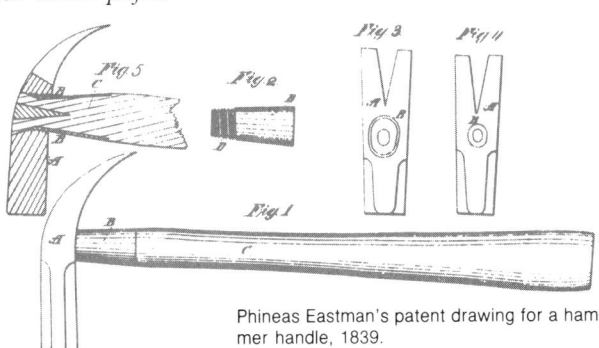

Phineas Eastman's patent drawing for a hammer handle, 1839.

85. CARPENTER'S CLAW HAMMER
by William Butterfield (at work 1849-1855), Canaan.

Marks: "BUTTERFIEL[D]"

One of the most prolific of Canaan's several nineteenth-century hammermakers, Butterfield had taken over the businesses established by Phineas Eastman and others by 1849. In the following year, his water-powered shop near Hart's Pond employed three men and consumed three tons of steel and ten tons of iron. The shop was capable of producing 12,000 hammers a year. The business was taken over in 1855 by Nathan Jones, who reportedly continued with simple manufacturing methods until forced out of business by the superior technology employed by competitors. This Butterfield hammer uses a type of handle reinforcement which was standard until the development of the "adze eye" hammer in the 1840s. Two iron straps are secured to the handle and pass through the eye, where their projecting ends are turned outward to prevent the head from loosening.

Materials: Steel, wrought iron, hickory handle.
Dimensions: L. 4⅜ in. (11.1 cm.)
W. 1¼ in. (3.0 cm.)
H. 12 in. (30.3 cm.)

Courtesy of Fred W. Courser, Jr.

86. AXLE GAUGE
by Harry Houston (1804-1865) of Concord.

Marks: "H.HOUSTON/ CONCORD NH."

Axle gauges of many forms were in widespread use throughout the nineteenth century. Their function was to guide the adjustment of carriage axle spindles in such a way that the bottom spokes of a properly dished wheel remained perpendicular to the road surface as the wheel revolved. Since Concord was the largest of New Hampshire's several centers of carriage manufacture, it is not surprising that this well-made gauge is the product of a local blacksmith. Harry Houston worked for the coach-building firms of Downing & Abbot, and J. S. & E. A. Abbot, from the 1830s until his death.

Materials: Wrought iron, wood (painted).
Dimensions: L. 66⅞ in. (169.8 cm.)
W. ⅞ in. (2.3 cm.)
H. 8⅜ in. (21.3 cm.)

New Hampshire Historical Society, purchase.

87. SELF-ADJUSTING CARRIAGE WRENCH
by Harry Walter Burleigh (1855-1927) of Franklin.

Marks: "H.W.BURLEIGH/ FRANKLIN, N.H." on flat side of wrench, "PAT. APL'D. FOR" on opposite side.

A farmer at the time he invented the wrench, Burleigh obtained a patent for the device in November 1889. The wrench has a pawl which is pulled by the index finger, opening the spring-loaded jaws. When the pawl is released, the wrench jaws close upon the wagon axle nut and the pawl engages a ratchet track within the handle, automatically locking the jaws over the nut. The wrench became sufficiently popular to be manufactured briefly by the prolific Goodell Company in Antrim, makers of cutlery, apple parers, and other hardware specialties.

Materials: Cast iron, birch (handle).
Dimensions: L. 8⅝ in. (21.9 cm.)
W. 5½ in. (14.1 cm.)
H. 1⅞ in. (4.5 cm.)

Courtesy of Fred W. Courser, Jr.

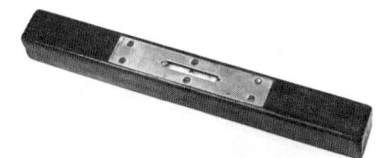

88. CARRIAGE WRENCH
by Adin Phillips Joy (1859-1940) of Newfields and/or Newmarket (Rockingham).

Marks: "A P JOY ROCKINGHAM N H" on lever, "PAT FEB 1 '98" on lever.

Patented in 1898, this is another of the many convenient wrenches invented during the nineteenth century for removing carriage wheels. This wrench uses a knurled nut for rough adjustment of the jaws, which are then quickly locked and unlocked by the eccentric cam lever. The wrench has a projecting handle for rapid threading and unthreading of the axle nut. Although Joy was a dry-goods peddler at the time he invented this wrench, his younger brother, Samuel Sumner Joy, was a manufacturer of carriage jacks in or near Rockingham and probably oversaw the production of the wrench.

Materials: Cast iron, wood handle (painted).
Dimensions: L. 9¾ in. (24.7 cm.)
W. 5 in. (12.8 cm.)
H. 2⅛ in. (5.2 cm.)
Courtesy of Marshall E. Merrill.

89. SPIRIT LEVEL
by Amos G. Atwood (at work 1841-1872), Nashua.

Marks: "A.G.ATWOOD./NASHUA" on brass plate, "A.G.ATWOOD." on end of level.

Several New Hampshire instrument makers manufactured carpenter's levels during the nineteenth century, but this example is the product of a Nashua machinist. Having the training and equipment for precise work, many New Hampshire machinists engaged in the small-scale manufacture of precision hand tools throughout the century, until forced out of business by the superior productivity of large-scale manufacturers.

Materials: Mahogany, brass.
Dimensions: L. 13⅜ in. (33.8 cm.)
W. 1⅜ in. (3.6 cm.)
H. 1⅜ in. (3.5 cm.)
Courtesy of Margaret Scott Carter.

90. COMBINATION TOOL
by Frank Ross Woodward (1845-1931) of Hill.

Marks: "THE WOODWARD TOOL/PAT. AUG. 24 75"

The nineteenth century abounded in multi-purpose inventions. A classic of the type was the Woodward Combination Tool, which performed the functions of glass cutter, cork screw, and knife sharpener. Woodward owned the New England Novelty Works in Hill, where he made knife sharpeners, can openers, washer cutters, ice picks, and various other edge tools. The rotary glass cutter, an important development which provided an inexpensive substitute for diamond cutters, was not Woodward's invention but became his specialty. After successfully disproving a charge of patent infringement brought by the cutter's purported inventor in 1875, Woodward continued to manufacture some 12,000 glass cutters a month. By 1880 his company employed between ten and sixteen people. Because the overall design of Woodward's Combination Tool was not protected by patent or copyright, many other companies in the United States and England manufactured products of nearly the same pattern.

Materials: Cast iron, steel.
Dimensions: L. 5¾ in. (14.4 cm.)
W. 1 in. (2.3 cm.)
H. 1⅝ in. (3.9 cm.)
Courtesy of Robert P. Nugent.

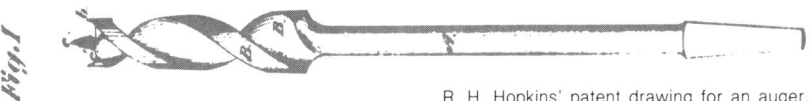

R. H. Hopkins' patent drawing for an auger, 1870.

The Tools

91. WATCHMAKER'S STAKING TOOL

by Kendrick & Davis Company (established 1876), Lebanon.

Marks: "K&D/SPECIAL," "1623"

Watchmaker's tools were among the many types of precision hand tools manufactured in New Hampshire. Several companies or individuals made such implements in the late nineteenth century, among them S. C. Smith of Claremont, Francis E. Allen of Keene, and Joseph Houghton of Manchester. This staking tool, used for such precise operations as punching or inserting jewels in watch plates, is the Kendrick & Davis No. 509 "Special" model, which sold for $25 during the early twentieth century. Still in operation, Kendrick & Davis began making such tools about 1895, having specialized previously in watch key manufacture. During the first decade of the twentieth century, Kendrick & Davis made several advances in the design of staking tools, and by 1909 had become the largest manufacturer of watchmaker's tools in the world. Their products usually bear the trademark "K&D."

Materials: Plated steel in cherry case with glass dome.
Dimensions: D. 6¾ in. (17.2 cm.) H. 7⅝ in. (19.5 cm.)

Courtesy of Charles J. Mitchell.

Instruments of Change

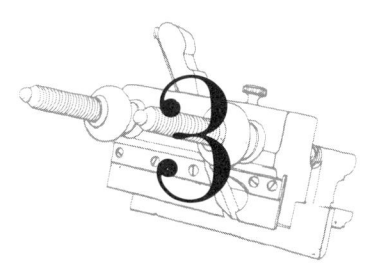

The Toolmakers

Blacksmith Shop, East Pembroke, N.H., c. 1890.

New Hampshire Toolmakers and Their Marks

OVER 1,000 *TOOLMAKERS* are known to have plied their various trades in New Hampshire between 1750 and 1900. Working in shops and factories, large and small, and in complex series of partnerships and firms, these craftsmen frequently applied their ingenuity to the improvement of existing technology. Included in the alphabetical listing which immediately follows are not only the state's makers of tools and parts of tools but also local inventors of improvements in tool design and methods of tool manufacturing.

This list of New Hampshire toolmakers was compiled from published town histories, state and county business directories, United States patent indexes, and manuscript industrial census returns. Additional information on individual toolmakers was obtained from published genealogies and biographical reviews; local and state directories; vital and cemetery records; manuscript population census returns; newspaper obituaries and advertisements; original patent records; and manuscript or published diaries, account books, and business records.

Included in the list are makers of most of the types of hand tools which were used to fabricate products likely to survive today. Makers of tools used in food and fiber production and processing are not included, except as they relate to the broader edge tool industry. Makers of certain simple machines and miscellaneous tool-related products are also listed.

Joiners, blacksmiths, machinists, founders, woodenware manufacturers, and other skilled craftsmen often made tools for sale, without actually specializing in tool manufacture. The numbers of such craftsmen in early New Hampshire preclude listing them in a work of this scale: before the end of the nineteenth century there had been about 100 blacksmiths working in the town of Weare alone. However, individual joiners, blacksmiths, and other general craftsmen are included when either business records or marked products survive as evidence of their toolmaking activity.

The goal has been to include in this catalogue all New Hampshire toolmakers whose careers began prior to 1900. Only in the case of the most significant toolmaking enterprises has early-twentieth-century evolution been traced in any detail.

Unless explained otherwise, the dates given following each toolmaker's name and town represent the earliest and latest dates of his tool production presently known. Future research may expand the date ranges given. The list of tools produced by each maker is not necessarily complete, but it reflects the terminology of the sources used.

The marks pictured are a selection representing the major toolmakers, as well as the most visually interesting marks of various types. Owing to limitations of space, no attempt has been made to record all known variations in a maker's marks.

Members of toolmaking partnerships are listed separately as well as under firm names if there is information available on the individuals themselves.

More detailed information on specific toolmakers is available by writing to the Index of New Hampshire Toolmakers at the New Hampshire Historical Society.

Abbott, J. R., & Co.; *probably John R. Abbott, principal; Antrim, c. 1874; brush handles.*

Abbott, John R.; *Antrim, c. 1860; brushes; probably also involved in J. R. Abbott & Co.*

Abbott, William; *Henniker, c. 1874; telescopic instruments.*

Adamascobite Company; *Winchester, c. 1885; whetstones.*

Adams & Rowell; *Penacook (Fisherville), 1846-1847; axes, hatchets; see also Ezekiel Adams.*

Adams, Charles A.; *Manchester, 1886-1929; manager of John B. Varick Company, hardware dealers; Adams's name (with town, preceded by "Vulcan Saw Works") appears on a rip saw.*

Adams, Ezekiel *(1811-1867); Hopkinton, 1849-1850; Webster, 1856-1867; edge tools, specializing in axes; "Adams's well known Chopping Axes," advertised in 1855 by Concord hardware dealer Gustavus Walker, probably his product.*

Adams, Harvey; *Lancaster, 1849-1857; edge tools (axes, forks, hoes).*

Aiken Brad Awl and Saw Set Manufacturing Company; *Franklin, c. 1879; brad awls and saw sets.*

Aiken, Francis Herrick *(1843-1876); Franklin, 1870-1876; saw sets, brad awls, wrenches (pocket), drills; succeeded father, Herrick Aiken, and continued to produce items patented by him.*

Aiken, Harriet A. (Colby), *variously called Hannah N. (1842-?); Franklin, 1877-1878; awls, saw sets, wrenches; carried on business of husband, Francis Herrick, after his death.*

Aiken, Herrick *(1797-1866); Franklin, 1838-1860; awls, saw sets, leather splitting machines, cutlery, carpenter's tools, shoe tools; patented leather splitting knife, 1823; saw set, 1830, 1835; leather splitting machine, 1835; tool handle, 1839; set of awls and tools, 1858; tool box, 1858; spiral brush.*

Aiken, Jonas Bradley *(1833-1903); Franklin, 1856-1895; machinist, known to have made railroad conductor's punches, 1878-1886; son of Herrick Aiken.*

Aiken, Walter Scott *(1831-1893); Franklin, 1853-1893; machinist, known to have made saw sets, c. 1878; son of Herrick Aiken.*

Akin, Samuel; *Warner, c. 1849; scythe snaths.*

Alcott & Co.; *partnership of William Alcott and John W. Moore; Nashua, 1864-1866; files.*

Alden & Kellog; *Lebanon, c. 1850; blacksmiths, specializing in picks.*

Aldrich, Moses; *Troy, c. 1808-1816; worked in partnership with William Barnard; scythes.*

Aldrich, Nathan; *Richmond, before 1884; scythe snaths.*

Alexander & Perkins; *apparently partnership of George E. Alexander and James M. Perkins; Sunapee, 1880-1900+; handles (fork, rake); succeeded Alexander, Perkins & Co. of Newport.*

Alexander & Purinton; *probably partnership of Lucius C. Alexander and John Purinton; Nashua, 1853-1856; wrenches.*

Alexander, Elkanah M.; *Newport, 1872-1879; worked alone and apparently in partnership or firm of Long & Alexander; handles (fork, hoe).*

Alexander, George E. *(1848-?); Newport, 1877-1878; Sunapee, 1880-1900+; worked alone and in partnerships or firms of Alexander, Perkins & Co. and Alexander & Perkins; handles (fork, hoe); son of Elkanah M. Alexander.*

Alexander, Perkins & Co.; *partnership of George E. Alexander and James M. Perkins; Newport, c. 1878; handles (hoe, fork).*

Alexander, Wesley *(1823-1890); Littleton, c. 1856-1860; scythes, crowbars; see also Henry C. Redington & Co.*

Allen, Amos Pratt *(1827-1867); Rindge, c. 1860; worked in partnership or firm of Oratio P. Allen & Son; sawhorses.*

Allen, Colburn & Co.; *Rindge, c. 1868; sawhorses; see also Oratio P. Allen & Son.*

Allen, Francis E.; *Keene, 1871-1875; watchmaker's tools, ring gauges; patented jeweller's combined calipers and poising tool, 1871.*

Allen, Oratio P., & Son; *partnership of Oratio P. and Amos Pratt Allen; Rindge, c. 1860; woodenware manufacturers, specializing in sawhorses.*

American Shearer Manufacturing Company; *Nashua, 1875-1900+; clippers (barber, horse, sheep); see also Joseph K. Priest.*

American Twist Drill Company; *Meredith, 1880-1887; Laconia, 1887-1893; drills, chuck jaws, machinist's tools.*

Amidon; *Hinsdale, c. 1886; worked in partnership or firm of Owen & Amidon; vises.*

Amoskeag Ax Company; *Manchester, 1862-1879; edge tools (axes, hatchets, adzes, mattocks, bush hooks, picks, hoes, etc.); formerly Blodgett Edge Tool Company; absorbed in 1879 by Underhill Edge Tool Company, which continued to use the Amoskeag name; see also Henry C. Reynolds, agent.*

Amoskeag Manufacturing Company Machine Shop; *Manchester, 1849-1856; heavy tools.*

Amsden, Downing; *Lebanon, 1807-1828; joiner, whose name appears on planes and moulding tools.*

Antrim Shovel Company; *Antrim, 1857-1861;* shovels; product based on patent of Jonathan White; business purchased by Treadwell & Co. of Boston, which may have continued to use the Antrim Shovel Company name, 1861-1864.

Applebee, Charles Henry *(1840-?); Littleton, 1882-1900+;* blacksmith, advertising production of stone tools, 1885.

Atherton & Goodrich; partnership of George Atherton and George Goodrich; *Chesterfield, 1849-1850;* augers and bits.

Atherton, George *(1817-1851); Chesterfield, 1849-1850;* worked in partnership of Atherton & Goodrich; augers and bits.

Atwood, Amos G.; *Nashua, 1841-1872;* machinist, whose name appears on spirit levels.

Atwood, D. G.; *Bedford, 1856-1857;* handles (fork, hoe).

Atwood, James; *Nashua, c. 1850;* axe helves.

Atwood, O. P.; *Nelson, c. 1870;* handles.

Atwood, Stephen; *Nashua, 1841-1875;* woodturner, known to have made ship handspikes, c. 1850.

Bachelder, James; *Lancaster;* patented currier's knife, 1825; machine for sharpening currier's knives, 1824.

Bachelder, Otis Freeman *(1800-1869); Bedford, 1825-1837;* tanner, known to have patented with John P. Houston a machine for shaving leather, 1825; moved to Littleton, 1837.

Bachelder; *see also* Batchelder.

Bailey, William; *Manchester, c. 1856;* edge tools.

Baker, C. S.; *Manchester;* patented with W. B. Noyes a saw set and gauge (also described as a combined gauge, square, and wrench for saws), 1868.

Balch, Dan Shaw *(1807-1888); Canaan, before 1849;* said to have made hammers with Phineas Eastman and Jonathan Kittredge; brother-in-law of latter.

Baldwin & White; apparently partnership of Isaac Baldwin and Jonathan White; *Antrim, c. 1833-1839;* hoes.

Baldwin & Whittemore; partnership of Samuel Baldwin, Amos Whittemore, and George Alfred Whittemore; *Bennington, 1853-1855;* cutlery (including draw, shoe, butcher, and bread knives).

Baldwin, Isaac *(1796-1872); Antrim, 1824-1839;* worked alone as blacksmith and in partnership or firm of Baldwin & White; hoes.

Baldwin, James, & Co.; *Manchester, 1859-?;* woodenware manufacturers, known to have made tool handles, 1877-1878.

Baldwin, Jedediah, variously spelled Jedidiah *(1768-1849); Hanover, 1793-1811;* clockmaker/silversmith, known to have made surveyor's instruments, protractors, and parts of scientific instruments (for Dartmouth students and faculty); account books in Dartmouth College Archives.

Baldwin, Josephus; *Nashua, 1856-1860;* axe handles.

Baldwin, Nathan H.; *Laconia, 1871-1874;* machinist's tools; patented saw filer's vise, 1871.

Baldwin, Samuel *(1802-1885); Bennington, 1826-1870;* blacksmith, known to have specialized in edge tools (axes, cutlery, drawshaves, shoe and butcher knives) and screwdrivers, 1849-1860; worked alone and in partnerships or firms of Baldwin & Whittemore and Samuel Baldwin & Co.; brother of Isaac Baldwin.

Baldwin, Samuel, & Co.; *Bennington, 1856-1857;* edge tools (cutlery).

Ball, Benjamin G.; *Nashua;* patented bench vise, 1856.

Ball, Thomas C.; *Walpole;* patented an improved scythe-fastening, 1856.

Ball, W. H.; *Washington, 1889-1899;* blacksmith, specializing in axes, 1889-1890.

Balser, Arthur W.; *Nashua, c. 1894;* worked in partnership or firm of Plaisted & Balser; blacksmith, advertising granite tools.

Barker, Andrew H. *(c. 1820-?); Manchester, c. 1874; Claremont, 1879-1880;* stencils.

Barnard, William; *Troy, c. 1808-1816;* worked in partnership with Moses Aldrich; scythes.

Barnett, Ezra; *Warner;* patented scythe, 1836.

Barr, Matthew, & Co.; *Nashua, c. 1865;* hardware dealers, whose name (with town) appears on planes.

Barrett, Edward H.; *Franklin, c. 1849;* scythe snaths.

Bartlett & Young; probably partnership of blacksmiths James Bartlett and Asa Young; *Portsmouth, c. 1812;* edge tools (axes, chisels, drawknives, hatchets, adzes, plane irons, stone tools).

Bartlett, Sylvanus; *Swanzey (Westport), c. 1874; Keene, c. 1882;* patented saw sets, 1874 and 1882.

Batchelder, Thomas; *Candia;* patented improvement in machinery for manufacturing the frames of wood saws, 1854.

Batchelder; *see also* Bachelder.

Bazin, Richard C.; *Portsmouth, c. 1821;* blocks.

Beck; *Newport, c. 1868;* worked in partnership or firm of Long & Beck; handles (fork, hoe).

Beck, Samuel; *Portsmouth, c. 1821;* blocks.

Beckwith, Alfred; *Stoddard, c. 1860;* saw frames.

Belknap, Amos *(1836-1898); Monroe;* blacksmith, known for his knife and shave blades.

Bell, Joseph; *Bedford, 1782-1798;* blacksmith, known to have made an eel hook, nib irons, and wedges for scythe tackling.

Bellows, Charles Cotesworth *(1813-1872); New Ipswich, 1866-1872;* leather creasing machines; patented machine for creasing, slicking, and skiving leather, 1866.

Bemis & Symonds; *Dublin, 1856-1857;* handles (fork, hoe).

Benton, W. W., & Co.; *Bristol, c. 1895;* handles (all kinds).

Berry, Oliver P.; *Hopkinton (Contoocook), 1888-1893;* axe handles.

Berry, Oliver P., Company; *Hopkinton (Contoocook), 1894-1895; Wolfeboro Falls, 1897-1900+;* handles (axe, adze, sledge, cant dog, pick, hammer); name given incorrectly in advertisement as O. B. Berry Company.

Bickford, Solomon E.; *Franklin;* patented with Frederick Flanders a graduated bevel square, 1867.

Bingham, Charles W.; *Gilsum, 1875-1879;* axe helves.

Bixby, Daniel *(1791-1870); Francestown;* cabinetmaker, known to have made knife handles; ledger (1839-1849) at Winterthur Museum (copy at New Hampshire Historical Society).

Blaisdell, John; *Gilford;* blacksmith, said to have made hoes and edge tools.

Blanchard's, Porter, Sons Company; *Nashua, 1891-1900+;* manufacturers of dairy equipment, known to have made butter scales and dairy thermometers, c. 1894; came to Nashua from Concord.

Blodgett Edge Tool Manufacturing Company; *Manchester, 1853-1862; edge tools (axes, adzes, hatchets, shaves); name changed to Amoskeag Ax Company in 1862; see also George Reynolds.*

Blodgett, Edwin; *Lisbon, 1855-1860; worked alone and probably in partnership or firm of Blodgett, Taylor & Wells; edge tools.*

Blodgett, George W.; *Monroe, 1884-1887; edge tools.*

Blodgett, Taylor & Wells; *probably Edwin Blodgett, principal partner; the part of Lisbon which later became Sugar Hill, c. 1860; edge tools.*

Bond, W. A. & C. B.; *Walpole, c. 1856; fork handles.*

Bourn, Reuben; *Richmond, before 1884; scythe snaths.*

Bowles, Thomas Salter *(1785-1851); Portsmouth, 1806-1825; mathematical instruments (surveying compasses, quadrants, sextants, telescopes, calipers, wantage rods, board rules); moved to Portland, Maine, in 1825.*

Boynton, L. D.; *Nashua, c. 1882; saws, carpenter's tools.*

Boynton, L. D., & Co.; *Nashua, 1883-1885; saws, carpenter's tools.*

Brandell, John; *Walpole; patented plane, 1898.*

Briard, Elisha *(?-1718); Portsmouth; blocks.*

Briard, Samuel *(?-1723); Portsmouth; blocks; son of Elisha Briard.*

Briggs, E.; *Keene, 18th century; one of several members of the woodworking Briggs family, whose name (with town) appears on planes; Eliphalet (1713-1780), Eliphalet, Jr. (1735-1776), and Elisha (c. 1738-1803) all came to Keene in the 1760s from Norton, Massachusetts, part of the early planemaking center surrounding Wrentham; Elisha Briggs was married in Wrentham in 1758.*

Briggs, Nathaniel *(1743-1777); Keene, c. 1773-1777; probably responsible for planes marked "N. BRIGGS" with no location given; lived both in Norton, Massachusetts, and Keene, N.H.; the second cousin of Elisha and Eliphalet Briggs, Jr.*

Brooks, George A. *(1826-1897); Alstead, 1864-1897; edge tools (axes, chisels, shaves, carpenter's tools, shovels); succeeded Hamlet L. Rice.*

Brooks, Henry O.; *Keene, 1882-1890; edge tools; apparently succeeded William H. Brooks.*

Brooks, Lebbeus *(1819-1858); Somersworth, 1853-1858; levels; patented a bar level, 1854; saw sets, 1856 and 1859 (the latter granted posthumously); owned one-tenth interest in the Great Falls Saw Set Company; "Brooks's mill saw sett" being manufactured c. 1860 by Tebbetts & Co. of Somersworth.*

Brooks, William H.; *Keene, 1879-1881; edge tools, stone tools (mill picks).*

Brown & Russell; *Chesterfield, before 1882; scythes.*

Brown & Stokes; *Manchester, c. 1870; cutlery.*

Brown, Calvin M.; *Andover, 1868-1870; handles.*

Brown, George; *Nashua, c. 1866; handles.*

Brown, George; *Nashua, c. 1866; edge tools; apparently worked for Underhill Edge Tool Company.*

Brown, Hial; *Newport, c. 1868; handles (hoe, fork).*

Brown, J. D.; *East Northwood, 1884-1886; edge tools.*

Brown, John; *Meredith Village and/or Center Harbor, c. 1887; edge tools.*

Brown, John Sleeper *(1797-1878); Auburn, 1837-?; worked alone and in partnership with brothers-in-law Flagg T. and Jay T. Underhill beginning in 1837; either John Sleeper and/or brother Nathaniel Brown worked in partnerships or firms of Underhill, Brown & Leighton, c. 1849, and Underhill & Brown, 1850-1856; edge tools; nephew of planemaker John Sleeper.*

Brown, Nathaniel *(1799-1877); Auburn; apprenticed to Jesse Johnson Underhill of that part of Chester which later became Auburn; appears to have worked alone, and either he and/or brother John Sleeper Brown worked in partnerships or firms of Underhill, Brown & Leighton, c. 1849, and Underhill & Brown, 1850-1856; edge tools; brother-in-law of Jay T. and Flagg T. Underhill.*

Brown, Oscar E.; *Middleton, 1870-1880; shoe tools, knives (carving, shoe, heel), axes.*

Brown, Peter S.; *Manchester, c. 1853; axe handles.*

Bryant; *Westmoreland, c. 1891; worked in partnership or firm of Farr & Bryant; axe handles.*

Buffum, James; *Richmond, before 1884; scythe snaths.*

Bugor, John; *Nashua, 1857-1866; edge tools; apparently worked for Underhill Edge Tool Company.*

Bunker, Nathaniel; *Moultonborough, 1872-1874; axe handles.*

Burgum, John *(1826-1907); Concord; coach painter, awarded diploma by American Institute of New York for improved try square in 1867 (also invented meat slicer, c. 1864, welder, and device for keeping meat under brine, 1866).*

Burleigh, Harry Walter *(1855-1927); Franklin; patented wrench, 1889; described in 1910 as a "manufacturer of hardware specialties"; wrenches of Burleigh's patent are found produced by the Goodell Company; account books at New Hampshire Historical Society.*

Burley, Thomas *(1723-1805); Epping; joiner, whose name (without town) is found on planes and moulding tools (including a group recently found in Rockingham County).*

Burlingame, William; *Exeter, c. 1868; machinist's tools; also proprietor of Exeter Machine Works.*

Instruments of Change

Burpee, Hamilton & Co.; *principal partners: Darius Burpee and Thomas Hamilton; Manchester, 1880-1882; edge tools (specializing in axes); two members of firm formerly with Amoskeag Ax Company; see also Charles E. Stearns.*

Burtis, R.; *East Acworth, c. 1868; handles (fork, hoe).*

Buss, Charles; *Marlborough; patented vise, 1856.*

Butterfield, John L. *(1831-?); Washington, 1854-1900 + ; sawmill operator, known to have made handles (spade, hoe), c. 1865-1870.*

Butterfield, William; *Canaan, 1849-1855; hammers; succeeded Phineas Eastman et al.*

Buxton, F.; *Lakeport (Lake Village); patented with George Crosby an edge plane for boots and shoes, 1868.*

Byron, George W.; *Stratford, c. 1855; edge tools.*

Call; *Acworth, 1884-1885; worked in partnership or firm of Kemp & Call; handles.*

Calley, Thomas *(1789-1814); Sanbornton; blacksmith, known to have made scythes.*

Campbell, William; *Gilsum; patented awl handle, 1836.*

Canney, Wesley J.; *Tuftonboro (Melvin Village), 1870-1872; edge tools (knives, axes).*

Carpenter & Co.; *Manchester, 1887-1890; brushes.*

Carpenter, O. C.; *Nashua, c. 1885; brushes.*

Carr, James; *Goffstown, 1768-1771; blacksmith, known to have made axes and bits.*

Carville; *North Sandwich, 1885-1896; worked in partnership or firm of Page & Carville; handles.*

Chamberlain, I. A.; *Dunbarton, c. 1877; scythe rifles.*

Champlin, John R.; *Laconia, 1878-1893; astronomical instruments (telescopes).*

Chandler, Abiel *(1807-1881); Concord; clockmaker, eventually specializing in "philosophical" instruments (surveyor's compasses and chains, plotting scales, protractors), 1844-1850.*

Chandler, Mary Burgin *(1842-?); Concord, 1880-1885; dressmaker, known to have patented an instrument for drafting patterns, 1883; daughter of Abiel Chandler.*

Chandler, Timothy *(1762-1848); Concord; clockmaker/silversmith, known to have made surveyor's compasses, 1792-1823 (apparently also quadrants, surveyor's chains, dividers, protractors, and scales).*

Chandler, William; *Henniker, 1878-1886; edge tools (apparently specializing in axes).*

Chapin, David B. *(1797-?); Newport, 1830-1860; worked alone and in partnership or firm of David B. Chapin & Co.; edge tools; learned his trade in Boston.*

Chapin, David B., & Co.; *Newport; blacksmiths, known to have "hired an experienced workman for shoeing & custom work," c. 1830, in order to "devote their time more exclusively to edge tools."*

Chase; *Weare, c. 1850; worked in partnership or firm of Currier & Chase; mechanic's tools, including augers.*

Chase & Drew; *Weare, c. 1855; edge tools.*

Chase & Smith; *see Smith & Chase.*

Chase, Aaron; *Woodstock, 1855-1857; edge tools.*

Chase, Amos *(1809-1884); North Weare; machinist, specializing in tanner's and currier's tools (fleshers, workers, slickers, arm boards), 1850-1860; patented a currier's grain or arm board, 1864.*

Chase, Charles F. *(1821-1884); North Weare; patented with brother John Winslow Chase a skiving machine, 1864.*

Chase, Charles J.; *Weare, 1855-1857; worked in partnership or firm of Smith & Chase; edge tools; made hay cutters, c. 1853.*

Chase, David G. *(1823-1887), listed variously as D. J. and David S.; North Weare, 1856-1887; edge tools (specializing in shoe knives), 1856-1872, 1885-1887; handles (file, knife, chisel), 1870-1881; brother of Amos Chase.*

Chase, E.; *North Weare, c. 1868; shoe knives.*

Chase, James *(1737-1812); the part of Gilmanton which later became Gilford, 1797-1812; joiner/cabinetmaker, known to have made and sold planes, plows, cooper's jointers, squares, mallets, yardsticks, and handles of all types; account books at New Hampshire Historical Society.*

Chase, John Winslow *(1813-1877); North Weare, 1846-1877; edge tool maker/machinist, known to have made hollow augers and tinner's punches, but specializing in currier's and boot and shoe manufacturer's tools (skiving machines, shoe knives); patented with J. A. Safford of Winchester, Massachusetts, and Charles F. Chase, respectively, two improved skiving machines, 1859, 1864; brother of Amos Chase.*

Chase, Joseph; *Nashua, c. 1864; edge tools; apparently worked for Underhill Edge Tool Company.*

Chase, Samuel; *Nashua, 1853-1858; worked for Underhill Edge Tool Company as forger.*

Cheever, William; *Alstead, c. 1878; edge tools.*

Childs, Amzi *(1817-?); Peterborough, 1872-1874; handles (fork, hoe).*

Church, Samuel *(1781-?); Newport; scythes; succeeded Ruel Keith.*

Claflin, John; *Campton, c. 1870; knives; see also John Coffren.*

Claremont Cutlery Company; *Claremont, 1853-1858; table cutlery.*

Claremont File Works; *Claremont, 1848-1892; files, rasps; see also Henry Nutt [& Co.], Samuel Richardson, and Charles H. Papps.*

Cleveland Stone Company; *Piermont, 1887-1890; scythe stones; absorbed by Pike Manufacturing Company.*

Clifford, Ebenezer *(1746-1821); Kensington, 1772-1793; Exeter, 1793-1808; joiner/architect, whose name appears on planes and moulding tools and who is known to have purchased hundreds of plane irons from Kensington blacksmith Jeremiah Fellows, 1772-1794.*

Clifford, George H.; *North Conway, 1885-1891; axes.*

Clifford, Marshall; *Alexandria, c. 1860; edge tools.*

Clough, C.H.; *Concord, 1868-1870; axe handles.*

Cobb, Isaac; *Walpole; patented machine for splitting skins, 1808.*

Coburn, Alonzo G. *(1858-1900); New Durham, 1870-1900; worked for father, Franklin Watson Coburn, as knife polisher (c. 1870) and later forger; possibly in partnership or firm of F. W. Coburn & Son; edge tools and shoe tools.*

Coburn, Franklin Watson *(1834-1911); New Durham (Coburnville), 1856-1910; worked alone and in partnership or firm of F. W. Coburn & Son; edge tools (axes, shave blades, shoe knives, cutlery), shoemaker's tools, hammers; apprenticed to brother-in-law James H. Fletcher; business continued by son as F. W. Coburn & Co.; undated catalogue at New Hampshire Historical Society.*

Coburn, Franklin Watson, Jr. *(1856-1918); New Durham, 1877-1914; worked for father, Franklin Watson Coburn, and probably in partnership or firm of F. W. Coburn & Son; continued father's business under firm name of F. W. Coburn & Co.; edge tools, shoemaker's tools; moved business to Farmington, c. 1915.*

Coburn, Franklin Watson, & Co.; *Franklin Watson Coburn, Jr., principal; New Durham, 1912-1914; edge tools (knives, shoe shaves); continued business of Franklin Watson Coburn after his death in 1911; moved to Farmington, c. 1915.*

Coburn, Franklin Watson, & Son; *partnership of Franklin Watson Coburn and one of his sons, Franklin W., Jr., or Alonzo G.; New Durham, 1887-1890; edge tools (shoe knives, shave blades).*

Coburn, Stillman; *Cornish, c. 1849; edge tools.*

Coffin, John T.; *Center Harbor, 1881-1892; worked alone and in partnership or firm of John T. Coffin & Son; edge tools (knives, shaves).*

Coffin, John T., & Son; *Center Harbor, 1884-1886; edge tools (knives, shaves).*

Coffren, John; *Campton, c. 1870; cutlery (butcher knives); possibly the same as John Claflin.*

Colburn; *Rindge, c. 1868; worked in partnership or firm of Allen, Colburn & Co.; sawhorses.*

Colby & Seaman; *New London, c. 1855; scythes.*

Colby, Anthony *(1792-1873); New London, 1835-1871; involved in partnerships or firms of Phillips, Messer, Colby [& Co.], Perkins, Messer, Colby & Co., and probably also Colby & Seaman; scythes; governor of New Hampshire, 1846-1847.*

Colby, John V.; *Concord, c. 1850; machinist, whose name (with town) is found on a cross-peen hammer; appears to have also worked in Nashua (Nashville), c. 1850.*

Cole & Trench; *Plainfield (Meriden), c. 1881; pruners.*

Cole, A. J.; *Concord, 1888-1890; edge tools (knife blades).*

Cole, I. H.; *Campton, c. 1860; edge tools.*

Coleman, Eben; *Wolfeboro, c. 1855; edge tools.*

Collins; *Claremont, 1868-1877; worked in partnerships or firms of Smith, Collins & Co. and Smith, Collins & Kempton; knives (chopping, mincing, shoe).*

Concord File Works; *Concord, 1874-1877; files, rasps; see also George Fantom and Henry G. Harrison.*

Constantine, S.W.; *Thornton, c. 1878; axes.*

Continental Construction Company; *Concord, c. 1882; tools; located in the former building of the New Hampshire State Prison.*

Cotter, Richard; *Portsmouth, c. 1771; cutler, who probably made, as well as repaired, small edge tools.*

Cotton, Nathaniel; *Nashua, c. 1860; wood turner, known to have made ship handspikes.*

Couch, John *(1780-1866); Salisbury, ?-1862; blacksmith, known for making edge tools.*

Couch, Samuel *(c. 1794-1865); Salisbury; blacksmith, known for his axes; said to have been taught welding and tempering by a former state prisoner; drawknife exhibited at Manchester Institute of Arts and Sciences, 1975.*

Crandall, C. H.; *Canaan, 1868-1870; pitchfork handles.*

Critchley & Whalley; *partnership of John Critchley and Nathan Whalley; Portsmouth, 1869-1881; machinists, known to have made expanding reamers.*

Critchley, John; *Portsmouth, 1865-1881; machinist, who worked alone and in partnership or firm of Critchley & Whalley; patented pipe expander, 1865.*

Crosby, George; *Lakeport (Lake Village); patented with F. Buxton an edge plane for boots and shoes, 1868.*

Crosby, Milo H.; *Bristol, 1892-1893; saws.*

Cross, Charles *(c. 1809-1895); Keene; Chesterfield; worked for Azel Wilder, for Benjamin Pierce, with Ezekiel P. Pierce, Jr. (c. 1835), and in partnership or firm of Pierce, Cross & Farr; augers, bits, gimlets.*

Cross, John; *Nashua, 1868-1872; worked in partnership or firm of Sargents & Cross; handspikes.*

Cross, Levi; *Swanzey, c. 1856; Keene, 1868-1874; worked in partnership or firm of Whitcomb & Cross; brush handles.*

Cummings; *Lebanon, c. 1860; worked in partnership or firm of Emerson & Cummings; scythes.*

Cummings & Young; *Sunapee, 1856-1857; handles (fork, hoe).*

Currier & Chase; *Weare, c. 1850; mechanic's tools, including augers.*

Currier Brothers; *partnership of Albert E. and F. Eugene Currier; Chesterfield, 1882-1886; augers, bits, gimlets, braces; came to Chesterfield from Newburyport, Massachusetts; succeeded Benjamin Pierce.*

Currier, H. G.; *Canaan, c. 1868; pitchfork handles.*

Currier, Moses F. *(1821-?); North Weare, 1850-1870; worked alone and with brother Daniel G. Currier (1825-?); augers, bits, screw plates, edge tools.*

Currier, Moses F. & Daniel G.; *partnership of two brothers; Weare, c. 1853; hollow augers, screw plates.*

Dame, Richard; *Hanover; patented tailor's measure, 1840.*

Damon, S. C.; *Bedford, 1868-1870; axe handles.*

Danforth, Jacob *(1766-1851); Jaffrey, 1792-1811; blacksmith, specializing in axes; learned blacksmithing from his brother David Danforth (1752-1827) in Amherst; returned to Amherst, 1811.*

Daniels, Albert H.; *Manchester; patented shears for cutting bale bands, 1869.*

Davis, Aaron *(1788-1857); Keene, 1812-1849; blacksmith/iron founder, known to have specialized in edge tools (axes, knives, hoes) in South Keene, 1824-1836.*

Davis, Eben; *Wentworth, c. 1850; saw frames.*

Instruments of Change

Davis, Fred A.; *Stoddard, c. 1885; scythe sticks.*

Davis, George W., & Co.; *partnership, until 1879, of George W. Davis and George A. Rollins; Nashua, 1863-1897; machinist's tools; succeeded George A. Rollins & Co.*

Davis, William F.; *Lebanon, 1876-1900 + ; worked in partnership or firm of Kendrick & Davis; watchmaker's tools.*

Day, Robert; *Peterborough, c. 1860; hoe handles.*

Dean, Hiram (1747-?); *Jaffrey, 1782-1802; steelyards; also lived in Rindge (1779-1781) and in several towns in Middlesex County, Massachusetts.*

Dearborn & Skinner; *partnership of Warren Dearborn and Elijah Skinner; Sandwich, 1828-1831; cabinetmaking partnership, known to have made and sold planes (jointer and smoothing stocks); records contained in Warren Dearborn's account book.*

Dearborn, Warren (1802-1863); *Sandwich, 1828-1862; worked alone and in partnership or firm of Dearborn & Skinner; cabinetmaker, known to have made planes (jointer and smoothing stocks), handles (all types), pulley blocks, yardsticks, rules, squares, saw frames; account books privately owned.*

Dearth, Lester A.; *Laconia; patented hand or jack plane, 1887.*

Decatur, N. J.; *New Durham, c. 1879; files.*

Demerse, Lewis; *East Alstead, 1875-1900 + ; scythe sticks.*

Dennis, George G.; *Manchester; patented bench plane guide, 1902.*

Dexter, David (?-1830); *Newport, 1780s and/or 1790s; Claremont, 1800-1824; worked with brother Stephen Dexter; scythes.*

Dexter, L. R.; *Whitefield; patented wrench ("more especially designed to be used in connection with wagons or carriages," but "applicable to other purposes"), 1869.*

Dexter, Stephen; *Newport, before 1787-1800; Claremont, 1800-1824; worked alone and with brother David Dexter; scythes.*

Dickerman; *Manchester, c. 1874; brushes; apparently succeeded William F. Robie.*

Dimick, Daniel B.; *Lyme, c. 1860; blacksmith, specializing in axes.*

Dimond, Ephraim, *variously recorded as Diamond (1797-1872); Goffstown, c. 1824; Antrim, 1825-1857; blacksmith, known for his edge tools (including scythes); probably the nephew of Israel Dimond.*

Dimond, Israel (1778?-1826?); *Goffstown; blacksmith, said to have made edge tools.*

Dodge; *Portsmouth and/or Bennington, 1868-1870; involved in partnership or firm of Woods, Dodge & Co.; cutlery.*

Dodge, Charles (1849-1912); *Piermont and Lisbon, 1878-1886; scythe stones; succeeded father, Corydon Dodge.*

Dodge, Corydon, *sometimes listed incorrectly as Croydon; Piermont and Lisbon, 1852-1878; scythe stones, scythe rifles.*

Dodge, Corydon, & Son; *probably partnership of Corydon and George Dodge; Piermont, c. 1868; scythe rifles.*

Dodge, George (1838-1877); *Piermont, 1868-1874; worked alone and probably in partnership or firm of Corydon Dodge & Son; whetstones, scythe rifles.*

Dodge, Leander F. (1822-?); *Newport, 1868-1886; worked alone and in partnership or firm of Leander F. Dodge & Co.; handles (fork, hoe); succeeded Jonathan M. Wilmarth.*

Dodge, Leander F., & Co.; *Newport, 1875-1878; handles (fork, hoe).*

Dodge, Simeon S.; *Sunapee; patented bench or hand plane, 1859.*

Doe, Charles O.; *Wolfeboro, c. 1894; cutlery.*

Dow, James (1792-1876); *Littleton, 1812-1876; joiner, possibly responsible for planes marked "J. DOW," with no location given; two of Dow's sons-in-law were planemakers—David Page Sanborn of Littleton and Franklin J. Gouch of Worcester, Massachusetts.*

Dow, Luther Thompson (1816-1898); *Littleton, 1871-1874; superintendent of the New Hampshire Scythe Company; scythes; brother-in-law of planemaker David Page Sanborn; learned scythemaking under the Redingtons.*

Dowse; *Lebanon, c. 1891; worked in partnership or firm of Merrill & Dowse; handles.*

Drake, J. L.; *Effingham, c. 1855; edge tools.*

Drew; *Weare, 1855-1857; worked in partnership or firm of Chase & Drew; edge tools.*

Drew, William E.; *Manchester, 1865-1900 + ; worked for Samuel Caldwell Forsaith from 1865, in partnership or firm of S. C. Forsaith & Co., and as agent of S. C. Forsaith Machine Company; saw sets, machinist's tools; had served his apprenticeship under Forsaith.*

Dudley, Joseph H.; *Milton, c. 1875; shoe knives; probably the same as Joseph H. Duntley.*

Dudley, Thomas D., & Co.; *Manchester, c. 1881; files.*

Dunlap, John (1746-1792); *Goffstown, 1768-1777; Bedford, 1777-1792; joiner/cabinetmaker, known to have made and sold a fork handle (1774), a sickle (1776), pulley blocks (1778-1782), scythes (1771-1782), a fore plane stock (1782), and a saw handle (1782); account book privately owned (copy at New Hampshire Historical Society).*

Dunlap, Samuel (1752-1830); *Goffstown and Bedford, 1773-1779; Henniker, 1779-1797; Salisbury, 1797-1830; joiner/cabinetmaker, known to have made and sold a bit stock (1794), a pair of compasses (1809), plane stocks (1800-1815), and a saw (1814); account book privately owned (copy at New Hampshire Historical Society).*

Duntley, Joseph H. (1847-1920); *Farmington, c. 1875; Milton, 1878-1881; Rochester, 1883-1900 + ; edge tools (shoe knives, shaves), special tools; see also Joseph H. Dudley.*

Dunton, William (1817-?); *Newport, 1842-1851; Lebanon, c. 1854; apparently worked alone in Newport and in partnership or firm of Sibley & Dunton; also worked for Phillips, Messer, Colby [& Co.] in Lebanon (apparently as foreman); scythes; came to Newport from Millbury, Massachusetts; also worked in Fitchburg, Massachusetts, and Canada.*

Durant, Edward J.; *Lebanon; patented lever-action railroad car mover, 1859.*

Durant, L. A., & Co.; *Claremont, c. 1880; handles.*

Durgin, Daniel (1792-1847); *Dover, 1830-1846; house carpenter, whose name (with town) appears on planes.*

Dustin, Jonathan; *Nashua, c. 1853*; machinist, who invented and manufactured a gold rolling machine for dentists and jewellers.

Eastman, George S.; *Canaan, c. 1849*; hammers.

Eastman, Phineas *(1772-1858)*; *Canaan, before 1849*; said to have made hammers with Dan Balch and Jonathan Kittredge; patented tool handle ("mode of making hammers and hatchets"), 1839.

Eaton; *Claremont, 1881-1884*; worked in partnership or firm of Graves & Eaton; handles (hoe, pitchfork).

Eaton, Albert; *South Hampton, c. 1870*; edge tools.

Eaton, E. & E.; possibly partnership of Edward and Edward Eaton, Jr.; *Enfield (Centerville), c. 1849*; edge tools.

Eaton, Edward; *Enfield, 1850-1860*; worked alone and possibly also in partnership or firm of E. & E. Eaton; edge tools (axes, chisels).

Eaton, Edward, Jr.; *Enfield, c. 1850*; hammers; worked alone and possibly also in edge tool making partnership or firm of E. & E. Eaton.

Eaton, Ephraim; *Penacook (Fisherville), c. 1852*; anvils.

Eaton, Hiram *(1817-?)*; *Antrim, 1841-1853*; worked in partnership or firm of White & Eaton; blacksmith, specializing in hoes, who claimed to have originated the idea of the "Antrim shovel," patented by partner Jonathan White, 1853.

Eayrs & Co.; *probably John Eayrs & Co. (apparently partnership of John and James Eayrs); Nashua, c. 1850*; lumber and emery manufacturers, probably responsible for planes and moulding tools marked: "EAYRS & CO./MAKERS/NASHUA, NH"; however, Eayrs & Co. name was also used, 1870-1881, by James Eayrs and family as proprietors of Pennichuck Drug Mill.

Edwards[s], Reuben J.; *East Alstead, c. 1875; Marlow, c. 1885*; scythe snath sticks.

Eggleston, William; *Cornish, mid-19th century*; woodenware manufacturers, known to have made axe helves.

Ellis & Olcott; *partnership of Thomas S. Ellis and Barzillai S. Olcott; Lancaster*; iron founders, 1875-1876, who are said to have owned and operated Lancaster File Works.

Ellis Brothers, apparently a partnership of R. J. and Thomas S. Ellis (1845-1909); *Lancaster, c. 1878*; files; probably owned Lancaster File Works, as R. J. Ellis was its proprietor in 1877 and T. S. in 1879.

Ellis, Austin A.; *Keene, 1893-1900 +*; brush handles.

Ely, Farr & Co.; *partnership of George W. Ely, George B. Redington, and John Farr; Littleton (Apthorp, formerly Scythe Factory Village), 1835-1842*; scythes.

Ely, George Warner *(1808-1876)*; *Littleton, 1835-1844*; worked in partnership or firm of Ely, Farr & Co.; scythes; moved to St. Johnsbury, Vermont, in 1844, where he made forks and hoes; brother-in-law of George B. and Henry C. Redington.

Emerson; *Lebanon, c. 1885*; worked in partnership or firm of Stearns & Emerson; snaths, etc.

Emerson; *Piermont*; worked in partnership or firm of Evans & Emerson; scythe stones.

Emerson & Cummings; *Lebanon, c. 1860*; scythes.

Emerson & Kimball; *Lebanon, c. 1868*; scythes.

Emerson & Ware; *partnership of Willis K. Emerson and Walter H. Ware; Milford, 1887-1895*; woodenware manufacturers, known to have specialized in tool chests, c. 1890.

Emerson Edge Tool Company; *East Lebanon, 1882-1900 +*; scythes, axes, shovels, hoes, hay knives, grass hooks, corn and straw knives; operated works also at Taftsville, Vermont, c. 1882.

Emerson, A. V.; *East Lebanon, 1894-1895*; edge tools.

Emerson, A. V. & M. W.; *Lebanon, c. 1868*; edge tools.

Emerson, E. V.; *Deerfield Center, c. 1878*; edge tools.

Emerson, Timothy *(1825-1905)*; *Barnstead Center, 1868-1870*; edge tools.

Emerton, Frank W., [& Co.]; *Rumney, c. 1860*; hoes, forks, knives (chopping, shoe).

Emerton, Joseph *(1804-1857)*, sometimes listed as Emerson; *Rumney, 1840-1860*; hoes, forks, manure hooks.

Estes, E. B., & Son; *Winchester (Ashuelot), c. 1893*; handles.

Eureka Wrench Company; *Eben N. Higley, agent; Somersworth (Great Falls), after 1882*; combination wrench and oiler; product based on patent of Prescott B. Kinsman and Josiah Merrill; advertising broadside at New Hampshire Historical Society.

Evans & Emerson; *Piermont*; scythe stones.

Evans & Libby; *Piermont*; scythe stones.

Evans & Risley; *Piermont, 1855-1857*; scythe stones; see also Lewis E. Risley, whose wife was an Evans.

Evans, William B.; *Campton, 1884-1887*; axes.

Exeter Machine Works; *Exeter, 1868-1894*; machinist's tools, vises, jeweller's tools; see also William Burlingame.

Fairbanks, Leonard O.; *Nashua*; patented a square and bevel attachment for planes and other bench tools, 1861.

Fantom, George; *Concord, c. 1877; Manchester, 1878-1886*; worked alone and in partnership or firm of George Fantom & Co.; proprietor of Concord File Works, c. 1877, and proprietor, agent, and/or foreman of Manchester File Works, 1882-1886; files and rasps.

Fantom, George, & Co.; *Manchester, c. 1882*; files and rasps; this partnership or firm served as agent or proprietor of Manchester File Works.

Farley, Benjamin; *Hollis, c. 1849*; cooper's edge tools.

Farnham, J. H.; *Manchester, 1887-1890*; worked alone and in partnership or firm of J. H. & W. J. Farnham; files.

Farnham, J. H. & W. J.; *Manchester, 1887-1888*; files.

Farr & Bryant; *Westmoreland, c. 1891*; axe handles; see also E. A. Farr & Co.

Farr, Alonzo *(1816?-1893?)*; *Chesterfield, after 1835*; worked in partnership or firm of Pierce, Cross & Farr; augers, bits, gimlets.

Farr, E. A., & Co.; *Westmoreland, c. 1893*; axe helves; probably succeeded Farr & Bryant.

Instruments of Change

Farr, John *(1810-1892); Littleton, 1835-1837; worked in partnership or firm of Ely, Farr & Co.; scythes; entered the law and, in 1871, became one of the organizers of the New Hampshire Scythe Company.*

Farr, Olin Ransom *(1855-?); West Chesterfield, 1877-1886; woodenware manufacturer, specializing in brush handles.*

Farr, Ora *(1786-1828); West Chesterfield; worked in partnership with brother-in-law John Snow; scythes, hoes.*

Farwell, C. & H.; *Harrisville, 1886-1890; brush handles.*

Farwell, John; *New Ipswich, before 1810; worked in partnership or firm of Ormsbee & Farwell; scythes; said to have moved to Fitchburg, Massachusetts, and carried on scythemaking on a larger scale.*

Fellows, Jeremiah *(1749-1837); Kensington, 1772-1832; blacksmith, known to have made and sold plane irons and a wide variety of other tools; account book privately owned.*

Fellows, Jonathan; *Concord, c. 1860; axes.*

Fellows, Samuel; *Wentworth, c. 1856; saw frames.*

Felton, S. A., & Co.; *Manchester, 1879-1885; brushes; succeeded L. H. Josselyn & Co.*

Felton, S. A., & Son; *Manchester, 1886-1892; brushes; succeeded S. A. Felton & Co.*

Felton, S. A., & Son Company; *Manchester, 1893-1900+; brushes; succeeded S. A. Felton & Son.*

Fernald, William [D.]; *Portsmouth, 1834-1860; worked alone and in partnership or firm of Martin & Fernald; blocks.*

Ferry, Joel; *Croydon, c. 1860; knives.*

Fessenden, James M.; *Rochester, 1850-1860; files.*

Fifield, George E.; *Newfields (South Newmarket), 1879-1890; machinist's tools, crank oilers.*

Fisher, C. V.; *Penacook (Fisherville), 1875-1886; East Pembroke, 1898-1900+; worked alone and in partnership or firm of Hiram M. Fisher & Sons; handles (axe, hammer, sledge); succeeded father, Hiram M. Fisher.*

Fisher, Hiram M. *(?-c. 1895); Penacook (Fisherville), 1868-1886; East Pembroke, c. 1894; worked alone and in partnership or firm of Hiram M. Fisher & Sons; handles (axe, hammer, sledge); estate continued to produce handles in Pembroke until c. 1897.*

Fisher, Hiram M., & Sons; *partnership of H. M., G. E., and C. V. Fisher; Penacook (Fisherville), 1875-1886; handles (axe, hammer, sledge).*

Fisherville Saw Company; *J. E. Marden and George Seldon Locke, proprietors; Penacook (Fisherville), 1882-1900+; saws (all types, including ice saws); succeeded Gage, Porter & Co.*

Fitts, J. E.; *Candia, c. 1881; saw frames.*

Fitzgerald, Rufus; *Nashua, 1886-1890; fishermen's ice augers, fishing rods.*

Flagg, Edward Hillary *(1864-1911); Dover, 1898-1911; worked in partnership or firm of Joshua G. Flagg & Son; knives, specializing in leather splitting knives; carried on business under same name after father's death.*

Flagg, Joshua Getchell *(1834-1907); Dover, 1874-1906; appears to have worked alone and in partnerships or firms of George W. Hobbs & Co. (Hobbs & Flagg) and Joshua G. Flagg & Son; knives, specializing in leather splitting knives.*

Flagg, Joshua Getchell, & Son; *partnership of Joshua Getchell and Edward Hillary Flagg; Dover, 1898-1909; knives, specializing in leather splitting knives; business carried on under same name by son after father's death in 1907; succeeded George W. Hobbs & Co.*

Flanders Hardware Company; *William Wallace Flanders, proprietor; North Weare, 1898-1900+; edge tools, knife handles.*

Flanders, Frederick; *Franklin; patented with Solomon E. Bickford a graduated bevel square, 1867.*

Flanders, John H. *(c. 1808-?); Penacook (Fisherville), c. 1850; apparently worked for Gage, Hubbard & Co.; saws.*

Flanders, William Wallace *(1870-1922); North Weare, 1892-1900+; worked alone and as proprietor of Flanders Hardware Company; handles; son-in-law of Peleg B. Thurston.*

Flanders, Winthrop B. *(c. 1832-?); Penacook (Fisherville), c. 1850; apparently worked for Gage, Hubbard & Co.; saws.*

Flather & Co.; *partnership of brothers Joseph and William J. Flather; Nashua, 1867-1900+; engine lathe manufacturers, who also made machinist's tools; brothers came to Nashua from England (after working elsewhere in America) and bought machine shop of Joseph K. Priest.*

Flather, Mark; *Nashua, c. 1888; machinist's tools.*

Flemaux, Joseph; *Wentworth, c. 1856; saw frames.*

Fletcher, George W.; *New Durham, 1872-1881; worked alone and in partnership or firm of George W. Fletcher & Co.; edge tools (cutlery, shoe knives).*

Fletcher, George W., & Co.; *New Durham, 1878-1879; shoe knives.*

Fletcher, James H.; *New Durham, 1850-1857; edge tools; brother-in-law of Franklin Watson Coburn, who was apprenticed to Fletcher, c. 1850.*

Fletcher, Tristram H. *(c. 1835-?); New Durham, c. 1870; Dover, c. 1880; boot and shoe knives and tools.*

Fonda, Isaac; *Laconia; patented saw clamp, 1872.*

Forbes, Nathan; *Plymouth, 1795-1805; gunsmith, known to have patented a machine for boring gun barrels, 1804.*

Forsaith, Hiram *(1820-1908); Manchester, 1864-1891; machinist, known to have made machinist's tools, 1870-1877.*

Forsaith, Samuel Caldwell *(1827-1885); Manchester, 1860-1885; machinist, who worked alone and in partnership or firm of S. C. Forsaith & Co.; later served as treasurer of S. C. Forsaith Machine Company; machinist's tools, lever saw sets; brother of Hiram Forsaith.*

Forsaith, Samuel Caldwell, & Co.; *partnership of Samuel C. Forsaith and William E. Drew; Manchester, 1872-1884; machinery and circular saw manufacturers, known to have manufactured lever saw sets and machinist's tools, 1879-1883; another partnership previously with same name (partnership of Samuel C. and Hiram Forsaith, c. 1865), not known to have made tools.*

Forsaith, Samuel Caldwell, Machine Company; *William E. Drew, agent; Manchester, 1884-1900+; machinery and circular saw manufacturers, known to have made lever saw sets, machinist's tools, 1884-1895; succeeded S. C. Forsaith & Co.*

Foss, Ivory; *Freedom, 1855-1857; edge tools.*

Foss, Obed; *Hillsborough Bridge, 1872-1874; shovel handles.*

Foss, Thomas *(1728?-?); said to have been a carpenter/joiner of Portsmouth; name (without town) appears on planes.*

Foss, William G.; *Hillsborough Bridge, 1874-1875; handles (fork, shovel).*

Foster, Orra I.; *Salem; patented sand-papering machine, 1872.*

Fowler, Cyrus; *Freedom, 1855-1857; edge tools.*

Fox, John M.; *Weare, 1886-1905; blacksmith, whose name (without town) appears on cooking forks and other utensils.*

Fox, Josiah F.; *Pelham, 1853-1877; edge tools, specializing in pruning shears.*

French, Frank L. *(1853-1924); Plainfield (Meriden), 1894-1895; wrenches.*

French, G. B.; *Dunbarton, 1868-1870; scythe rifles.*

French, Nathaniel; *Hollis, 1884-1885; axe handles.*

French, P.; *Bedford, c. 1856; forks.*

Frost, H. N.; *Plaistow, c. 1872; axes.*

Fuller, Levi; *Marlborough, 1892-1897; handles.*

Fury, James *(?-1873); Concord, 1867-1872; blacksmith, said to have made ice picks, saws, hammers, axes.*

Gage, Calvin *(1811-1889); Penacook (Fisherville); lumber manufacturer, also a member of partnerships or firms of Gage, Hubbard & Co. and Gage, Porter & Co., 1849-1880; saws.*

Gage, Hiram; *Penacook (Fisherville), c. 1850; machinist, who advertised bench screws.*

Gage, Hubbard & Co.; *Calvin Gage, John Chandler Gage, Sherman D. Hubbard, and Hermon M. Rolfe, proprietors; Penacook (Fisherville), 1849-1854; saws (cross-cut, pit, felloe, turning, veneering, billet, wood cutter's, web, pruning, butcher's, chest, hand, panel, ripping), plasterer's trowels; succeeded Porter & Rolfe.*

Gage, Isaac Kimball *(1818-1894); Penacook (Fisherville), 1854-1882; managing partner of Gage, Porter & Co.; saws; cousin of Calvin Gage.*

Gage, John Chandler *(1814-1895); Penacook (Fisherville); lumber manufacturer, also a member of partnerships or firms of Gage, Hubbard & Co. and Gage, Porter & Co., 1849-1880; saws; brother of Calvin Gage.*

Gage, John H. *(1815-1862); Nashua, 1838-?; worked alone (in machine shop of Nashua Manufacturing Company) and in partnership or firm of Gage, Warner & Whitney; his shop is said to have been "the first establishment in the United States devoted exclusively to the manufacture of machinists' tools"; also served as first president of the Underhill Edge Tool Company.*

Gage, Porter & Co.; *Isaac Kimball Gage, Calvin Gage, John Chandler Gage, George Porter, and Hermon M. Rolfe, proprietors; Penacook (Fisherville), 1854-1882; saws (cross-cut, pit, wood, and others); succeeded Gage, Hubbard & Co.*

Gage, Warner & Whitney; *partnership of John H. Gage, David A. G. Warner, and George H. Whitney; Nashua, 1851-1864; machinist's tools, planes.*

Gale, Elijah B.; *Nashua, 1857-1889; edge tools; worked for Underhill Edge Tool Company.*

Gannett, William H.; *Piermont, 1874-1887; scythe stones.*

Gannon, George; *Raymond, 1883-1884; stencils.*

Garland, J. H.; *Enfield (Centerville), c. 1849; hoes.*

Garnsey, Cyrus; *Richmond, before 1884; scythe snaths.*

Garnsey, William; *Richmond, before 1884; scythe snaths.*

Gee, Asa; *Sutton, 1855-1857; edge tools.*

George, Currier; *Danville, c. 1850; Sandown, 1855-1857; edge tools (including axes).*

George, William F. *(1818?-1865); Pittsfield, c. 1860; blacksmith, known to have made edge tools; born in Sandown and possibly related to Currier George; said to have learned his trade in New York State.*

Gerould, Richardson & Skinner; *Keene, 1868-1870; stencils.*

Gerrish, Stephen *(1770-1815); Boscawen; blacksmith, said to have invented the "attachment of the screw to the pod-auger" and an auger for boring logs and wooden pumps; a fleshing knife with horn handles found in Boscawen bears his initials and date, 1804.*

Gerry, Eben G.; *Wolfeboro, c. 1855; edge tools.*

Gibson, Francis Newton *(1839-1905); New Ipswich, 1875-1885; leather creasing machines.*

Gilford, Tyler *(c. 1827-?); Penacook (Fisherville), c. 1850; apparently worked for Gage, Hubbard & Co.; saws.*

Gilkey; *Colebrook, c. 1883; worked in partnership or firm of Graham & Gilkey; spades.*

Gilman, Benjamin Clark *(1763-1835); Exeter, 1791-1835; clockmaker/silversmith, who also made mathematical instruments (surveying and navigational instruments, carriage odometers).*

Gilman, Josiah; *apparently worked in partnership with brother Winthrop Gilman; Gilford; blacksmith, said to have made small tools.*

Gilman, Winthrop; *apparently worked in partnership with brother Josiah Gilman; Gilford; blacksmith, said to have made small tools.*

Gilmore, Hiram *(?-1862); Claremont, 1826-1856; worked alone and in partnership with brother Leonard Gilmore; edge tools (axes, scythes, etc.); moved to Montreal in 1858, where he specialized in augers and bits.*

Gilmore, John; *Bedford, 1764-1771; blacksmith, known to have made butcher and jackknives.*

Gilmore, Leonard *(?-1876); Claremont, 1826-1841; worked in partnership with brother Hiram Gilmore; edge tools (axes, scythes, etc.).*

Globe Tool Works; *Hampstead, c. 1871; shoe tools.*

Goodall, Frank P.; *Deering; patented tree pruning knife, 1859.*

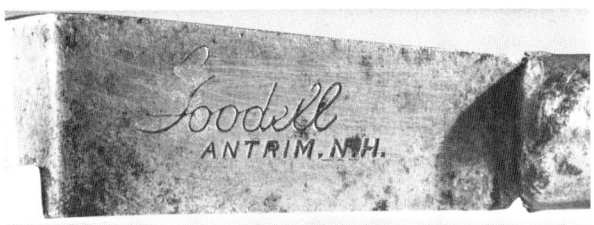

Goodell Company; *formed by consolidation of operations of David Harvey Goodell and Woods Cutlery Company; Antrim, 1875-1900+; Bennington, 1879-1900+; cutlery (table, butcher's, skinning, hunting, sticking, cigar, apple, broom, budding, putty, carver's, and shoe knives), file and knife handles, wrenches; also made apple, peach, and potato parers, cherry stoners, seed sowers, pencil pointers, and can openers; operated six factories at Antrim and Bennington by 1908.*

Goodell, David Harvey (1834-1915); *Antrim, 1857?-1915; Bennington, 1872-1915; edge tools (shovels, cutlery); treasurer/agent of Antrim Shovel Company, 1857?-1861+; worked alone and in partnership of D. H. Goodell & Co. (1865-1867) manufacturing seed sowers, apple parers (which he patented, 1864), and knife handles, c. 1874; helped organize the Woods Cutlery Company in Bennington, 1872; founded the Goodell Company, 1875, and served as its manager; governor of New Hampshire, 1889-1891.*

Goodnow, L. F.; *Marlow, c. 1868; fork handles.*

Goodrich, George (1822-1884); *Chesterfield, ?-1855; worked alone and in partnership or firm of Atherton & Goodrich; bits, augers.*

Goodwin, Joseph; *Nashua, 1851-1857; brushes (floor, furniture, whitewash, paint, grainer's and blender's).*

Gordon, Edward F. (1842-?); *Concord, 1879-1887; worked in partnership or firm of Hobbs, Gordon & Co.; machinist's tools; patented lubricator for planes, 1879.*

Graham & Gilkey; *Colebrook, 1876-1891; iron founders/machinists, known to have made spades, c. 1883.*

Granite File Works; *Benjamin S. Stokes, proprietor; Manchester, 1851-1881; files and rasps, "from the finest article used by the watchmaker, to the largest rasp for wood work."*

Graves & Eaton; *Claremont, 1881-1884; handles (hoe, pitchfork); see also Bela Graves.*

Graves, Bela; *Claremont, 1879-1884; worked alone and apparently in partnership or firm of Graves & Eaton; handles (fork, hoe).*

Graves, Caleb S.; *Chesterfield, (Factory Village), c. 1849; bits, augers.*

Great Falls Saw Set Company; *Somersworth (Great Falls), c. 1858; saw sets; see also Lebbeus Brooks and William Orne Rust.*

Green, John; *Portsmouth, c. 1755; blocks.*

```
F  M GREENLEAF
      LITTLETON
              N H
MAKER
```

Greenleaf, Florence M., *variously called "Flossie," "Flossa" (1882-?); Littleton, ?-1916; log calipers; daughter of William Gardner Greenleaf; later worked in Belmont, Massachusetts, and Jacksonville, Alabama.*

Greenleaf, William Gardner, *sometimes spelled Greenlief (1834-1916); Littleton, 1868-1916; woodworker/carriagemaker, known to have spent his retirement (c. 1903-1916) in the manufacture of log calipers.*

Greenleaf, William P.; *Washington; patented mode of fastening scythes to snaths, 1855.*

Greenwood, Samuel (1790-1858?); *New London, 1842-1858; involved in partnership or firm of Phillips, Messer, Colby & Co.; scythes.*

Griffin, Francis B.; *Hinsdale, 1883-1900+; involved in partnership or firm of Jennings & Griffin Manufacturing Company; chisels, drawknives, etc.*

Griffin, George Washington (1839-1913); *Franklin, 1879-1908?; worked in partnership or firm of George W. Griffin & Co.; saws; said to have invented several machines used in saw manufacture.*

Griffin, George Washington, & Co.; *partnership of George Washington Griffin and Parker Cross Hancock; Franklin, 1879-1908; scroll and fret saw manufacturers, who eventually also made other types of saws (hack, jeweller's, coping); also made rug machines.*

Griffin, George Washington, Company; *Franklin, 1908-1979; saws (hack, jeweller's, coping); also scroll saws; succeeded G. W. Griffin & Co.; business records and company scrapbooks at New Hampshire Historical Society.*

Grover, John B.; *Nashua, 1892-1894; worked in partnerships or firms of Ridge & Grover and John B. Grover & Co.; files and rasps.*

Grover, John B., & Co.; *partnership of John B. Grover and Louis B. Ames; Nashua, 1893-1894; files and rasps (including horse rasps); proprietors of Nashua Rasp Company; succeeded Ridge & Grover.*

Haines & Wallace; *partnership of Joseph A. Haines and Andrew C. Wallace; Manchester, c. 1872; machinist's tools.*

Hale, Franklin W. (1851-?); *Henniker; storekeeper/traveling merchant whose name (with town) appears as maker on yardsticks.*

Haley Manufacturing Company; *Concord, 1887-1893; brush wire.*

Hall, Andrew J.; *Farmington; patented shoe knife, 1873.*

Hall, Elma E.; *Barrington, c. 1894; axe handles.*

Hall, Frank P.; *Concord, 1874-1878; stencils, steel stamps, dies.*

Hall, J. H.; *Shelburne, 1855-1857; edge tools.*

Hall, James H.; *Lancaster, c. 1849; edge tools, including forks.*

Hall, James Horace *(1842-1937); Nashua, c. 1880-1890; planes; "sole manufacturer and proprietor of Warren's improved mitre plane."*

Ham, Ephraim; *Portsmouth, 1757-1772; blocks.*

Hamilton, M.; *see Matthew Harvey Milton.*

Hamilton, Thomas; *Manchester, 1871-1900 + ; worked in partnership or firm of Burpee, Hamilton & Co., 1880-1882; also worked (as overseer) for Amoskeag Ax Company, 1871-1879; for Manchester Axe Company, 1883-1884; and (as handlemaker and foreman) for B. H. Piper [&] Co., 1886-1900 + ; edge tools and handles.*

Hammond, John McCurdy *(1826-?), incorrectly recorded in 1868 as John C. McHammond; Dunbarton, 1858-1868; scythe rifles; his brother, James Mills, may have worked with him, c. 1858.*

Hancock, Parker Cross *(1843-1908); Franklin, 1879-1908; worked in partnership or firm of George W. Griffin & Co.; saws; brother-in-law of George Washington Griffin.*

Hannaford, Taylor P.; *New Hampton, c. 1850; saw frames.*

Hanson, Daniel *(1837-1907); North Weare, 1877-1906; skiving machines; succeeded John Winslow Chase, from whom he learned his trade.*

Hanson, James; *Weare, c. 1850; currier's tools; probably the James Hanson who died in Weare in 1854 and who, although a carriagemaker by trade, was the father of skiving machine maker Daniel Hanson.*

Hardy Brothers; *Rumney Depot, c. 1879; handles; see also Baxter P. Hardy.*

Hardy, Baxter P.; *Rumney Depot, 1879-1892; worked alone and apparently in partnership or firm of Hardy Brothers; handles (including fork, ice hook).*

Hardy, David P.; *Hebron, c. 1872; edge tools.*

Hardy, E. D.; *Hebron, c. 1886; butcher's knives.*

Hardy, Ephraim L. *(1801-1870); Brookline, 1841-1870; edge tools (axes, shaves), specializing in cooper's tools; came to Brookline from Hollis.*

Harris, Luke *(1781?-1865?); Richmond, before 1884; scythe snaths.*

Harrison, Henry G.; *Concord, 1872-1875; files and rasps; proprietor of Concord File Works, c. 1874.*

Harrison, John; *Webster, 1868-1870; axes.*

Hart, William *(1734-1812); Portsmouth, 1757-1809; mathematical instruments (surveyor's and mariner's compasses, quadrants, sextants, plotting and Gunter's scales, gauging rods, rulers, perspective, time, and spy glasses, etc.); account books at New Hampshire Historical Society; see also Michael Whidden.*

Hartshorn & Co.; *partnership of Charles Hartshorn, Cyrus Eastman, and Samuel Alden Edson; Littleton, 1862-1870; scythes; succeeded Wesley Alexander.*

Hartshorn, Anson, *listed variously as Anderson and A. H.; Nashua, 1853-1858; edge tools; apparently worked for Underhill Edge Tool Company as axe grinder.*

Hartshorn, Charles *(1817-?); Littleton; principal member of the partnership or firm of Hartshorn & Co.; also known to have served as treasurer of New Hampshire Scythe Company, 1874-1875; scythes, axes.*

Hartwell, Ephraim *(1745-1816); New Ipswich, before 1800-?; scythes; came to New Ipswich from Princeton, Massachusetts, c. 1782; see also John Putnam.*

Haselton, Hermon R.; *variously spelled Herman Hazelton, Hazeltine, Hezelton, etc. (1856-1939); Groton, 1877-1878; Hopkinton (Contoocook), 1881-1924; worked alone and in partnership or firm of Rufus B. Haselton & Son; log calipers, board and wood measures, wine gauges, outing sticks, yardsticks, glazier's rules; son of Rufus B. Haselton; after father's death, continued to mark product with father's name rather than his own.*

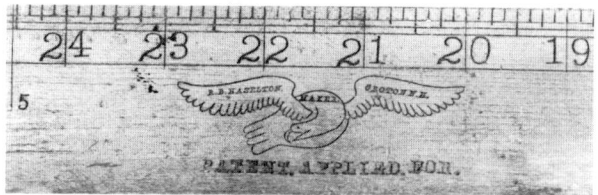

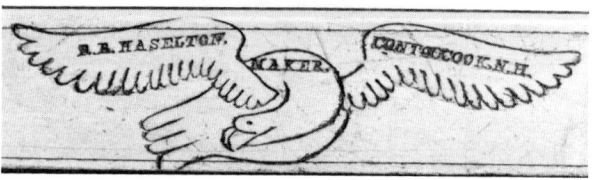

Haselton, Rufus B. *(1828-1879); Groton, 1847-1878; Hopkinton (Contoocook), 1872-1874; worked alone and in partnership or firm of Rufus B. Haselton & Son; rules (board, bench, log, school, and bookkeeper's), yardsticks, calipers, gauges, squares, wantage rods; living in Warner, 1875.*

Haselton, Rufus B., & Son; *partnership of Rufus B. and Hermon R. Haselton; Groton, 1877-1879; log calipers, squares, yardsticks, bookkeeper's, glazier's, and board rules.*

Hasham, Stephen, *variously called Hassam (c. 1764-1861); Charlestown, 1787-1844; clockmaker, whose name (with town) has been found on a surveyor's semi-circumferenter dated 1788; also said to have constructed his own carriage odometer; came to Charlestown from Massachusetts.*

Hastings, William N., & Son; *Nashua, c. 1891; "microscopists."*

Hathorn, Ebenezer *(?-1819); Jaffrey, 1770-1819; blacksmith, specializing in steelyards; came to Jaffrey from Wilmington and Andover, Massachusetts.*

Haven, B. T.; *Newport (Northville), c. 1849; fork handles.*

Haven, Benjamin F. *(1819-?); Newport; believed to have been listed incorrectly c. 1855 as a hone maker; actually a hame maker.*

Haven, James; *Newport; patented lathe for turning rake, etc., handles, 1835.*

Hawkins, Floyd F.; *Acworth, c. 1880; handles (axe, pick).*

Hayden, Henry W.; *Concord, 1888-1907; worked alone as granite polisher and in partnership or firm of Nutting & Hayden; granite worker's and stone cutter's tools; born in Quincy, Massachusetts.*

Hayes Brothers; *partnership of Seth W., George, and Augustus Hayes; New Durham, 1885-1910; cutlery, specializing in shoe knives; said to have learned their trade in Haverhill, Massachusetts.*

Hayes, Israel; *Farmington; shoe manufacturer, known to have patented a shoe shave, 1864.*

Heald & Co.; *Addison Heald, principal; Nashua, c. 1856; described as "manufacturer of tools" and probably responsible for planes found marked "A. HEALD & CO." (without town).*

Heald, Addison (1817-1895); *Nashua, c. 1856; Hudson, c. 1868; Milford, 1868-1895; worked alone and in partnerships or firms of Heald & Co., Warren & Heald, and Addison Heald & Son; planes and cooper's tools; apparently learned planemaking from Cyrus and/or William Warren.*

Heald, Addison, & Son; *partnership of Addison and Daniel Milton Heald; Milford, 1873-1906; bench planes and cooper's tools; also made toy planes; after death of Addison Heald in 1895, business continued under same name by son.*

Heald, Daniel Milton (1852-1929); *Milford, 1873-1906; worked in partnership or firm of Addison Heald & Son; bench planes and cooper's tools; patented bench plane, 1878.*

Heald, Paul; *Atkinson, 1849-1860; machinist, specializing in edge tools by 1856.*

Healey, W. W.; *Hampton Falls, 1882-1886; bolt cutters.*

Hemenway, Luther (1780-1870); *Sullivan, c. 1828; Gilsum, 1832-?; patented awl handle, 1828; apparently manufactured awls as well.*

Hewes' Mill; *Richmond, before 1884; hoes, scythes.*

Heywood, Simeon; *Claremont, 1856-1857; handles (fork, hoe).*

Higley, Eben N. (1843-1920); *Somersworth (Great Falls), 1869-1912; machinist, known to have served as agent of the Eureka Wrench Company, after 1882, and as manager of the Self-Holding Pruner Company, c. 1912; wrenches, pruners; learned his trade in Lakeport (Lake Village).*

Hildreth, John Caldwell (1808-1905); *New Ipswich, 1839-1884; blacksmith, known to have sold tools, 1847.*

Hildreth, Solomon, & Son; *Plainfield, c. 1860; axe handles.*

Hill, John (?-c. 1762); *Portsmouth; blocks.*

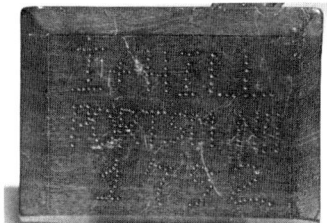

Hill, John; *Portsmouth, c. 1803; joiner, probably responsible for moulding tools marked "I + HILL" (with town given) — one of which is dated 1792 (probably made for joiner's own use).*

Hillard, George W.; *Lisbon, 1855-1857; edge tools.*

Hinsdale Machine and Tool Company; *Hinsdale, 1885-1890; tools.*

Hinton, George (c. 1824-?); *Penacook (Fisherville), c. 1850; apparently worked for Gage, Hubbard & Co.; saws.*

Hinton, John; *Nashua, 1860-1875; saws; seems to have specialized in circular saws by 1874.*

Hobart, George W. L. (1824-1913); *Brookline, 1855-1881; blacksmith, specializing in edge tools.*

Hobbs & Flagg; *see George W. Hobbs & Co.*

Hobbs, George W. (1827-1903); *Dover, 1867-1895; worked alone and in partnership or firm of G. W. Hobbs & Co. (Hobbs & Flagg); edge tools, specializing in knives (including currier's and shoe knives); learned the business of manufacturing knives in Massachusetts.*

Hobbs, George W., & Co. *(also known as Hobbs & Flagg); partnership of George W. Hobbs and Joshua Getchell Flagg; Dover, 1880-1895; edge tools, specializing in knives (including leather splitting knives); the two firm names apparently used interchangeably, particularly between 1884 and 1890.*

Hobbs, Gordon & Co.; *partnership of Horatio Hobbs and Edward F. Gordon; Concord, 1883-1887; machinist's tools (including saw gummers/sharpeners); located in the former building of the New Hampshire State Prison.*

Hoit, Josiah; *Sandown, 1855-1857; edge tools.*

Holbrook, Enos (1772-?); *Richmond, 1805-1830; scythes, hoes; born in Uxbridge, Massachusetts; moved to Illinois, 1834.*

Holman & Merriman; *partnership of J. R. Holman and C. D. Merriman; Hinsdale, 1868-1885; machinists, known to have made jack, bench, and press screws, c. 1868.*

Holmes, Charles W.; *Bristol, 1893-1894; machinist, known to have made vises and jack screws.*

Holmes, William; *Winchester; patented twisted screw auger for boring guns, 1820.*

Holt Brothers; *partnership of A. Frank, Benjamin, Harrison W., and Charles H. Holt; Concord; carriage stock manufacturers, known to have made handles, 1878-1879.*

Holt, C. F.; *Antrim, 1882-1885; handles (knife, etc.).*

Holt, Henry A.; *Wilton; patented carpenter's plane, 1872.*

Homans, L. W.; *Bristol, 1889-1893; blacksmith, who advertised, in 1892, "tool making a specialty."*

Hook, Abraham (c. 1805-?); *Penacook (Fisherville), c. 1850; apparently worked for Gage, Hubbard & Co.; saws.*

Hopkins & Pierce; *partnership of Richard Henry Hopkins and Fred B. Pierce; Chesterfield, 1868-1870; augers and bits.*

Hopkins, Richard Henry (1831-1877); *Chesterfield, 1855?-1870; Hinsdale, 1870-1873; machinist, known to have worked for Benjamin Pierce and in partnerships or firms of Hopkins & Pierce, Howe & Hopkins, and Wilder & Hopkins; may also have worked alone; augers and bits, edge tools (chisels, drawknives), and hatchels; patented auger or bit, 1870; said to have learned his trade in Hinsdale, apparently under Cyrus S. Tolman.*

Hopkins, William (?-1761); *Portsmouth; blocks.*

Houghton, Joseph *(c. 1851-1901); Manchester, 1883-1901; watchmaker's tools; previously employed by Elgin Watch Company of Elgin, Illinois; said to have invented several watchmaker's tools.*

House, Charles D.; *Lakeport (Lake Village); patented an apple cutting and coring knife, 1869.*

Houston, Harry; *Concord, 1830-1864; blacksmith, whose name (with town) appears on an axle gauge, and who is known to have worked as a blacksmith for successive Abbot-Downing carriage-making firms.*

Houston, James; *Bedford, 1759-1787; blacksmith, known to have made a jackknife blade, axe, [scythe] nibs and wedges, eel hooks, picks.*

Houston, John P.; *Bedford; patented with Otis Freeman Bachelder a machine for shaving leather, 1825.*

Howard Brush Company; *Claremont, c. 1886; brushes.*

Howard, J. B.; *Claremont, c. 1868; handles.*

Howard, Joseph B.; *Alstead (Paper Mill Village), c. 1849; fork handles.*

Howard, W. B.; *Claremont, 1856-1857; handles (fork, hoe).*

Howe & Hopkins; *partnership of Richard Henry Hopkins and Horace Howe; Chesterfield, before 1870; woodenware manufacturers, known to have made hatchels.*

Howe, Horace *(?-1870); Chesterfield; worked in partnership or firm of Howe & Hopkins; hatchels.*

Hoyt; *Grafton, c. 1856; worked in partnership or firm of Lang & Hoyt; axes.*

Hoyt, Thomas Rowell *(1776-1861); Goffstown; patented shoemaker's clamp, 1817.*

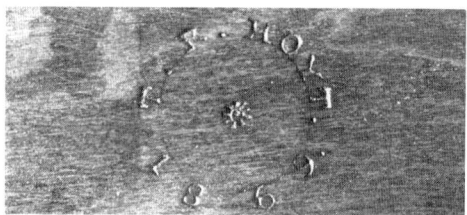

Hoyt, Thomas Rowell *(1811-1898); Goffstown, 1845-1886; mathematical instruments (calipers, board and wood rules, gauging rods, yardsticks, etc.); son of above.*

Hubbard, Sherman D. *(c. 1822-?); Penacook (Fisherville), 1849-1854; worked in partnership or firm of Gage, Hubbard & Co.; saws.*

Huggins, Oliver B.; *Chesterfield, c. 1835-1851; worked in partnership or firm of Richardson & Huggins; bits, augers, gimlets.*

Humphrey Machine Company; *Keene, 1874-1920; founders/machinists, known to have made machinist's tools and log calipers (1882-1904); also known to have made axe helve lathes, 1882-1886; succeeded John Humphrey & Co.*

Humphrey, John, & Co.; *partnership of John Humphrey & Lewis Herrick; Keene, 1868-1872; machinists, whose name (with town) appears on log calipers and who are known to have made machinist's tools.*

Huntington, Gurdon *(1763-1804); Walpole, 1789-1804; clockmaker/silversmith, who advertised surveyor's compasses in 1795; came to Walpole from Windham, Connecticut.*

Huntley, Oli & Eli; *Marlow, c. 1860; knife handles.*

Hurd, A. A.; *East Northwood, 1884-1886; edge tools.*

Hurd, William; *Dover, c. 1881; brushes.*

Hutchins, Levi *(1761-1855); Concord, 1784-1838; clockmaker, who advertised in 1804 that he made compasses and other instruments for surveying.*

Hutchinson Brothers; *probably a partnership of Arthur and Homer Harden Hutchinson; Bristol, 1895-1897; woodenware manufacturers, known to have made handles, saw bucks, carriage and wagon jacks.*

Hutchinson, Arthur *(1860-1898); Bristol, 1886-1897; worked alone and in partnership or firm of Hutchinson Brothers; handles, saw bucks, and carriage jacks.*

Hutchinson, Charles H.; *Manchester, 1875-1900+; founder/machinist, known to have made jack screws (c. 1892).*

Ingalls, Eleazer F.; *Nashua (Dunstable), 1810-1822; blacksmith, known to have made axes, hammers, hatchets, hoes.*

Jackson, Aura; *Sutton, c. 1820; scythes and scythe snaths.*

Jackson, Daniel; *Troy, c. 1850; blacksmith, known to have made axes.*

Jackson, Daniel; *Portsmouth, c. 1755; blocks.*

Jackson, Elisha *(?-c. 1760); Portsmouth; blocks.*

Jameson, John *(1750-1806); Dunbarton; blacksmith, known for his axes.*

Jenness, Herbert E. *(c. 1852-?); New Durham, c. 1870; apparently worked for Tristram H. Fletcher as knife finisher.*

Jennings & Griffin Manufacturing Company *(apparently also known as C. [E.] Jennings & Co.); Charles E. Jennings, president; Francis B. Griffin, secretary/treasurer; George S. Wilder, manager; Hinsdale, 1883-1900+; carpenter's and edge tools (chisels, drawknives), boring implements (with a specialty of ship augers); a second factory at Yalesville, Connecticut (specializing in household cutlery; possibly making boring implements as well); succeeded George S. Wilder of Hinsdale and L'Hommedieu Hardware Company of Connecticut; office in New York City.*

Jennings, Charles [E], & Co.; *see Jennings & Griffin Manufacturing Company.*

Johnson & Smith *(also known as Charles B. Smith & Co.); Haverhill (Woodsville), 1870-1878; shovel handles.*

Johnson, Thomas B.; *Portsmouth, 1860-1870; cutlery.*

Johnson, William *(1832-1906); Hampstead; patented three improvements in tools for chamfering the soles of boots and shoes, 1858 and 1859 (April and June); later lived in Haverhill, Massachusetts and Cleveland, Ohio.*

Jones, Daniel; *Exeter, 1786-1798; blacksmith, known to have sold plane irons, chisels, picks, and shovels.*

Jones, J.; *Hampstead, c. 1849; edge tools.*

Jones, Nathan *(1818-1894); Canaan, 1855-1880; hammers (nail, shoe, blacksmith's, farrier's); succeeded William Butterfield.*

Josselyn & Marston; *partnership of Lewis H. Josselyn and C. L. Marston; Manchester, c. 1875; brushes (boot, shoe, factory); apparently succeeded Dickerman.*

Josselyn, Lewis H., & Co.; *Manchester, 1876-1879; brushes; succeeded Josselyn & Marston; also manufactured furniture until the 1890s.*

Joy, Adin Phillips, *variously called Aden Phillip Joy (1859-1940); Newfields (Rockingham); patented wrench, 1898; brother of Samuel Sumner Joy.*

Joy, James *(1778-1857); Durham, ?-1820; Pittsfield, 1820-?; blacksmith/entrepreneur, specializing in the manufacture of scythes.*

Joy, Samuel Sumner *(1861-1941); Newfields (Rockingham), 1898-1900+; carriage jacks; brother of Adin Phillips Joy.*

Keene Manufacturing Company; *Keene, 1892-1894; hacksaw frames.*

Keith, Ruel *(1769-1842); Newport, c. 1800-?; blacksmith, specializing in scythes; succeeded Stephen Dexter; came to Newport from Uxbridge, Massachusetts.*

Kellog; *Lebanon, c. 1850; worked in partnership or firm of Alden & Kellog; picks.*

Kelly, E. L., *variously spelled Kelley; West Lebanon, 1875-1900+; axe helves.*

Kemp & Call; *Acworth, 1884-1885; handles.*

Kemp Brothers; *Acworth, c. 1882; handles.*

Kemp, O. R.; *Acworth, 1868-1885; worked alone and apparently in partnerships or firms of Kemp Brothers and Kemp & Call; handles (hoe, fork).*

Kempton; *Claremont, 1875-1877; worked in partnership or firm of Smith, Collins & Kempton; mincing knives.*

Kendall, P. A.; *Nashua, 1885-1900+; saws; succeeded L. D. Boynton & Co.*

Kendrick & Davis; *partnership of Frank Brown Kendrick and William F. Davis; Lebanon, 1876-1909; watch key manufacturers, eventually specializing in watchmaker's tools; incorporated as Kendrick & Davis Company in 1909.*

Kendrick & Davis Company; *Lebanon, 1910-present; watchmaker's tools.*

Kendrick, Frank Brown *(1845-?); Lebanon, 1867-1910+; worked in partnership or firm of Kendrick & Davis; watchmaker, eventually manufacturing watch keys and watchmaker's tools; first president of Kendrick & Davis Company.*

Kennard, John *(1782-1861); Newfields (South Newmarket), 1812-?; clockmaker, whose name (with town) appears as maker on quadrants of Phinehas Merrill's invention; learned his trade in Portsmouth; also lived in Nashua and Concord prior to 1812.*

Kennedy, James; *Bedford, 1754-1762; blacksmith, known to have made plane irons, hay fork, beetle rings, and gunsmith's bit.*

Kenny, George; *Nashua; carriagemaker, who patented a gauge and dividers, 1870.*

Kidder, Daniel; *North Groton, 1887-1890; edge tools.*

Kidder, E. P.; *Alstead, 1884-1890; handles (shovel, etc.).*

Kilburn, Edward; *Littleton, c. 1856; bits, augers.*

Kimball; *Lebanon, c. 1868; worked in partnership or firm of Emerson & Kimball; scythes.*

Kimball, Caleb Jewett *(1817-1896); Milford, c. 1841-1849; Wilton, 1849-1851; Bennington, 1851-1894; worked alone and in partnership or firm of C. J. Kimball & Son; blacksmith, specializing by 1860 in edge tools (hoes, drawknives, shaves); learned his trade from his father, Isaac Kimball; drawknife marked "MILFORD" known.*

Kimball, Caleb Jewett, & Son; *partnership of Caleb Jewett and George Edward Kimball; Bennington, 1873-1894; carpenter's and edge tools (axes, hoes, cutlery, drawknives, shaves, shoe and butcher knives, tanner's fleshers).*

Kimball, Caleb Jewett, Company; *partnership or firm of Fred Hastings Kimball, Charles Herbert Kimball, and William H. Odell; Bennington, 1894-1900+; edge tools (cutlery, drawknives); continued business of Caleb Jewett Kimball after his retirement.*

Kimball, Charles Herbert *(1848-1912); Bennington, 1894-1900+; helped to continue father's business under firm name of C. J. Kimball Company; edge tools.*

Kimball, Fred Hastings *(1857-1917); Bennington, 1894-1900+; helped to continue father's business under firm name of C. J. Kimball Company; edge tools.*

Kimball, George Edward *(1842-1913); Bennington, 1873-1894; worked in partnership or firm of C. J. Kimball & Son; edge tools.*

Kimball, Isaac *(1789-1881); Greenville (Mason Village), ?-1829; Temple, 1829-?; blacksmith, known for making axes and other edge tools.*

Kimball, John *(1739-1817); Manchester (Derryfield), c. 1762; Concord, 1764-1814; joiner, known to have made hoe, fork, and auger handles, 1790-1803; account book at New Hampshire Historical Society.*

Kimball, L.; *Nashua, 1868-1870; stencils.*

Kimball, S. S.; *Newport, 1877-1878; machinist's tools.*

King, Henry; *Alstead (Paper Mill Village), 1856-1860; handles (shovel, hoe, fork).*

Kinsman, Prescott B. *(1847-1930); Somersworth (Great Falls); patented with Josiah Merrill a carriage wrench (1882), which was manufactured by the Eureka Wrench Company.*

Kittredge, Jonathan *(1793-1864); Canaan, before 1849; lawyer/temperance advocate, said to have been involved with Phineas Eastman and Dan Balch in the manufacture of hammers; brother-in-law of latter.*

Knowlton & Stone; *partnership of William H. Knowlton and Charles H. Stone; Keene, 1870-1900 + ; hardware dealers, whose name appears on tools.*

Ladd, Jeremiah; *probably either Alexandria or Lee; patented tanner's beaming machine, 1801.*

Laighton; *see Leighton.*

Lakin, Taylor D.; *Hancock; patented cutlery handle, 1866.*

Lancaster File Works; *Lancaster, 1875-1879; files and rasps (mill saw, flat, round, half-round); see also Moody & Co.; Moody & Cave; Moody, Carr & Ellis; Ellis Brothers; Ellis & Olcott.*

Lang & Hoyt; *Grafton, c. 1856; axes; see also Gilman L. Lang.*

Lang & Sleeper; *see Long & Sleeper.*

Lang, Gilman L. *(c. 1826-?), variously recorded as E. L., E. G., L. G., and G. E. Lang (or Long); Grafton, 1856-1865; Andover, 1865-1880; worked alone and apparently in partnership or firm of Lang & Hoyt; edge tools, specializing in axes; moved to Iowa.*

Larned & Sibley; *partnership of Sylvanus Larned and Ezra Taft Sibley; North Newport (Northville), 1845-1848; scythes.*

Larned, Sylvanus *(?-1848); North Newport (Northville), 1842-1848; worked alone and in partnership or firm of Larned & Sibley; scythes.*

Laskey, L. B., & Co.; *Dover, c. 1882; brushes.*

Lawrence, Artemas *(1781-1841); Jaffrey; blacksmith, specializing in axes.*

Laws, Ebenezer; *Washington, c. 1849; fork handles.*

Lawson, John H.; *Manchester, c. 1886; proprietor of Manchester File Works; files, rasps.*

Leavitt & McDaniel; *Penacook (Fisherville), 1848-1849; saws (all kinds, "for cutting wood, iron, brass, or stone"), plasterer's trowels, try square and scraper blades.*

Leavitt, Dudley; *Gilford; blacksmith, known to have made axes, farm tools.*

Leavitt, Eben J.; *Milford, c. 1853; chisel handles.*

Lebanon Machine Works; *Lebanon, c. 1870; woodworking tools.*

Leighton & Lufkin; *partnership of William W. Leighton and Jacob Lufkin; Auburn, 1856-1860; edge tools.*

Leighton & Son; *probably partnership of William W. and Charles O. Leighton; Manchester, c. 1885; proprietors of Manchester Axe Works; axes.*

Leighton, Andrew; *probably Andrew P. Leighton (1793-1882); Manchester, c. 1854; worked in partnership or firm of William W. Leighton & Co.; edge tools; father of William W. Leighton.*

Leighton, Charles O. *(1851-?); Manchester, 1880-1882 and 1885; worked alone and apparently in partnership or firm of Leighton & Son as proprietors of Manchester Axe Works; edge tools; son of William W. Leighton.*

Leighton, George H.; *Portsmouth, c. 1835; blocks.*

Leighton, John; *Portsmouth, 1821-1827; blocks.*

Leighton, Littleton M.; *Portsmouth, 1834-1857; worked alone and in partnership or firm of Samuel Leighton & Son; blocks.*

Leighton, Luke M.; *Portsmouth, 1802-1827; blocks.*

Leighton, Mark; *Portsmouth, 1802-1821; blocks; patented rollers for block sheaves, 1810.*

Leighton, Paul; *Portsmouth, 1802-1827; blocks.*

Leighton, Samuel; *Portsmouth, 1821-1834; worked alone and in partnership or firm of Samuel Leighton & Son; blocks.*

Leighton, Samuel, & Son; *partnership of Samuel and Littleton M. Leighton; Portsmouth, c. 1834; blocks.*

Leighton, William, Jr.; *Portsmouth, c. 1834; blocks.*

Leighton, William F.; *Portsmouth, c. 1839; blocks.*

Leighton, William M.; *Portsmouth, c. 1834; blocks.*

Leighton, William W. *(1815-1885); Auburn, c. 1849; Manchester, 1850-1856; Auburn, 1856-1865; Manchester, 1866-1885; worked alone and in partnerships or firms of Underhill, Brown & Leighton, c. 1849; William W. Leighton & Co., c. 1854; Leighton & Lufkin, 1856-1860; and probably Underhill & Leighton and Leighton & Son, c. 1885; also worked (as toolmaker and foreman) for Amoskeag Ax Company, 1866-1879; for the Underhill Edge Tool Company, Nashua (as foreman), c. 1881; for the Manchester Locomotive Works, 1881-1883; and for S. C. Forsaith & Co., 1884; became proprietor with son, Charles O., of Manchester Axe Works, c. 1885; said to have been apprenticed in Boston to Samuel Graham Underhill from Chester.*

Leighton, William W., & Co.; *partnership of Andrew and William W. Leighton; Manchester, c. 1854; edge tools.*

Leland & Co.; *Milford, c. 1853; axe helves.*

Libby; *Piermont; worked in partnership or firm of Evans & Libby; scythe stones.*

Libby, Marvin W.; *Manchester; machinist, specializing in tools, c. 1894.*

Lincoln, Josiah S. *(c. 1821-?), variously called Isaiah; Canaan, c. 1862-1870; awls (boot and shoe manufacturer's tools); also worked in Brockton, Massachusetts, where he had learned his trade from his father, Charles Lincoln, said to be "one of the first manufacturers of pegging awls in the United States."*

Little, Alfred; *Nashua, c. 1866; apparently worked for Underhill Edge Tool Company; edge tools.*

Littleton Hone Stone Company; *Littleton, 1887-1890; hone and scythe stones; apparently succeeded Littleton Scythe Stone Company.*

Littleton Scythe Stone Company; *Littleton, 1883-1886; hone and scythe stones.*

Locke & Marden; *partnership of George Seldon Locke and J. E. Marden; Penacook (Fisherville), 1882-1887; proprietors of Fisherville Saw Company; saws.*

Locke, George Seldon *(1852-1923); Penacook (Fisherville), 1867-1900 + ; worked for Gage, Porter & Co. and became proprietor (both alone and as member of partnership of Locke & Marden) of Fisherville Saw Company, the successor to Gage, Porter & Co.; saws.*

Long & Alexander; *probably partnership of Leander Long and Elkanah M. Alexander; Newport/Sunapee, c. 1872; fork handles.*

Long & Beck; *Newport, c. 1868; handles (fork, hoe); see also Leander Long.*

Long & Sleeper, *variously recorded as Lang & Sleeper; probably partnership of Leander Long and Benjamin R. Sleeper; Sunapee, 1879-1880; handles (fork, hoe).*

Long, Gilman L.; *see Gilman L. Lang.*

Long, Isaac *(1764-1840); Hopkinton, 1797-1825; joiner, possibly responsible for planes marked "I LONG" with no location given; Isaac Long's probate inventory included 4 sets bench planes, 70 moulding planes, other planes, 6 bench planes, 9 cornice moulding tools, 6 smoothing planes, and numerous other tools; Long was related to planemaker Joshua Morse through the marriage of their children.*

Long, Leander *(1812-?); Newport/Sunapee, 1868-1880; apparently worked alone and in partnerships or firms of Long & Beck, Long & Alexander, and Long & Sleeper; handles (fork, hoe); previously a cabinetmaker.*

Lougee, John; *Somersworth (Great Falls), 1868-1870; glazier's points.*

Lovejoy & Webster; *Abbott Lovejoy, principal partner; Bristol, 1829-?; blacksmiths, specializing in edge tools.*

Lovejoy, Abbott *(1800-1879); Alexandria, 1821-1823; Bristol, 1824-c. 1865; worked alone and in partnership or firm of Lovejoy & Webster; blacksmith, known to have made edge tools, 1824-1849; learned his trade from his brother, Stephen, in Hebron; drawknife marked "A. LOVEJOY" exhibited at Manchester Institute of Arts and Sciences, 1975.*

Loveland, Isaac; *Gilsum, 1860-1875; axe handles.*

Loveland, Lewis [H.]; *Rumney, 1891-1900+; handles (hoe, fork).*

Lowell, A. H.; *Manchester; founder/machinist, known to have made jack screws, c. 1884.*

Lucier, Alfred; *Nashua, 1864-1870; apparently worked for Underhill Edge Tool Company; edge tools.*

Lucier, Eben N.; *Nashua, 1894-1900+; apparently worked for Underhill Edge Tool Company; edge tools.*

Lucier, Eleazer; *Nashua, c. 1866; apparently worked for Underhill Edge Tool Company; edge tools.*

Lucier, George [A.]; *Nashua, 1885-1892; apparently worked for Underhill Edge Tool Company; edge tools.*

Lucier, Jeremiah; *Nashua, 1868-1872; apparently worked for Underhill Edge Tool Company; edge tools and handles.*

Lucier, Joseph; *Nashua, 1868-1870; apparently worked for Underhill Edge Tool Company; edge tools.*

Lucier, Nector; *Nashua, c. 1870; apparently worked for Underhill Edge Tool Company; edge tools.*

Lucier, Olin P.; *Nashua, 1894-1896; apparently worked for Underhill Edge Tool Company; edge tools.*

Lucier, Paul [Ammi]; *Nashua, 1864-1900+; worked for Underhill Edge Tool Company (foreman, c. 1877); edge tools.*

Lufkin, Jacob *(1825-1872); Auburn, 1856-1860; worked in partnership or firm of Leighton & Lufkin; edge tools.*

Luther, Jabez *(1776-?); Cornish; said to have invented a shave used in making grain cradles.*

Mack, Andrew *(c. 1808-?); Nashua, 1843-1858 and c. 1866; Hillsborough, c. 1860; worked alone and for Underhill Edge Tool Company (c. 1858 and c. 1866); blacksmith, specializing in edge tools; a farmer in Alstead by 1870.*

Mack, John *(c. 1698-1753); Londonderry; yeoman, said to have made an axe, c. 1740, exhibited at Londonderry's 150th anniversary in 1869.*

Magoon, Stephen S., *variously spelled Magoun; New Hampton, 1807-1850; joiner, possibly responsible for plow marked "S. MAGOUN" with no location given.*

Manchester Axe Company, *variously called Manchester Axe Works; Manchester, 1883-1885; edge tools (specializing in axes and axe wedges); succeeded Burpee, Hamilton & Co.; also made "boys' axes"; see also Leighton & Son and Charles E. Stearns.*

Manchester File Works; *Manchester, 1882-1891; files, rasps; probably succeeded Granite File Works; see also George Fantom [& Co.] and John H. Lawson.*

Manchester Locomotive Works; *Manchester, 1853-1900+; engine manufacturers/founders, known to have made tools, 1855-1860.*

Manley, Josiah; *Washington, 1868-1870; handles.*

Mann, Thomas W.; *Chesterfield, c. 1830; scythes.*

Manning, George W.; *Hollis, 1880-1886; cooper's tools.*

March, Isaac; *Nashua (Dunstable), c. 1822; scythes.*

Marsh, Gilman, *variously called Mash; Gilmanton, 1802-1809; blacksmith, known to have made hammer, hoe, pitchfork, and sash plane iron.*

Marshall & Trickey; *partnership of Christopher J. Marshall and William P. Trickey; Portsmouth, c. 1864; blacksmiths/shipsmiths, who advertised edge tools.*

Marshall, Ansel, *variously spelled Ansil; Dunbarton, 1878-1890; axe handles.*

Marshall, Nathaniel; *Portsmouth, c. 1739; blocks.*

Marshall, Obediah; *Portsmouth, c. 1739; blocks.*

Marston; *Farmington, 1884-1888; worked in partnership or firm of Morgan & Marston; edge tools.*

Marston & Stearns *(also known as Leonard Stearns & Co.); probably partnership of David W. Marston and Leonard Stearns; Lebanon, 1860-1880; scythe snaths.*

Marston Patent Scythe Company; *Lebanon, 1887-1892; scythes and snaths; product apparently based on patent of David W. Marston.*

Marston, C. L.; *Manchester, c. 1875; worked in partnership or firm of Josselyn & Marston; brushes.*

Marston, David W.; *Lebanon, 1860-1880; apparently worked in partnership or firm of Marston & Stearns (L. Stearns & Co.); patented improvement in method of uniting scythes and snaths, 1867; probably also involved in Marston Patent Scythe Company; "Marston's Patent Snaths" also manufactured by G. W. & M. L. Stearns.*

Martin & Fernald; *partnership of William Martin and William [D.] Fernald; Portsmouth, 1834-1857; blocks.*

Martin, B. Franklin; *Portsmouth, 1860-1912; apparently worked alone and at Portsmouth Navy Yard; blocks.*

Martin, C. H., & Co., *Concord, c. 1874; brushes; described as brush manufacturers; advertised only as brush dealers.*

Martin, James; *Bedford, 1773-1789; blacksmith, known to have made a shave and drill.*

Martin, William; *Portsmouth, 1834-1868; worked alone and in partnership or firm of Martin & Fernald; blocks.*

Martin, William M.; *Portsmouth, c. 1827; blocks.*

Martin, William R.; *Portsmouth, 1860-1875; blocks.*

Mascoma Edge Tool Company; *Lebanon, 1870-1890; scythes; see also Martin V. [B.] Purmort.*

McCord, Edward *(?-c. 1899); Nashua, 1883-1899; files.*

McCulloch, Eppie J.; *Manchester; patented bench plane, 1893.*

McDaniel; *probably John; Penacook (Fisherville), 1848-1849; worked in partnership or firm of Leavitt & McDaniel; saws, etc.*

McDaniel, T. D.; *Canterbury, 1899-1900+; axe handles.*

McHammond, John C.; *see John McCurdy Hammond.*

Melcher, Daniel; *Portsmouth, c. 1802; blocks.*

Merrill & Dowse; *Lebanon, c. 1891; handles.*

Merrill & Wilder; *partnership of Pliny Merrill and George Sheldon Wilder; Hinsdale, c. 1860?; mechanic's tools (chisels, drawknives, gouges); the Merrill & Wilder name continued to be stamped on tools made after 1883 by the Jennings & Griffin Manufacturing Company.*

Merrill, Benjamin F.; *West Lebanon; patented shaft key gauge, c. 1868.*

Merrill, George H.; *Littleton, c. 1878; stencils.*

Merrill, Jacob *(1763-1841); Plymouth, 1784-1812; carpenter/cabinetmaker, known to have made and sold handles (file, scythe, hoe), mallets, and planes (smoothing, fore, rabbet); account book at New Hampshire Historical Society.*

Merrill, James O.; *Chichester, 1860-1880; handles (axe, hammer).*

Merrill, John B.; *Hinsdale, c. 1849; edge tools (hoes).*

Merrill, Josiah; *Somersworth (Great Falls); carriage manufacturer/wheelwright ("Berwick side"), who patented with Prescott B. Kinsman a carriage wrench (1882), which was manufactured by the Eureka Wrench Company.*

Merrill, Lewis Lovejoy *(1805-1870); Littleton, 1845-1851; blacksmith, specializing in hammers and edge tools.*

Merrill, P., & Co.; *probably Pliny Merrill, principal; Hinsdale, c. 1856; chisels (socket firmer and framing).*

Merrill, Pardon-Haynes *(1788-1879); Hinsdale, 1820-1850; "expert iron worker," known to have patented a hoe, 1820; came to Hinsdale from Shelburne, Massachusetts; said to have become "wealthy in the manufacture of farming implements"; and to have moved to Wisconsin, c. 1848.*

Merrill, Phinehas *(1767-1815); Stratham; surveyor/author, who invented a quadrant manufactured by John Kennard of Newfields after 1812 and advertised by Timothy Chandler of Concord, 1815.*

Merrill, Pliny *(1800-?); Hinsdale, 1840-1868; blacksmith/founder, specializing in edge tools (chisels, drawknives, and gouges); worked alone, with nephew George Sheldon Wilder, and probably in partnerships or firms of P. Merrill & Co. and Merrill & Wilder;*

brother of Pardon-Haynes Merrill; "Merrill chisels" advertised in 1875 by George Sheldon Wilder.

Merriman, C. D.; *Hinsdale, 1868-1885; worked in partnership or firm of Holman & Merriman; jack, bench, and press screws.*

Messer Brothers; *partnership of Frank D. and C. H. Messer; East Alstead, 1881-1890; woodenware manufacturers, known to have made handles (knife, shovel) and scythe nibs.*

Messer, Augustus S. *(1834-?); Lebanon, c. 1855; scythes; agent of Phillips, Messer, Colby [& Co.]; son of Richard Heath Messer.*

Messer, Frank D. *(1858-1907); East Alstead, 1881-1900+; worked alone and in partnership or firm of Messer Brothers; woodenware manufacturer, known to have made handles (knife, shovel) and scythe nibs; also operated blacksmith shop; son of William H. Messer.*

Messer, Richard Heath *(1807-1872); New London, 1835-1872; worked in partnership or firm of Phillips, Messer, Colby [& Co.]; apparently also involved in Perkins, Messer, Colby & Co.; scythes; learned scythemaking in Fitchburg, Massachusetts.*

Messer, William H. *(c. 1823-1881), variously recorded as W. A. and H[op] Messer; East Alstead (New Alstead), 1862-1881; woodenware manufacturer, known to have made scythe nibs after 1870; occasionally listed as making edge tools (scythes).*

Miller, Henry J.; *Nashua, c. 1868; worked in partnership or firm of Whiting & Miller (Henry J. Miller & Co.); boot brushes/jacks.*

Miller, Henry J., & Co.; *see Whiting & Miller.*

Milliken, Adams; *Charlestown, c. 1830; blacksmith, who advertised the making of edge tools (axes).*

Milton, Joseph *(1789-1864); Canaan, 1818-?; cabinetmaker, known to have made planes.*

Milton, Matthew Harvey *(1819-1905), listed incorrectly in 1849 as M. Hamilton; Canaan, ?-1854; cabinetmaker, known to have specialized in joiner's planes, c. 1850; son of Joseph Milton, from whom he learned his trade; became a merchant after 1854; father and son may have worked together, as their marks have been found both on the same plane.*

Moody & Cave; *probably partnership of George Moody and George E. Cave; Lancaster, c. 1875; files; proprietors of Lancaster File Works.*

Moody & Co.; *partnership of George Moody and George E. Cave; Lancaster; files; said to have operated Lancaster File Works; probably the same as Moody & Cave.*

Moody & Ellis; *probably George Moody, principal partner; Lancaster, 1877-1879; files.*

Moody, Carr (Cave?) & Ellis; *probably George Moody, principal partner; Lancaster, c. 1876; files; possibly operating Lancaster File Works.*

Moore & Co.; *probably John W. Moore, principal; Hudson, 1868-1870; files.*

Moore, Daniel; *Bedford, 1764-1768*; blacksmith, known to have made plow plates and a shave.

Moore, James, & Sons; partnership of James, Byron, and Ira B. Moore; *Concord, 1872-1883*; hardware dealers, whose name (with town) appears on planes; advertised as agents for joiner's tools.

Moore, John W.; *Nashua, 1864-1866 and c. 1870*; *Hudson, 1866-1870*; apparently worked alone and in partnerships or firms of Alcott & Co., Moore & Co., and C. H. Papps & Co.; files.

Moore, Orrin (1811-1894); *Goffstown, 1854-1885*; worked alone and in partnership or firm of Orrin Moore & Sons; said to have worked in company with his brother; scythe rifles, whetstones; also manufactured vehicles and woodenware.

Moore, Orrin, & Sons; *Goffstown, 1875-1879*; scythe rifles and whetstones.

Morgan & Marston; *Farmington, 1884-1888*; edge tools.

Morrill & Wilson; probably O. F. Morrill, principal partner; *Croydon, c. 1850*; knives.

Morrill, George Peverly (1844-?); *Canterbury, 1881-1900 +*; *West Concord, 1908 +*; axe handles, specializing in wedges; by 1908, advertised as "the only manufacturer of steel axe and hammer wedges in the world."

Morrill, O. F.; *Croydon, 1849-1850*; worked alone and apparently in partnership or firm of Morrill & Wilson; knives.

Morse, Joshua (1774-1826); *Hopkinton*; joiner, known to have advertised bench and moulding tools for joiners, cabinetmakers, and coopers, 1816-1819.

Morse, William H. (c. 1807-?); *Penacook (Fisherville), c. 1850*; apparently worked for Gage, Hubbard & Co.; saws.

Moses, William P.; *Exeter*; patented currier's knife, 1860.

Moss, F.; *Thornton, 1855-1857*; edge tools.

Mussey, Frank; *New Durham, c. 1875*; pruning shears; possibly the same as Henry F. Muzzey.

Muzzey, Henry F. (1836-?), variously recorded as Mussey; *New Durham, 1870-1876*; blacksmith, known to have specialized in edge tools, c. 1875; possibly the same as Frank Mussey.

Nashua Edge Tool Company; see Underhill Edge Tool Company.

Nashua File Company; *Nashua, c. 1870*; files; see also Charles H. Papps & Co.

Nashua File Works; *Nashua, 1877-1889*; files, rasps (specializing in mill and saw files); see also Edwin Ridge & Co., Ridge & Co., and John Ridge.

Nashua Hand Rock Drill Company; *Nashua, 1885-1886*; rock drills.

Nashua Iron Foundry; see Charles Williams.

Nashua Manufacturing Company Machine Shop; *Nashua, 1845-?*; machine shop, in which axes, hoes, etc., were manufactured, apparently by a variety of makers.

Nashua Rasp Company; *Nashua, 1892-1894*; files, rasps (including horse rasps); see also Ridge & Grover and John B. Grover & Co.

Neil, Joseph; *Auburn*; worked for (and was possibly apprenticed to) Jesse Johnson Underhill, of that part of Chester which later became Auburn; edge tools.

Neville, George D. (1812-1892); *New Boston, 1849-1890*; edge tools (specializing in axes but also making knives, shaves, etc.); a native of Nova Scotia.

New England Flint; see Wiggin & Stevens.

New England Novelty Works, occasionally referred to as New England Novelty Company; Frank Ross Woodward, proprietor; *Hill, 1877-1893*; glazier's tools (glass cutters), combination tools, washer cutters, ice picks, knife sharpeners, can openers.

New Hampshire Iron Factory Company; *Franconia, 1805-1860*; ironworks/foundry, with blacksmith shop, said to produce axes, drills, shovels, crowbars, and pod augers.

New Hampshire Scythe Company; *Littleton (Apthorp, formerly Scythe Factory Village), 1871-1884*; scythes, axes; succeeded Hartshorn & Co.; see also Charles Hartshorn, Luther Thompson Dow, John Farr, James H. Witherell, and George B. and Henry C. Redington.

New London Scythe Company; *New London (Elkins, formerly Scytheville), 1871-1888, and Wilmot, 1882-1886*; scythes, hay knives, axes; succeeded Phillips, Messer, Colby & Co.

Newcomb; *Nelson, c. 1860*; worked in partnership or firm of Welch & Newcomb; shovel handles.

Newcomb & Wilder; apparently partnership of Everett Newcomb and Azel Wilder; *Keene, ?-1836*; screw gimlets, bits, augers.

Newcomb, Everett (1786-1836); *Keene, c. 1833*; carpenter, involved in manufacturing screw gimlets, according to the invention of his brother Gideon Newcomb; said to have worked successively with George Page and Azel Wilder at their shops; see Newcomb & Wilder.

Newcomb, Gideon (1795-1838); *Roxbury*; blacksmith, said to have invented and made screw gimlets; manufactured on a larger scale by brother Everett Newcomb in Keene.

Newcomb, John (1782-1825); *Roxbury/Chesterfield*; blacksmith, said to have made the first twisted gimlet; brother of Gideon Newcomb.

Newell, Ezra; *Greenville (Mason Village), c. 1810*; blacksmith, known to have made scythes and axes.

Newmarket Machine Company; *Newmarket, incorporated 1847*; cotton machinery and tools, c. 1849.

Newton, Henry E.; *Manchester, 1866-1868*; worked in partnerships or firms of Robie & Newton and Henry E. Newton & Co.; brushes; patented blacking brush, 1868.

Newton, Henry E., & Co.; *Manchester, c. 1868*; brushes.

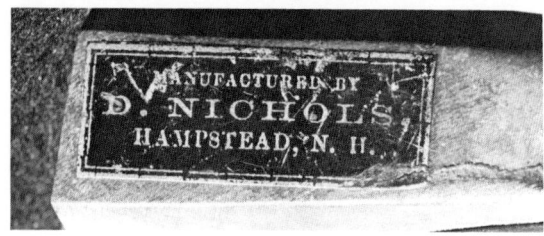

Nichols, Daniel *(1811-1885)*; *Hampstead, 1856-1885*; shoe tools (specializing in chamfering tools).

Nichols, Hiram; *Hampstead, c. 1856*; chamfering tools; later made shoe tools in Haverhill, Massachusetts; brother of Daniel Nichols.

Noble, Moses; *Portsmouth, c. 1763*; blocks.

Noyes, Person *(1800-1827)*; *Haverhill*; worked with father, Timothy Noyes; scythe stones; said to have discovered local source of scythe stones, c. 1821, and to have sold them locally.

Noyes, Simon C.; *Lisbon/Landaff, 1889-1890*; rules (caliper, board).

Noyes, Timothy *(1745-?)*; *Haverhill*; worked with son, Person Noyes; scythe stones; said to have been the "first manufacturers of scythe stones in New Hampshire."

Noyes, W. B.; *Manchester*; patented with C. S. Baker, a saw set and gauge (also described as a combined gauge, square, and wrench for saws), 1868; also patented removable points for saw teeth, 1869; see also Walter B. Noyes.

Noyes, W. O.; *Derry, c. 1888*; stone and potato forks.

Noyes, Walter B.; *Dorchester*; patented saw jointer, 1868; possibly the same as W. B. Noyes of Manchester.

Nutt, Henry; *Claremont, 1850-1860*; worked alone and in partnership or firm of Henry Nutt & Co.; files and rasps.

Nutt, Henry, & Co.; *Claremont, c. 1850*; files and rasps; probably first proprietors of Claremont File Works, established 1848.

Nutting & Hayden; *partnership of Luther M. Nutting and Henry W. Hayden; Concord, 1888-1908*; granite worker's and stonecutter's tools (bush hammers a specialty); name also found on blacksmith's tongs.

Nutting, Harris O.; *Rumney, 1880-1888*; worked alone and in partnership or firm of T. P. & H. O. Nutting; handles (hoe, hay fork).

Nutting, Luther M.; *Concord, 1881-1908; Canterbury, c. 1899*; apparently worked alone and in partnerships or firms of Luther M. Nutting & Co. and Nutting & Hayden; stone tools.

Nutting, Luther M., & Co.; *East Concord, 1881-1888*; granite worker's and stonecutter's tools (bush hammers, etc.).

Nutting, T. P.; *Rumney, 1886-1890*; worked alone and in partnership or firm of T. P. & H. O. Nutting; handles (hoe, hay fork).

Nutting, T. P. & H. O.; *Rumney, 1886-1888*; handles (hoe, hay fork).

O'Dell, Francis; *Milford, c. 1868*; handles.

Odiorne, Thomas *(1799-?)*, name changed to Odion; *Portsmouth, 1821-1875*; blocks.

Odiorne, Thomas Henry *(1828-1883)*, name changed to Odion; *Portsmouth, 1851-1856*; blocks.

Ormsbee & Farwell; *partnership of Oliver Ormsbee and John Farwell; New Ipswich, before 1810*; scythes; succeeded Ephraim Hartwell and John Putnam.

Ormsbee, Oliver; *New Ipswich, before 1810*; worked in partnership or firm of Ormsbee & Farwell; scythes.

Orr, James; *Bedford, 1774-1777*; worked for Nathan Shed; blacksmith, known to have made branding iron and nippers.

Osgood, H. Melville; *East Sullivan, 1868-1870*; handles (hoe, fork).

Otterson, Jotham Dutton *(1805-1880)*; *Nashua, 1864-1880*; iron founder, who advertised spoke shaves in 1866.

Owen & Amidon; *probably David A. Owen, principal partner; Hinsdale, c. 1886*; vises.

Owen, David A.; *Hinsdale, 1886-1891*; worked alone and apparently in partnership or firm of Owen & Amidon; vises, carpenter's tools.

Page & Carville; *Joel R. Page, principal partner; North Sandwich, 1885-1896*; handles.

Page, George; *Keene, 1825-1838*; machinist and manufacturer of pumps and mortising machines; also known to have made screw gimlets, in association with Everett Newcomb; patented chisels, 1833, 1835; spiral bit with countersink for setting screws, 1836; geared drill-stock, 1838; also patented mortising machines, 1833, 1836.

Page, Joel [R.]; *North Sandwich, 1885-1900+*; handles, including shovel and rake.

Paige, A. H.; *Manchester, 1872-1882*; stencils, steel stamps, dies, brands, seals.

Palmer, Freeman *(c. 1793-?)*; *Littleton, 1824-1850*; blacksmith, who patented a currier's knife, 1826; later lived in New York, Ohio, and Wisconsin.

Palmer, G.; *Lyme, c. 1894*; fork handles.

Palmer, Lorenzo D.; *Haverhill and/or Piermont, 1855-1857*; scythe stones.

Papps, Charles H.; *Nashua, c. 1870; Claremont, 1886-1900+*; worked alone and in partnership or firm of C. H. Papps & Co.; files; proprietor of Claremont File Works, 1886-1892.

Papps, Charles H., & Co.; *partnership of Charles H. Papps and John W. Moore; Nashua, c. 1870*; files; proprietors of Nashua File Company.

Parker, C. S.; *Amherst, 1882-1894; axe handles.*

Parker, George A.; *Sutton, 1892-1894; axe handles.*

Parmelee, Henry; *Claremont, c. 1856; handles (hoe, fork).*

Parmelee, John *(1778-1839); Newport, ?-1839; blacksmith, specializing in scythes; learned his trade from Stephen Dexter.*

Patten, Matthew *(1719-1795); Bedford, 1754-1773; woodworker, known to have made and sold handles (including axe, saw, and scythe) and planes (including smoothing, fore, rabbet, ogee, cooper's jointers, and plows); manuscript diaries at New Hampshire Historical Society.*

Pearl, Ellsworth; *Rochester, 1898-1909; blacksmith, who patented a spring-loaded punch, 1900.*

Pease, Daniel *(1808-1883); North Strafford (Blue Hill), 1860-1875; worked alone and in partnership or firm of Daniel Pease & Son; blacksmiths, specializing in edge tools.*

Pease, Daniel, & Son; *partnership of Daniel and Daniel H. Pease; North Strafford, c. 1875; blacksmiths, specializing in edge tools.*

Pendergast, Isaac S. *(1804-1892); Barnstead; patented shoemaker's paring knife, 1841.*

Perkins, James M.; *Newport, c. 1878; Sunapee, 1880-1900+; worked in partnerships or firms of Alexander & Perkins and Alexander, Perkins & Co.; handles (hoe, fork).*

Perkins, Joseph; *Seabrook; chamfering tools; possibly Joseph Perkins (c. 1859-?), son of a shoe factory worker.*

Perkins, Messer, Colby & Co.; *Lebanon, 1849-1850; scythes; possibly same as Phillips, Messer, Colby [& Co.] of Lebanon and New London.*

Perkins, Wheeler, & Brother; *Weare, c. 1841; axe handles.*

Peverly, Herbert *(c. 1850-?); New Durham, c. 1870; apparently worked for Franklin W. Coburn as knife polisher.*

Phelps, Peter; *Jaffrey, before 1881; brushes.*

Philbrook, Alfred S. *(c. 1802-?); Claremont, 1865-1875; carpenter, known to have made handles; patented a machine for bending scythe snaths, 1865.*

Phillips, Joseph E. *(1811-1896); New London, 1835-1869; worked in partnership or firm of Phillips, Messer, Colby [& Co.]; apparently also involved in Perkins, Messer, Colby & Co.; scythes; apprenticed to Asa P. Cowdin of Fitchburg, Massachusetts.*

Phillips, Messer & Colby; *partnership of Joseph E. Phillips, Richard Heath Messer, and Anthony Colby; New London (Elkins, formerly Scytheville), 1835-1842; scythes; succeeded by Phillips, Messer, Colby & Co.; business records privately owned; see also Ezra Taft Sibley.*

Phillips, Messer, Colby & Co.; *partnership of Joseph E. Phillips, Richard Heath Messer, Anthony Colby, and Samuel Greenwood; New London (Elkins, formerly Scytheville), 1842-1871; scythes; succeeded Phillips, Messer & Colby; reorganized in 1871 as the New London Scythe Company; business records privately owned.*

Phillips, Messer, Colby [& Co.]; *Augustus S. Messer, agent; Lebanon, 1854-1856; scythes; apparently a branch of the New London operation; see also Perkins, Messer, Colby & Co. and William Dunton.*

Pierce Brothers; *East Haverhill, c. 1875; scythe stones; probably the same as, or successor to, R. & C. G. Pierce.*

Pierce, Benjamin *(1814?-1899); Chesterfield, 1851-1882; bits, augers, braces, other boring tools; succeeded Richardson & Huggins, for which he had previously worked as salesman; also involved (as superintendent/salesman) in a chisel factory (probably Pliny Merrill's) at Hinsdale, 1852-1865; widely known for the manufacture of spinning wheel heads; account book at New Hampshire Historical Society; see also Barton Skinner and Frederick Benjamin Pierce.*

Pierce, Cross & Farr; *partnership of Ezekiel P. Pierce, Jr., Charles Cross, and Alonzo Farr; Chesterfield, after 1835; bits, augers, gimlets.*

Pierce, Ezekiel Porter *(1785-1865); Chesterfield, 1820-?; spinning wheel head manufacturer, said to have been engaged to some extent in the manufacture of bits and augers; appears to have been associated with Richardson & Huggins; apparently not related to Benjamin Pierce and family.*

Pierce, Ezekiel Porter, Jr. *(1814-?); Chesterfield, c. 1835-?; worked with Charles Cross and in partnership or firm of Pierce, Cross & Farr; augers, bits, gimlets.*

Pierce, Frederick Benjamin *(1845-1928); Chesterfield, 1868-1900; South Keene, 1901+; worked for father, Benjamin Pierce, managing his business, 1870-1882 (son often listed under his own name at end of this period) and in partnerships or firms of Hopkins & Pierce and F. B. Pierce [&] Co.; augers, bits, braces, edge tools and, after 1876, brush handles (paint, varnish); from 1882, manufactured brush handles and spinning wheel heads exclusively.*

Pierce, Frederick Benjamin, & Co.; *Chesterfield, 1899-1900; brush handles.*

Pierce, Frederick Benjamin, Company; *South Keene, 1903+; brush handles.*

Pierce, Levi; *Hollis, c. 1872; mechanic's tools (cooper's and carpenter's).*

Pierce, R.; *Haverhill, 1870-1877; worked alone and probably in partnership or firm of R. & C. G. Pierce; scythe stones.*

Pierce, R. & C. G.; *Haverhill, 1870-1872; scythe stones; see also Pierce Brothers.*

Pike & Pike; *partnership of Alonzo Franklin and Joseph Pike; East Haverhill, c. 1870; scythe stones.*

Pike Manufacturing Company; *East Haverhill (Pike), 1889-1900+; Littleton, 1902+; scythe stones, oilstones, whetstones; succeeded Alonzo Franklin Pike Manufacturing Company after absorbing the eastern business and quarries of the Cleveland Stone Company; operated quarries and mills around the country.*

Pike, Alonzo Franklin *(1835-1891), variously listed as A. W. and H. F. Pike; East Haverhill (Pike), 1860-1883; worked alone and in partnerships or firms of Pike & Pike and A. F. Pike Manufacturing Company; scythe stones, whetstones; continued and expanded the business of his father, Isaac Pike.*

Pike, Alonzo Franklin, Manufacturing Company; *East Haverhill (Pike), 1884-1889; scythe stones, whetstones; quarries in Haverhill, Piermont, and Lisbon, as well as in Vermont and New York; continued business of Alonzo F. Pike; name changed in 1889 to Pike Manufacturing Company.*

Pike, Benjamin *(1745-1824); Hampton Falls; blacksmith, said to have made axes, scythes, knives; came to Hampton Falls from Salisbury, Massachusetts, by the 1780s.*

Pike, Isaac *(1799-1860); East Haverhill (Pike), 1823-1860; scythe stones, whetstones (quarried originally in Piermont); in 1827, married the widow of Person Noyes, discoverer of the quarry.*

Pillsbury, John D.; *Chatham, 1872-1874; edge tools.*

Pillsbury, Oliver M. *(c. 1820-?); Claremont, c. 1875; stencil dies.*

Piper & Reynolds; *see Benjamin H. Piper & Co.*

Piper, A. M.; *Wolfeboro; name (with town) appears on planes.*

Piper, Benjamin H. *(?-1899); Manchester, 1867-1899; worked in partnership[s] or firm[s] of Benjamin H. Piper [&] Co. (Piper & Reynolds); handles; frequently listed or advertised under his own rather than the firm name.*

Piper, Benjamin H., & Co. *(also known, before 1877, as Piper & Reynolds); partnership of Benjamin H. Piper and Henry C. Reynolds; Manchester, 1867-1890; handles (axe, pick, sledge, hatchet, hammer); also manufactured spokes.*

Piper, Benjamin H., Company; *Manchester, 1890-1900 + ; handles (axe, pick, sledge, hatchet, hammer); also manufactured spokes and baseball bats.*

Piper, Rufus *(1791-1874); Dublin; carpenter, whose name (with town) appears on planes.*

Pitman, Nathaniel; *Portsmouth, c. 1821; blocks.*

Plaisted & Balser; *partnership of Alberto C. Plaisted and Arthur W. Balser; Nashua, c. 1894; blacksmiths, advertising granite tools.*

Poole, Jonathan; *Northumberland, 1855-1857; edge tools.*

Porter & Rolfe; *partnership of George Porter and Hermon M. Rolfe; Concord, 1843-1853; hardware dealers, said to have made saws in Penacook (Fisherville), c. 1849; succeeded Leavitt & McDaniel in saw business.*

Porter, George; *Penacook (Fisherville), 1849-1855; worked in partnerships or firms of Porter & Rolfe and Gage, Porter & Co.; saws.*

Porter, J. H.; *Lyme, c. 1877; edge tools.*

Porter, Roger W.; *Nashua, 1864-1867; handles; patented combination pruning hook, knife, chisel, and saw, 1867.*

Portsmouth Machine Company; *Portsmouth; brass and iron founders/machinists, known to have made machinist's tools, 1887-1890.*

Pratt, Captain *(probably Solomon); Conway, 1800-1820; blacksmith, said to have employed several men making axes, scythes, etc.*

Prescott Company; *Franklin, 1893-1894; fishing rods.*

Prescott, Charles B.; *Franklin, 1894-1895; appears to have worked alone and in partnership or firm of Prescott Company; fishing rods.*

Price, Edwin; *Nashua, 1849-1857; files and rasps.*

Priest & Wellington; *partnership of Joseph Priest and George P. Wellington; Hinsdale, 1868-1870; woodenware manufacturers, who advertised handles (paint, varnish, sash tool, framing, and firmer chisel).*

Priest, Joseph K. *(1824-?); Nashua, 1863-1891; superintendent, and eventually president, of American Shearer Manufacturing Company; clippers (barber, horse, sheep); patternmaker/machinist, said to have invented the first barber's clipper, 1873; also first powered sheep-shearing and horse-clipping machines.*

Prince, George Stanley *(1850-1915); West Salisbury; patented a circular saw jointer, 1874; later a lumber mill superintendent in Littleton.*

Proctor, Amos *(1783-1844); Exeter, 1805-1830; blacksmith, known for his axes, of " 'silver steel' — his own invention"; moved to New York.*

Proctor, James *(1777-1847); the part of Salisbury which later became Franklin, 1809-?; edge tools (scythes, axes, etc.); learned edge tool making at Claremont; also lived in Andover.*

Pryor & Matthews; *partnership of Frank L. Pryor and Edward C. Matthews; Portsmouth, 1881-1900 + ; hardware dealers, whose name (with town) appears on tools.*

Purmort, Martin V. [B.] *(c. 1841-?); Lebanon, 1875-1889; apparently worked alone and as proprietor of Mascoma Edge Tool Company (1875-1879); scythes.*

Putnam, John; *New Ipswich, before 1800-?; scythes; said to have worked under the patronage of Ephraim Hartwell.*

Quint, George; *Dover, c. 1877; handles.*

Radford, Cass M.; *East Concord, 1886-1890; telescopes.*

Raitt, James W.; *Portsmouth, 1860-1900 + ; blacksmith/shipsmith, who advertised edge tools in 1864.*

Rand, John A.; *Swanzey, 1883-1885; axe helves.*

Randall, Lewis W.; *Claremont, 1877-1879; handles.*

Read, Silas; *Plainfield, late 19th century; worked with Sam Spaulding; said to have had a blacksmith shop and to have made tools.*

Redington, George Benjamin *(1808-1888); Littleton, 1835-1856; worked in partnerships or firms of Ely, Farr & Co. and Henry C. Redington & Co.; scythes; also on first board of directors of New Hampshire Scythe Company, founded in 1871.*

Redington, Henry Cornelius *(1816-1889); Littleton, 1842-1856; worked in partnership or firm of Henry C. Redington & Co.; scythes; also involved in organization of New Hampshire Scythe Company in 1871.*

Redington, Henry Cornelius, & Co.; *partnership of brothers Henry Cornelius and George Benjamin Redington; Littleton (Apthorp, formerly Scythe Factory Village), 1842-1856; scythes; succeeded Ely, Farr & Co.; after 1856 the firm concentrated on the lumber business and leased the scythe shop to Wesley Alexander.*

Reed, James M. *(c. 1822-?); East Acworth, 1870-1884; handles.*

Reed, Joseph Mason *(1826-?); Keene, c. 1855 and 1881-1903; jack screws (c. 1855); later a box manufacturer, known to have made chisel boxes, c. 1888; also made boxes in Swanzey (Westport).*

Reynolds, George; *Manchester, 1856-1860; superintendent of Blodgett Edge Tool Manufacturing Company; edge tools; patented a machine for making axe polls, 1858.*

Reynolds, Henry C. *(1829-1877); Manchester, 1855-1877; worked for Amoskeag Ax Company (after 1863, as agent); also involved in partnership or firm of Benjamin H. Piper & Co. (Piper & Reynolds); edge tools and handles; patented a "mode of manufacturing the cutting-edges of common chopping-axes and other edge-tools," 1865, and a machine for shaving axes, 1867; probably the son of George Reynolds; one of the Reynoldses (probably Henry*

C.) was apparently also responsible for "Reynolds's patent combination hatchet—a shingling & claw hatchet & claw hammer combined," which was advertised by the Amoskeag Ax Company, 1869.

Reynolds, J., *variously spelled Raynolds; Wakefield, 1882-1886; edge tools.*

Rhoades, C. W.; *Amherst; said to have made planes.*

Rice Manufacturing Company; *New Durham, 1889-1900+; wire brushes; also known for manufacturing steam packing.*

Rice, Edward E. *(1863-?); New Durham, 1888-1900+; worked alone and as founder/manager of the Rice Manufacturing Company; wire brushes.*

Rice, Hamlet L.; *Alstead (Paper Mill Village), 1842-1864 and c. 1878; edge tools (axes, carpenter's tools).*

Richards, Romance; *Clarksville, 1878-1886; edge tools (axes, knives).*

Richardson; *Keene, 1868-1870; worked in partnership or firm of Gerould, Richardson & Skinner; stencils.*

Richardson & Huggins; *partnership of Joshua Richardson and Oliver B. Huggins; Chesterfield, c. 1835-1851; bits, augers, gimlets; see also Ezekiel Porter Pierce.*

Richardson, Alpha; *North Enfield; patented leather splitting machine, 1851.*

Richardson, E. B.; *Mason, c. 1875-1897; handles.*

Richardson, Joshua *(1807-?); Chesterfield, c. 1835-1851; worked in partnership or firm of Richardson & Huggins; bits, augers, gimlets; lived in Iowa by 1874.*

Richardson, Samuel *(1841-?); Claremont, 1872-1885; files, rasps; agent/proprietor of Claremont File Works; sometimes listed under his own name as well.*

Richardson, William, & Co.; *Mason, c. 1870; brush handles.*

Richardson, Wyman *(1746-1839); Swanzey, 1780-1800; sickles.*

Ridge & Co., *variously called John Ridge & Co.; partnership of John and Rebecca (widow of Edwin) Ridge; Nashua, 1881-1883; files, rasps; succeeded Edwin Ridge & Co. as proprietors of Nashua File Works.*

Ridge & Grover; *partnership of John Ridge and John B. Grover; Nashua, c. 1892; rasps; proprietors of Nashua Rasp Company.*

Ridge, Edwin, & Co.; *partnership of Edwin Ridge and George Dow; Nashua, 1877-1879; files and rasps; proprietors of Nashua File Works; advertised in 1879 "having had thirty years' experience both in England and America."*

Ridge, John; *Nashua, 1881-1892; worked alone and in partnerships or firms of Ridge & Co. (John Ridge & Co.) and Ridge & Grover; files, rasps; both alone, and in partnership, served as proprietor of Nashua File Works, 1881-1889.*

Riggs, A. L.; *Portsmouth, c. 1856; edge tools.*

Risley, Lewis E.; *Piermont, c. 1856; scythe stones; probably also involved in partnership or firm of Evans & Risley, 1855-1857; married an Evans.*

Robb, Samuel *(1821-1873); South Stoddard, 1856-1860; handles (hoe, fork).*

Robbins & Flint; *Antrim, 1839-1841?; hoes (?); succeeded Baldwin & White.*

Roberts, Thomas; *New Durham, c. 1860; edge tools.*

Robie & Newton; *partnership of William F. Robie and Henry E. Newton; Manchester, c. 1866; brushes; succeeded Henry G. Wilson.*

Robie, Hiram; *Thornton, 1855-1860; edge tools.*

Robie, William F.; *Manchester, 1866-1872; worked alone and in partnership or firm of Robie & Newton; brushes.*

Robinson, Daniel B.; *Candia, c. 1875; edge tools.*

Robinson, Samuel R.; *Antrim; patented saw-setting apparatus, 1900.*

Robinson, Thomas Stewart, *variously called Stuart Robinson; Deerfield, 1849-1850; worked alone and in partnership or firm of T. S. Robinson & Co.; blacksmith, specializing in screwdrivers, hoes, and deckscrapers.*

Robinson, Thomas Stewart, & Co.; *South Deerfield, c. 1849; hoes.*

Robinson, William K.; *Charlestown, 1830-?; watch and clock maker, who advertised that he made mathematical and surveying instruments; served his apprenticeship in London.*

Roby; *see Robie.*

Rogers, F. J.; *Marlow, c. 1868; knife handles.*

Rolfe, Hermon M., *variously spelled Herman; Penacook (Fisherville), 1849-1854; worked in partnerships or firms of Porter & Rolfe and Gage, Hubbard & Co.; saws.*

Rollins, George Augustine *(1827-?); Nashua, 1854-1900+; worked in partnerships or firms of George A. Rollins & Co. and George W. Davis & Co.; machinist/engine manufacturer, known to have made machinist's tools, 1858-1879; learned his trade in Manchester.*

Rollins, George Augustine, & Co.; *Nashua, 1854-1863; machinists/engine manufacturers, known to have made machinist's tools, 1858-1860; succeeded in 1863 by George W. Davis & Co.; firm name resumed in 1879, but apparently as engine rather than tool manufacturers.*

Rowell; *Penacook (Fisherville), 1846-1847; worked in partnership or firm of Adams & Rowell; axes, hatchets.*

Royal, H. E.; *Lyme Center, c. 1878; handles (hoe, fork).*

Rugg, Elias *(1803-1882); Keene, 1850-1879; carpenter/patternmaker, probably responsible for planes marked "E. RUGG."*

Russell; *Chesterfield, before 1882; worked in partnership or firm of Brown & Russell; scythes.*

Russell, Levi; *Rindge, c. 1860; woodenware manufacturer, known to have made sawhorses.*

Rust, William Orne *(1822-1885); Somersworth (Great Falls); patented saw set, 1854; apparently involved with Lebbeus Brooks in the Great Falls Saw Set Company.*

Sanborn & Weeks; *partnership of Francis Davidson Sanborn and Minot Weeks; Littleton, 1869-1873; carpenter's tools (planes), log calipers, board rules; also made churns, washing machines, patent models, etc.*

Sanborn, David Page *(1810-1871); Littleton, c. 1841 and 1850-1870; worked alone and in partnership or firm of D. P. & F. D. Sanborn; planes and moulding tools; listed under edge tools as well as planes, 1855-1857; worked in Worcester, Massachusetts, alone and in partnership with brother-in-law Franklin J. Gooch, 1845-1848; probably in Worcester firm of Sanborn & Co. as well; also made churns and other woodwork; see also James Dow.*

Sanborn, David Page & Francis Davidson; *Littleton, c. 1866; planes (bench, smoothing, fore); also made churns and washing machines.*

Sanborn, Francis Davidson *(1834-1880); Littleton, 1866-1875; worked alone and in partnerships or firms of D. P. & F. D. Sanborn and Sanborn & Weeks; woodenware manufacturer, known to have made planes, board rules, yardsticks, sawhorses, bench screws, mallets, handles (auger, chisel, knife); son of David Page Sanborn; does not seem to have made planes except in partnerships.*

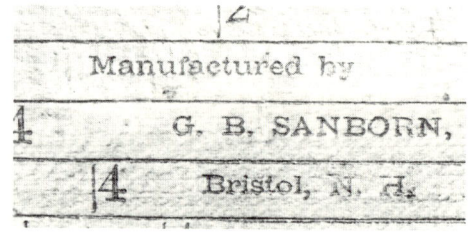

Sanborn, Gustavus B. *(1848-1902); Bristol, 1877-1890; log calipers, rules (lumber, wood, bark, tally board); patented a monkey wrench, 1884; applied for patent on log calipers, c. 1884; was married in Groton, N.H., and may have learned rulemaking from Rufus B. Haselton; moved to Ballard, Washington.*

Sanborn, Israel *(1767-1848); Gilford, 1806-1833; joiner/cabinetmaker, known to have sold rules (two-foot and joint) and a sawhorse; account book at New Hampshire Historical Society.*

Sanders, F. E., Tool Company; *Nashua, 1889-1890; machinists, known to have made belt punches, awls, screwdrivers, and machinist's tools.*

Sanders; *see also Saunders.*

Sargent, Dana *(1818-1884); Hudson, c. 1840; Manchester, 1840s; Nashua/Hudson, 1860-1879; worked alone and in partnership or firm of Sargents & Cross; hardware and lumber dealer (Manchester, Nashua, and Lawrence, Massachusetts), said to have made carpenter's planes in Hudson in his youth (where he probably learned planemaking from Cyrus Warren); name appears on planes (together with either Nashua or Manchester); lumber partnership in which he was involved made handspikes and serving mallets.*

Sargent, Jacob T.; *Sutton; patented garden hoe, 1853.*

Sargent, John; *Manchester, c. 1866; tools.*

Sargent, John G.; *Manchester, 1866-1869; tools.*

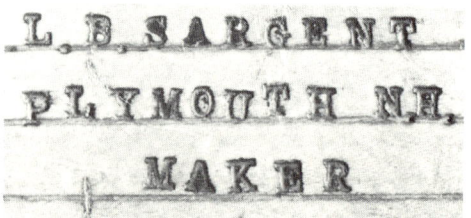

Sargent, L. B.; *Plymouth; Lincoln; log calipers.*

Sargent, L. N.; *Enfield Center, c. 1892; fishing rods.*

Sargent, Philip *(1790-1858); Concord, 1827-1858; joiner/house carpenter, specializing in making planes by 1844; a relatively*

high percentage of surviving tools used originally by carriagemakers.

Sargents & Cross; *partnership of Benjamin F. Sargent, Dana Sargent, and John Cross; Nashua, 1868-1872; lumber dealers, known to have made handspikes and serving mallets.*

Saunders, A. H.; *Nashua, c. 1868; machinist's tools.*

Saunders, John, *variously spelled Sanders (1791-1877); Jaffrey, 1850-1857; blacksmith, specializing in axes; also worked as blacksmith in Dublin and Peterborough.*

Saunders; *see also Sanders.*

Savory, A. G., & Co.; *Sunapee, 1868-1870; handles (fork, hoe).*

Sawtell, Aaron Servetus, *variously called Selvetus or Sevetus Sawtell (1823-?); Rindge, 1849-1885; woodenware manufacturer, known to have made sawhorses, 1860-1875.*

Sawyer, David; *Cornish; patented scythe nib (or scythe snath thole), 1849.*

Seaman; *New London, c. 1855; worked in partnership or firm of Colby & Seaman; scythes.*

Shackford, John *(c. 1678-1738); Portsmouth; worked in partnership with brother Samuel; blocks.*

Shackford, John *(c. 1708-1766); Portsmouth; blocks; son of blockmaker John Shackford.*

Shackford, Samuel *(c. 1675-c. 1730); Portsmouth; worked in partnership with brother John; blocks.*

Shattuck & Wells; *Samuel Shattuck, principal partner; Nashua, c. 1860; turners, whose product included ship handspikes.*

Shed, Nathan *(1747-1809); Bedford, 1774-1780; Goffstown, 1780-1785; Merrimack, 1785-1788; New Boston, 1788-c. 1800; Stoddard, c. 1800-c. 1809; blacksmith, known to have made and sold beetle rings (1775), scythes (1778), and axes (1780-1787); came to New Hampshire from Roxbury, Massachusetts; see also James Orr.*

Shelters, Leonard; *Manchester; patented combined calipers, dividers, square, and rule, 1867.*

Shillaber, Joseph; *Portsmouth; blacksmith, who advertised edge tools (scythes, axes, hoes, etc.), c. 1768; came to Portsmouth from Salem, Massachusetts.*

Sibley & Dunton; *partnership of Ezra Taft Sibley and William Dunton; North Newport (Northville), 1848-1851; scythes; succeeded Larned & Sibley.*

Sibley Scythe Company; *partnership of Ezra Taft and Frank Arthur Sibley; North Newport (Northville), 1873-1900 +; scythes; also "sole manufacturers of Humphrey's patent toothed hoe"; after retirement of Ezra T. Sibley in 1891, business carried on alone by son Frank A.*

Sibley, Amos *(1783-1863); Troy, 1816-1844; scythes; learned his trade from his brother in Athol, Massachusetts; succeeded Moses Aldrich and William Barnard; lived briefly in Oxford, Sutton, and Dudley, Massachusetts.*

Sibley, Ezra Taft *(1817-1909); North Newport (Northville), 1845-1891; worked alone and in partnerships or firms of Larned & Sibley, Sibley & Dunton, and Sibley Scythe Company; scythes; son of scythemaker Ezra Sibley (1787-1830) of Millbury (Sutton) and Auburn, Massachusetts; learned scythemaking from Hale & Whipple in Millbury, Massachusetts; before coming to Newport, worked in Chelmsford, Massachusetts, and New London, N.H. (the latter for nine years), probably for Phillips, Messer, Colby [& Co.].*

Sibley, Frank Arthur *(1851-1909); North Newport (Northville), 1873-1909; worked in partnership or firm of Sibley Scythe Company; scythes and toothed hoes; son of Ezra Taft Sibley.*

Simonds, C.; *Antrim; cooper's croze, said to be made by him, exhibited at the Manchester Institute of Arts and Sciences, 1975.*

Simonds, Frederick *(1828-1899); Canaan, c. 1863-?; worked for Josiah S. Lincoln; awls.*

Simonds; *see also Symonds.*

Simons, Arad *(1754-1836); Lebanon, c. 1785-1836; joiner/carpenter, whose name (without town) appears on planes and moulding tools; came to Lebanon from Mansfield, Connecticut.*

Skinner; *Keene, 1868-1870; worked in partnership or firm of Gerould, Richardson & Skinner; stencils.*

Skinner, Barton *(1801-1865); Chesterfield, 1851-1853; augers and bits; said to have "carried on the . . . business for Benjamin Pierce, who furnished the stock, etc."*

Skinner, Elijah *(1786-1871); Sandwich; machinist/inventor, involved in partnership or firm of Dearborn & Skinner, 1828-1831; planes.*

Slayton, Stephen D.; *Lebanon, c. 1860; edge tools.*

Sleeper, Benjamin R., *sometimes listed incorrectly as R. B. Sleeper; Sunapee, 1879-1900 +; worked alone and apparently in partnerships or firms of Long & Sleeper and B. R. Sleeper & Co.; handles (fork, hoe).*

Sleeper, Benjamin R., & Co.; *Sunapee, c. 1881; handles (probably fork); apparently succeeded Long & Sleeper.*

Sleeper, John *(1754-1834); Chester, 1814-1825; planes and moulding tools; came to Chester from Newburyport, Massachusetts; town not given on surviving products; distinctively shaped "Sleeper-type" wedge, so named by collectors.*

Small, David; *Manchester, c. 1856; stencils.*

Smalley, J. F., *variously spelled Smally; Hanover, c. 1850; blacksmith, known to have made axes.*

Smart, L. T.; *Ossipee; patented saw set, 1868.*

Smith; *Hill, 1856-1857; edge tools.*

Smith & Chase, *listed variously as Chase & Smith; partnership of Reuben Smith and Charles J. Chase; Weare, 1855-1857; edge tools; made hay cutters, c. 1853.*

Smith, Aaron W.; *Manchester; patented bit stock, 1866.*

Smith, Ballard *(1774-1863); Nashua (Dunstable); blacksmith; either he and/or Benjamin Smith probably responsible for axes and drawknives marked "SMITH/DUNSTABLE"; apparently the son of Benjamin Smith (c. 1736-1821).*

Smith, Barnard H.; *Laconia and/or Sanbornton, 1872-1874; axes.*

Smith, Benjamin *(c. 1736-1821); Nashua (Dunstable); blacksmith, believed to have made and sold axes, c. 1766; see also Ballard Smith.*

Smith, Benjamin *(?-1805); Tilton (Sanbornton Bridge), 1788-1805; worked in partnership or firm of Tilton & Smith; scythes.*

Smith, Charles B. *(1814-1880); Haverhill (Woodsville), 1870-1878; worked in partnership or firm of Johnson & Smith (Charles B. Smith & Co.); shovel handles; business often referred to under his own rather than firm name.*

Smith, Charles B., & Co.; *see Johnson & Smith.*

Smith, Charles H. V. *(1845-?); Milford; lumber dealer, known to have manufactured brush backs.*

Smith, Collins & Co.; *Claremont, 1868-1875; meat chopping and shoe knives.*

Smith, Collins & Kempton; *Claremont, 1875-1877; mincing knives; succeeded Smith, Collins & Co.*

Smith, David M.; *Gilsum; patented awl hafts,1832 and 1836.*

Smith, Elias F.; *Rochester, 1885-1900+; worked alone and in partnership or firm of Wadleigh & Smith; handles (axe, pick, sledge); son-in-law of partner Warren Wadleigh.*

Smith, John; *Concord, 1868-1874; cutlery (pocket and pen knife blades, razors, scissors, shears).*

Smith, John B.; *Sunapee, 1868-1887; machinist, known to have specialized in telescopes and object glasses by 1882.*

Smith, Julius; *Lyman, c. 1856; bits and augers; listed as a machinist in 1868.*

Smith, Perley; *Lyman, c. 1849; bits and augers; also a gunsmith.*

Smith, Reuben; *Weare, 1855-1857; worked in partnership or firm of Smith & Chase; edge tools; made hay cutters, c. 1853.*

Smith, S. C.; *Claremont, c. 1872; watchmaker's tools.*

Smith, Schuyler E.; *Newport; believed to have been listed incorrectly c. 1855 as a hone maker; actually a hame maker.*

Snow, John *(1778-1829); West Chesterfield; worked in partnership with brother-in-law Ora Farr; scythes, hoes.*

South Lancaster Lumber Company; *Lancaster, c. 1878; saws.*

Spaulding, E. R.; *Plainfield, c. 1875; axe handles.*

Spaulding, I. W.; *Plainfield, c. 1881; knives.*

Spaulding, Sam; *Plainfield, late 19th century; worked with Silas Read; said to have had a blacksmith shop and to have made tools.*

Spiller, Joseph D.; *Concord, 1856-1857; mechanic, known to have patented saw set, 1857.*

Sprague, Moses F.; *Nashua, 1864-1900+; patternmaker/machinist, who advertised squares, triangles, and drawing boards, 1864-1872; also made patent models.*

Stacy, Byron *(1837-1875); Goshen, c. 1860; fork handles.*

Staples, Alvah, *variously called Alna (?-c. 1865); Nashua, 1856-1858; worked for Underhill Edge Tool Company as axe temperer.*

Star Stamp Company; *Dover, c. 1893; Manchester, 1898-1927; stencils, punches, dies, steel and rubber stamps, seals, brands.*

Starrett, Charles Hammond, *variously called Hammon[d] Starrett (1800-1869); Francestown, 1831-?; blacksmith, specializing in axes; had become a machinist in Nashua by 1845; eventually moved to Gray, Maine.*

Stearns & Emerson; *Lebanon, c. 1885; snaths, etc.; apparently succeeded G. W. & M. L. Stearns.*

Stearns & Sons; *Lebanon, c. 1880; scythe snaths.*

Stearns Manufacturing Company; *Milo Leonard Stearns, proprietor; Lebanon, 1886-1890; snaths, etc.; apparently succeeded Stearns & Emerson.*

Stearns, Charles E.; *Manchester, 1880-1884; worked in partnerships or firms of Burpee, Hamilton & Co. and Manchester Axe Company; edge tools (specializing in axes); worked previously for Amoskeag Ax Company.*

Stearns, George W. *(1814-?); Lebanon, 1877-1884; worked in partnership or firm of G. W. & M. L. Stearns; scythe snaths.*

Stearns, George W. & Milo Leonard; *partnership of father and son; Lebanon, 1877-1884; scythe snaths ("Marston's patent and common snaths"); for information on patent see David W. Marston.*

Stearns, Leonard *(1804-1885); Plainfield (Meriden), c. 1849; Enfield, c. 1850; Lebanon, 1860-1880; worked alone in Plainfield and Enfield and in partnership or firm of Marston & Stearns (Leonard Stearns & Co.) in Lebanon; scythe snaths; brother of George W. Stearns.*

Stearns, Leonard, & Co.; *see Marston & Stearns.*

Stearns, Milo Leonard; *Lebanon, 1877-1887; worked in partnership or firm of G. W. & M. L. Stearns, and as proprietor of Stearns Manufacturing Company, 1886-1887; probably also in partnership or firm of Stearns & Emerson; scythe snaths; son of George W. Stearns.*

Stevens, William S.; *Dover, 1867-1874; worked in partnership or firm of Wiggin & Stevens; sandpaper.*

Stockwell Brothers; *Croydon, 1885-1890; handles (hoe, fork).*

Stokes; *Manchester, c. 1870; worked in partnership or firm of Brown & Stokes; cutlery.*

Stokes, Benjamin S.; *Manchester, 1851-1881; files and rasps; proprietor of Granite File Works; often listed under his own rather than business name; moved to Boston, c. 1885.*

Stokes, Septimus C.; *Manchester; patented combined knife sharpener and glass cutter, 1872.*

Stone, John *(1777-1853); Jaffrey, after 1798; blacksmith, specializing in axes.*

Stowell, G. H.; *Claremont, 1868-1870; axe handles.*

Stowell, Sylvester; *Newport, c. 1860; edge tools.*

Straw, Alonzo; *Farmington, c. 1850; tools.*

Sullivan Machine Company; *Claremont, 1868-1892; machinists/founders, known to have made jack screws, wagon jacks,*

Instruments of Change

and "tools"; branch at Rutland, Vermont; succeeded by Sullivan Machinery Company.

Swamscot Machine Company; *Newfields (South Newmarket), 1846-1897; machinists/founders, known to have made machinist's tools, 1855-1894.*

Swan, Benjamin; *Dunbarton, 19th century; scythes.*

Swan, Robert; *Richmond, before 1884; scythe snaths.*

Symonds; *Dublin, 1856-1857; worked in partnership or firm of Bemis & Symonds; handles (fork, hoe).*

Symonds; *see also Simonds.*

Taft, Herbert O.; *Fitzwilliam, c. 1885; brush handles.*

Tarbell, Wendell Phillips *(1854-?); Milford, 1888-1891; "mechanic," known to have manufactured clamps and screws, c. 1891; patented cabinetmaker's hand screw clamp, 1888; employed, 1895-1900 +, by furniture manufacturers, French & Heald.*

Tash, Edwin S., & Co.; *Dover, c. 1892; boot and shoe tools.*

Taylor; *the part of Lisbon which later became Sugar Hill, c. 1860; worked in partnership or firm of Blodgett, Taylor & Wells; edge tools.*

Tebbets & Co.; *Somersworth (Great Falls), c. 1860; hardware dealers, known to have manufactured "Brooks's mill saw sett"; see also Lebbeus Brooks.*

Thayer, Elihu *(1802-1834); Manchester (Goffe's Falls), c. 1830; apprenticed to Jesse Johnson Underhill, c. 1822, in that part of Chester which later became Auburn, as well as in Boston; edge tools; brother-in-law of George W. Underhill, et al.*

Thayer, Nelson; *Richmond, 1849-1878; edge tools (axes, drawknives).*

Thomas, W. S.; *Laconia, 1882-1884; machinist's tools.*

Thompson; *Hinsdale, c. 1868; worked in partnership or firm of Wilder & Thompson; chisels, drawknives.*

Thompson & Hoague; *partnership of Willis D. Thompson and Edgar C. Hoague; Concord, 1890-1902 +; hardware dealers, whose name appears on tools; became Thompson & Hoague Company by 1904.*

Thompson, A. S.; *Conway, c. 1879; blacksmith, whose name (together with "N. CONWAY") appears on a pipe wrench.*

Thompson, E. G.; *Antrim, c. 1870; wood turner, whose product included knife handles.*

Thompson, H.; *possibly Horace; Concord, c. 1874; edge tools.*

Thompson, Levi; *Epping, 1868-1870; axes.*

Thompson, Luke; *Antrim, c. 1874; knife handles.*

Thompson, William D.; *Littleton, c. 1874; edge tools.*

Thurston, Franklin R.; *Marlborough, 1849-1857; blacksmith/machinist, specializing in edge tools (axes).*

Thurston, Peleg B. *(1835-?); North Weare, 1888-1894; handles.*

Tilton and Smith; *partnership of Jeremiah Tilton and Benjamin Smith; Tilton (Sanbornton Bridge), 1788-1805; scythes.*

Tilton, Jeremiah *(1762-1822); Tilton (Sanbornton Bridge), 1788-1805; worked in partnership or firm of Tilton & Smith; scythes.*

Tolman, Cyrus S. *(c. 1818-?); Hinsdale, 1849-1850; machinist, known to have made bench and jack screws.*

Tolman, J. C. *(c. 1816-?); Hinsdale, 1856-1860; machinist, known to have made jack, bench, and clamp screws; had become a machinist in Keene by 1868.*

Tomkinson, J. & R., *variously recorded as Tomlinson, Tompkinson, and Tomkins; Plymouth and/or Holderness, 1870-1880; files.*

Tompkins, G.; *Newport, c. 1849; hoe handles.*

Towns, Carleton J., *variously spelled Towne[s]; Nashua, 1864-1872; machinist, known to have made machinist's and woodworker's tools, 1870-1872.*

Trafton Brothers; *partnership of Alfred S. and Timothy J. Trafton; Portsmouth, 1860-1874; blacksmiths, who advertised edge tools.*

Trafton, Alfred S., & Son; *partnership of Alfred S. and George A. Trafton; Portsmouth, 1879-1882; blacksmiths/shipsmiths, who advertised edge tools.*

Trafton, George A.; *Portsmouth, 1879-1900 +; worked alone and in partnership or firm of A. S. Trafton & Son; blacksmith, who advertised edge tools; son of Alfred S. Trafton.*

Trafton, W. P.; *Portsmouth, 1868-1870; stencils.*

Treadwell & Co.; *Antrim, 1861-1864; shovels; a Boston firm, which purchased and operated the Antrim Shovel Company.*

Trench; *Plainfield (Meriden), c. 1881; worked in partnership or firm of Cole & Trench; pruners.*

Trickey, William P.; *Portsmouth, c. 1864; worked in partnership or firm of Marshall & Trickey; blacksmith, advertising edge tools.*

Tripp, William; *Epsom; patented saw buck (sawhorse), 1868.*

Trumbull, Walter S.; *Andover (Potter Place), 1885-1900 +; fishing rods.*

Trundy, John *(1800-1873); Portsmouth, c. 1850; mathematical instruments (including surveyor's compasses).*

Trussell, Moses *(1837-?); Webster (West Boscawen), 1859-c. 1865; axes; worked in sawmill by 1865.*

Tucker, Daniel *(c. 1780-1843); Laconia (Meredith Bridge), c. 1810-?; blacksmith, said to have made axes, knives, shaves, and scythes.*

Turner, John; *Hudson, after c. 1860; files; worked in former shops of Warren planemakers.*

Tuttle, A. D.; *possibly Alexis D. (1839-?); Nottingham; name (with town) appears as manufacturer on leatherworker's tools.*

Tyler, Benjamin and John; *Claremont; patented improvement in scythe factory machine, 1817; wooden bellows, 1817.*

Tyler, John; *see Benjamin and John Tyler.*

The Toolmakers

Tyler, Merrill A.; *New Durham; patented heel shave, 1874 (patent assigned to Franklin W. Coburn).*

Tyler, P.; *name (without town) appears on planes and moulding tools said to have been made in Marlow.*

Underhill & Brown; *Auburn, 1850-1856; edge tools (axes, chisels, shears, hatchets); see also Nathaniel and John Sleeper Brown.*

Underhill & Leighton; *Manchester; possibly a partnership of William W. Leighton and Hazen R. Underhill, both in Manchester, c. 1852; edge tools.*

Underhill Brothers; *partnership of Hazen R. and Samuel Graham Underhill; Boston, Massachusetts, c. 1853-1867; edge tools.*

Underhill Edge Tool Company; *sometimes referred to, especially in early years, as the Edge Tool Company or the Nashua Edge Tool Company; George W. Underhill, superintendent; John H. Gage, first president; Nashua (Edgeville), 1852-1890; edge tools (axes, hatchets, chisels, picks, adzes, brick hammers, hooks, mattocks, scrapers, froes, stone sledges, carpenter's, butcher's, and cooper's tools); absorbed the Amoskeag Ax Company in 1879; in 1890 the American Axe and Tool Company, a national conglomerate, purchased and closed the Nashua operation but continued to use the Underhill name.*

Underhill, Brown & Leighton; *Auburn, c. 1849; edge tools; see also William W. Leighton and Nathaniel and John Sleeper Brown.*

Underhill, Flagg Temple *(1804-1850); Auburn, 1835-?; Manchester, c. 1848; worked alone in Manchester and in partnership with Jay Temple Underhill in that part of Chester which later became Auburn, 1835-1839; edge tools.*

Underhill, George Washington *(1815-1882); Nashua, 1839-1852; worked alone and with Rufus K. Underhill, making tools for Samuel G. Underhill of Boston; superintendent of the Underhill Edge Tool Company, 1852-1875 (worked in Boston prior to 1839); edge tools (axes, chisels, and hatchets).*

Underhill, George Washington, & Co.; *Nashua; a name appearing (with town) on tools and possibly used by George Washington and Rufus K. Underhill while working together 1840-1852; edge tools.*

Underhill, Hazen R. *(1821-1898); Auburn, c. 1842-1849; Manchester, c. 1852; Nashua, c. 1853, probably working for Underhill Edge Tool Company; Derry, 1867-1898; worked alone and in partnership or firm of Hazen R. Underhill & Co., 1887-1888, and Underhill Brothers in Boston, c. 1853-1867; edge tools (axes, butcher's tools, carpenter's tools, cutlery, plane irons).*

Underhill, Hazen R., & Co.; *Derry, 1887-1888; edge tools (axes).*

Underhill, Jay Temple *(1802-1839); Chester, 1828-1835; Auburn, 1835-1839; worked alone in Chester and in partnership with Flagg Temple Underhill in that part of Chester which later became Auburn; edge tools (worked in Boston from 1822 while still apprenticed to Jesse Johnson Underhill).*

Underhill, Jesse Johnson *(1784-1860); Manchester, c. 1813; the part of Chester which later became Auburn, ?-1822, 1826-1829, 1832-? (worked in Boston at other times); worked alone and with Samuel G. Underhill briefly in 1832; edge tools.*

Underhill, Josiah *(1758-1822); the part of Chester which later became Auburn; blacksmith, known to have made edge tools (scythes, axes, hoes, etc.); said to have been apprenticed to E. Fitts.*

Underhill, Rufus K. *(1819-1894); Nashua, 1840-1853; worked with George W. Underhill making tools for Samuel G. Underhill of Boston; edge tools.*

Underhill, Samuel Graham *(1809-1885); Auburn, c. 1832; worked briefly with Jesse Johnson Underhill in that part of Chester which later became Auburn; edge tools (worked in Boston at other times).*

Union Toy Turning Works; *Claremont, 1886-1890; handles.*

Union Wood Turning Company; *Newport, c. 1891; handles (brush, tool, file), hand vises, scythe snath nibs; appears to have succeeded Union Toy Turning Works of Claremont.*

United States Tool Company; *Newfields (South Newmarket), 1883-1890; edge tools.*

Upton, Alvan; *Mont Vernon, c. 1860; edge tools.*

Varick, John B., Company; *Manchester, 1884-1900+; hardware dealers, whose initials appear on tools; succeeded John B. Varick [& Co.].*

Virgin, Simeon *(1781-1838); Concord, 1803-1837; carpenter/furniture maker, known to have made planes (smoothing, plow, and double-iron jointer) and handles (fork, etc.); account book at New Hampshire Historical Society.*

Vogler, J. S., & Co.; *Concord, 1868-1870; brushes.*

Vulcan Saw Works; *see Charles A. Adams.*

Wadleigh & Smith; *partnership of Warren Wadleigh and Elias F. Smith; Rochester, 1885-1890; handles (axe, pick, sledge).*

Wadleigh, Warren *(1807-?); Sanbornton; Hill; Tilton (Sanbornton Bridge), c. 1860; Lakeport (Lake Village); Alton, 1870-1871;*

Rochester, 1871-1890; worked alone and in partnership or firm of Wadleigh & Smith; handles (axe, pick, sledge); patented machine for turning irregular forms, 1856.

Walker, Gustavus (1830-1902); Concord, 1855-1883; hardware dealer, whose name (with town) appears on tools; advertised as agent for Gage, Porter & Co. saws and [Ezekiel] Adams axes.

Walker, Richard; Portsmouth; patented file cutting machine, 1847.

Walker, Saladin A. (c. 1827-?); Bennington, c. 1860; knives.

Walker, Stephen H.; Portsmouth, c. 1821; blocks.

Wallace, Andrew C.; Manchester, c. 1872; worked in partnership or firm of Haines & Wallace; machinist's tools.

Walton, Samuel, [& Son]; Samuel Walton (c. 1817-1892), principal partner; Hudson, 1877-1891; files; individual and partnership names used alternately; worked in former shops of Warren planemakers.

Warde, Humphrey & Dodge; partnership of David A. Warde, Stillman Humphrey, and Howard A. Dodge; Concord, 1870-1874; hardware dealers, whose name (with town) appears on tools.

Ware, Walter H.; Milford, 1887-1890; worked in partnership or firm of Emerson & Ware; tool chests.

Warner & Whitney; partnership of David A. G. Warner and George H. Whitney; Nashua, 1866-1879; machinist's tools; succeeded Gage, Warner & Whitney.

Warner, David A. G. (?-c. 1873); Nashua, 1851-1872; worked in partnerships or firms of Gage, Warner & Whitney and Warner & Whitney; machinist's tools.

Warner, Jethro W. (1847-1875); Dover, 1871-1874; shoemaker, who patented lasting hammer, 1869.

Warren & Heald; *partnership of Addison Heald and one or more of the Warrens (Cyrus, William, and/or George Henry); Nashua, c. 1860; planes.*

Warren, Cyrus (1804-1888); Hudson, c. 1836-1857; Nashua, 1857-1875; worked alone and with brother William in Hudson; planes and moulding tools.

Warren, George Henry (1829-1900); Hudson, 1850-1857; apparently worked alone and in association with uncle William Warren; known products all marked "NASHUA" rather than "HUDSON", apparently for name recognition; son of Cyrus Warren.

Warren, George Henry and William; apparently incorrectly recorded as C. H. & Wm. Warren; Hudson, c. 1853; planes.

Warren, William (1818-1861); Hudson, 1853-1860; at various times, worked alone, with brother Cyrus, and with nephew George H. (c. 1853); planes; known products all marked "NASHUA" rather than "HUDSON", apparently for name recognition.

Warren, Wilson; Hudson; believed to have been listed incorrectly in 1860 as a planemaker instead of William Warren.

Waukewan Manufacturing Company; Meredith; name (with town) appears on hacksaws.

Way, Charles A. (1836-1909); North Charlestown, 1865-1900; fishing rods.

Weare, Jonathan (1781-1848); East Andover; edge tools (shovels, forks, hoes, scythes, chopping and broad axes, drawknives).

Weare, Leonard F.; Laconia, 1882-1884; worked in partnership or firm of Woodman & Weare; machinist's tools.

Weaver, Cyrus; Hudson; believed to have been listed incorrectly in 1849 as a planemaker instead of Cyrus Warren.

Weaver, William; Nashua, 1872-1875; marble worker's and stonecutter's tools.

Webster; Bristol, 1829-?; worked in partnership or firm of Lovejoy & Webster; blacksmith, specializing in edge tools.

Webster, Stephen C. (1779-1850); Salisbury, 1804-1843; joiner, known to have made and sold planes (jointer, smoothing) and other tools; account book privately owned.

Webster, Wilbur (1839-1905); East Jaffrey, 1873-1894; boot and shoe knives; previously made cutlery in Brockton, Massachusetts; business sold to C. J. Kimball Company of Bennington in 1894.

Weeks, Benjamin; Portsmouth, 1821-1877; blocks.

Weeks, George (?-c. 1875); Dover, 1837-1874; blacksmith, whose name (with town) appears on broad axe.

Weeks, Minot (1841-1873); Littleton, 1869-1873; worked in partnership or firm of Sanborn & Weeks; planes, measuring tools; son-in-law of David Page Sanborn.

Welch & Newcomb; Nelson, c. 1860; woodenware manufacturers, whose product included shovel handles.

The Toolmakers

Welch, Daniel; *Canaan; patented grinding tools, hammers, etc., 1833.*

Weld, Elbridge G.; *Orford, 1830-1839; worked in partnership with Francis Weld; scythes.*

Weld, Francis; *Orford, 1830-1839; worked in partnership with Elbridge G. Weld; scythes.*

Wellington, George P.; *Hinsdale, 1868-1870; worked in partnership or firm of Priest & Wellington; handles.*

Wells, *variously known as Welds; Goffstown, c. 1785; blacksmith, known to have made augers.*

Wells; *the part of Lisbon which later became Sugar Hill, c. 1860; worked in partnership or firm of Blodgett, Taylor & Wells; edge tools.*

Wells; *Nashua, c. 1860; worked in partnership or firm of Shattuck & Wells; ship handspikes.*

West, Robert L.; *Manchester, 1884-1885; brushes.*

Weston, Charles H.; *Nashua; patented spokeshave, 1858.*

Whalley, Nathan; *Portsmouth, 1869-1881; worked in partnership or firm of Critchley & Whalley; machinists, known to have made expanding reamers.*

Wheeler, C. A.; *Peterborough, 1872-1881; churn thermometers.*

Wheeler, Edgar L.; *New London (Elkins, formerly Scytheville); patented scythe, 1873.*

Wheeler, John F.; *East Jaffrey, 1885-1892; saw frames.*

Wheeler, Robert H.; *Langdon, c. 1880; scythe snath sticks.*

Wheeler, W. A.; *Littleton; name (with town) appears as maker on log calipers.*

Whidden, Michael *(c. 1695-1773); Portsmouth, 1716-1773; joiner, known to have made compass boxes and quadrant cases for mathematical instrument maker William Hart, 1757-1772.*

Whitaker, Luther; *Conway, c. 1850; blacksmith, known to have made edge tools.*

Whitcomb & Cross; *partnership of Alanson S. Whitcomb and Levi Cross; Swanzey, c. 1856; Keene, 1868-1874; brush handles (paint, varnish, French, common sash, stencil marking, etc.).*

Whitcomb, Alanson S. *(1822-?); Swanzey, c. 1856; Keene, 1868-1891; worked alone in Keene and in partnership or firm of Whitcomb & Cross; brush handles.*

White & Eaton; *partnership of Jonathan White and Hiram Eaton; Antrim, 1841-1853; shovels and cast steel and concave hoes; partners together responsible for development of the "Antrim shovel."*

White, Edwin B., [& Co.]; *Nashua, 1853-1855; screw chucks.*

White, George; *Walpole, c. 1800; name (with town) appears as maker on a surveyor's compass.*

White, Jonathan *(1814-1864); Antrim, c. 1833-1856; worked alone and in partnerships or firms of Baldwin & White and White & Eaton; shovels, hoes; patented "improvement in uniting shovel-blades to the handle-straps," 1853; served his apprenticeship with Isaac Baldwin.*

White, Samuel G. *(1842-1906); Peterborough, 1874-1900+; machinist, known to have made machinist's tools.*

Whitehouse, George Leighton *(1797-1887); Farmington, Dover; surveyor's compasses; patented a leveling rod, 1876.*

Whiting & Miller *(also known as Henry J. Miller & Co.); partnership of Benjamin Whiting and Henry J. Miller; Nashua, c. 1868; boot brushes/jacks.*

Whiting, Seth; *Rindge, ?-1836; brushes; later of Boston.*

Whiting, Stephen, & Co.; *Bath, c. 1810; whetstones.*

Whitney; *Mason; cooper's sun plane, said to be made by him, exhibited at Manchester Institute of Arts and Sciences, 1975.*

Whitney, George H. *(?-c. 1895); Nashua, 1851-1892; worked alone and in partnerships or firms of Gage, Warner & Whitney and Warner & Whitney; machinist's tools.*

Whittemore, Amos *(1802-1881); Bennington, 1853-1860; worked in partnerships or firms of Baldwin & Whittemore and Amos & George Alfred Whittemore (Amos Whittemore & Co.); cutlery.*

Whittemore, Amos & George Alfred; *partnership of two brothers (apparently also known as Amos Whittemore & Co.); Bennington, c. 1860; edge tools (cutlery, specializing in shoe and butcher knives).*

Whittemore, George Alfred, *variously known as Alfred (1807-?); Bennington, 1853-1860; worked in partnerships or firms of Baldwin & Whittemore and Amos & George Alfred Whittemore (Amos Whittemore & Co.); cutlery.*

Whittemore, Winslow; *Marlow, 1870-1872; sawmill operater/turner, whose product included handles (trowel, knife).*

Wiggin & Stevens; *partnership of Russel B. Wiggin and William S. Stevens; Dover, 1858-1900+; glue manufacturers, known to have made sandpaper ("New England Flint" brand) in Dover, 1867-1874; by 1890 the Dover plant was devoted exclusively to the manufacture of glue to be used in the production of sandpaper, etc., at Wiggin & Stevens's Malden, Massachusetts, factory.*

Wight, George H.; *Laconia, c. 1881; machinist's tools.*

Wilder & Hopkins; *partnership of Richard Henry Hopkins and George Sheldon Wilder; Hinsdale, 1870-1873; edge tools (chisels, drawknives); apparently succeeded Wilder & Thompson.*

Wilder & Thompson; *probably George Sheldon Wilder, principal partner; Hinsdale, c. 1868; chisels, drawknives.*

Wilder, Azel *(1788-1860); Keene, c. 1836; apparently worked alone and in partnerships or firms of Newcomb & Wilder and Azel Wilder & Co.; bits, augers, gimlets; also made spinning wheels, vehicles, and furniture.*

Wilder, Azel, & Co.; *partnership of Azel Wilder, Rufus Gates, and Henry Thompson; Keene, 1836-?; augers, spur bits, gimlets; succeeded Newcomb & Wilder; also made spinning wheels and wheel heads.*

Wilder, Charles *(1836-1900); North Peterborough, 1860-c. 1903; thermometers and barometers; business continued for three years after his death by his sons (Frank Jones and John Maryatt), in accord with his will.*

Wilder, George Sheldon *(1828-1900); Hinsdale, 1844-1891; worked alone, with uncle Pliny Merrill, and in partnerships or firms of Merrill & Wilder, Wilder & Thompson(?), and probably*

Wilder & Hopkins; edge tools (chisels, drawknives), carpenter's tools, planes; business under his own name succeeded in 1883 by Jennings & Griffin Manufacturing Company, of which he became Hinsdale manager.

Wilder, Josiah Prescott (1801-1873); New Ipswich; chairmaker, who also made handles of all types; day books and ledger privately owned; son of Peter Wilder.

Wilder, Peter (1761-1841); Keene, 1781-1799; chairmaker, who advertised scythe snaths in 1798; later of New Ipswich.

Wilder, William; Manchester, 1858-1868; blacksmith's bellows.

Williams, Charles; Nashua, c. 1870; iron founder, known to have produced "small tools;" agent of Nashua Iron Foundry.

Williams, William (?-c. 1721); Portsmouth, c. 1707; blocks.

Willoughby, Edwin; Hudson, 1877-1878; files.

Wilmarth, George; Sandwich, c. 1872; handles.

Wilmarth, George E. (1834-?); Newport; handles (fork, hoe); nephew of Jonathan M. Wilmarth.

Wilmarth, Jonathan M. (1796-?); Newport, 1839-1860; handles (fork, hoe).

Wilson; Croydon, c. 1850; worked in partnership or firm of Morrill & Wilson; knives.

Wilson, Andrew, & Co.; Portsmouth, 1867-1878; hackles (hemp and flax).

Wilson, George W. (1821-1910); Concord, 1864-1901; mathematical, surveyor's, and engineer's instruments (including lenses and spirit levels).

Wilson, Henry G.; Manchester, 1854-1864; brushes.

Wilson, Joseph, variously spelled Willson (1770-1838); Marlborough and Keene; blacksmith, said to have invented the potato hook and been the first in his vicinity to manufacture the twisted auger and bit; patented pronged hoe, 1827; lived on town line.

Wilson, Joseph; Pembroke, after 1843; knives and hammers.

Wilson, Leonard, variously spelled Willson; Derry, 1850-1856; edge tools (axes).

Wilson, Stillman; Swanzey, c. 1860; edge tools.

Wilson, Thomas; Hillsborough, c. 1849; fork handles.

Winslow; Haverhill (Woodsville), c. 1875; worked in partnership or firm of Wyman & Winslow; axe helves.

Winslow, Benjamin A. (1852-?); Northfield Depot, c. 1894; axe handles.

Wiswell, Andrew; Exeter; patented tailor's square, 1832.

Witherell, James H.; Littleton, 1880-1888; scythes and axes; manager of New Hampshire Scythe Company, 1880-1885, apparently under firm name of James H. Witherell & Co.; said to have "held a copyright on a name and style of scythes and axes that had met with large sales."

Witherell, James H., & Co.; Littleton (Apthorp, formerly Scythe Factory Village), 1880-1888(?); axes, scythes; apparently managers of New Hampshire Scythe Company, 1880-1885.

Woodbury, Isaac & Jacob; partnership of two brothers; Newport, c. 1860; edge tools.

Woodbury, Levi; Concord, c. 1887; cutlery.

Woodman & Weare; partnership of Eben F. Woodman and Leonard F. Weare; Laconia, 1882-1884; machinist's tools.

Woodman Brothers; partnership of Addison L. and Edward S. Woodman; Concord, 1874-1880; machinist's tools, jack screws, granite worker's tools.

Woodman, B. F.; Fremont, 1872-1882; carpenter, whose name (with town) appears as maker on planes.

Woods Cutlery Company; Bennington, 1872-1875; knives; probably succeeded W. D. & E. F. Woods, although recorded dates overlap slightly; office at Antrim; was combined in 1875 with the operations of David Harvey Goodell to form the Goodell Company.

Woods, Charles; Hudson, c. 1850; handles.

Woods, Dodge & Co.; Portsmouth, 1868-1870; Bennington, c. 1870; cutlery.

Woods, Eben F. (c. 1835-?); Bennington, 1860-1874; forger in knife factory, 1860 (apparently worked for either Samuel Baldwin or A. & G. A. Whittemore); worked in partnership or firm of W. D. & E. F. Woods, 1868-1874; cutlery.

Woods, Walter D. (c. 1830-?); Bennington, 1868-1874; worked in partnership or firm of W. D. & E. F. Woods; edge tools (knives); patented table cutlery, 1868, and knife handle, 1870; also worked alone making sandpaper, c. 1853.

Woods, Walter D. & Eben F.; partnership of two brothers (apparently also known as W. D. Woods & Co.); Bennington, 1868-1874?; edge tools (shoe and table knives); see also Woods Cutlery Company.

Woodward, Frank Ross (1845-1931); Hill, 1873-1900+; novelty manufacturer, known to have produced ice picks, washer cutters, can openers, knife sharpeners, and combination tools, but specializing in glazier's tools (glass cutters); patented rotary cutter for use on paper, leather, pasteboard, textiles, glass, etc., 1875; listed interchangeably (between 1877 and 1893) under his own name and that of the New England Novelty Works, of which he was proprietor; published briefs from patent dispute against Woodward (1876), available at New Hampshire Historical Society.

Worster, George; Allenstown, 1868-1870; machinist, known to have made shoe knives.

Worster, Isaac (1801-?); Milton, 1849-1850; apparently worked alone and in partnership or firm of Isaac & George Worster; forks and hoes; moved to Rochester.

Worster, Isaac & George, also recorded incorrectly as J. G. Worster; partnership of two brothers; Milton, c. 1849; forks and hoes.

Wright, William; Brookline, c. 1881; edge tools.

Wyman & Winslow; Haverhill (Woodsville), c. 1875; axe helves.

Yeaton, Benjamin; Portsmouth, 1802-1821; blocks.

Yeaton, William; Portsmouth, c. 1765; blocks.

York, V. P.; Landaff, c. 1860; edge tools.

Young; Sunapee, 1856-1857; worked in partnership or firm of Cummings & Young; handles (fork, hoe).

Young, Acanthus, variously spelled Arcanthas (c. 1815-1877); Center Barnstead, 1868-1870; edge tools.

Young, Asa; Portsmouth, 1812-1821; blacksmith, believed to have worked in partnership or firm of Bartlett & Young; edge tools.

Young, E. P.; Hampton, c. 1856; edge tools.

List of Toolmakers by Town

Acworth
Burtis, R.
Hawkins, Floyd F.
Kemp & Call
Kemp Brothers
Kemp, O. R.
Reed, James M.

Alexandria
Clifford, Marshall

Allenstown
Worster, George

Alstead
Brooks, George A.
Cheever, William
Demerse, Lewis
Edward[s], Reuben J.
Howard, Joseph B.
Kidder, E. P.
King, Henry
Messer Brothers
Messer, Frank D.
Messer, William H.
Rice, Hamlet L.

Alton
Wadleigh, Warren

Amherst
Parker, C. S.
Rhoades, C. W.

Andover
Brown, Calvin M.
Lang, Gilman L.
Trumbull, Walter S.
Weare, Jonathan

Antrim
Abbott, J. R., & Co.
Abbott, John R.
Antrim Shovel Company
Baldwin & White
Dimond, Ephraim
Goodell Company
Holt, C. F.
Robbins & Flint
Robinson, Samuel R.
Simonds, C.
Thompson, E. G.
Thompson, Luke
Treadwell & Co.
White & Eaton
White, Jonathan

Atkinson
Heald, Paul

Auburn
Brown, John Sleeper
Brown, Nathaniel
Leighton & Lufkin
Leighton, William W.
Underhill & Brown
Underhill, Brown & Leighton
Underhill, Flagg Temple
Underhill, Hazen R.
Underhill, Jay Temple
Underhill, Jesse Johnson
Underhill, Josiah
Underhill, Samuel Graham

Barnstead
Emerson, Timothy
Pendergast, Isaac S.
Young, Acanthus

Barrington
Hall, Elma E.

Bath
Whiting, Stephen, & Co.

Bedford
Atwood, D. G.
Bachelder, Otis Freeman
Bell, Joseph
Damon, S. C.
Dunlap, John
French, P.
Gilmore, John
Houston, James
Houston, John P.
Kennedy, James
Martin, James
Moore, Daniel
Patten, Matthew
Shed, Nathan

Bennington
Baldwin & Whittemore
Baldwin, Samuel
Baldwin, Samuel, & Co.
Goodell Company
Kimball, Caleb Jewett
Kimball, Caleb Jewett, & Son
Kimball, Caleb Jewett, Company
Walker, Saladin A.
Whittemore, Amos & George Alfred
Woods Cutlery Company
Woods, Dodge & Co.
Woods, Walter D.
Woods, Walter D. & Eben F.

Boscawen (See also Penacook)
Gerrish, Stephen

Bristol
Benton, W. W., & Co.
Crosby, Milo H.
Holmes, Charles W.
Homans, L. W.
Hutchinson Brothers
Hutchinson, Arthur
Lovejoy & Webster
Lovejoy, Abbott
Sanborn, Gustavus B.

Brookline
Hardy, Ephraim L.
Hobart, George W. L.
Wright, William

Campton
Claflin, John
Coffren, John
Cole, I. H.
Evans, William B.

Canaan
Balch, Dan Shaw
Butterfield, William
Crandall, C. H.
Currier, H. G.
Eastman, George S.
Eastman, Phineas
Jones, Nathan
Kittredge, Jonathan
Lincoln, Josiah S.
Milton, Joseph
Milton, Matthew Harvey
Welch, Daniel

Candia
Batchelder, Thomas
Fitts, J. E.
Robinson, Daniel B.

Canterbury
McDaniel, T. D.
Morrill, George Peverly
Nutting, Luther M.

Center Harbor
Brown, John
Coffin, John T.
Coffin, John T., & Son

Charlestown
Hasham, Stephen
Milliken, Adams
Robinson, William K.
Way, Charles A.

Chatham
Pillsbury, John D.

Chester (See also Auburn)
Sleeper, John
Underhill, Jay Temple

Chesterfield
Atherton & Goodrich
Brown & Russell
Currier Brothers
Farr, Olin Ransom
Farr, Ora
Goodrich, George
Graves, Caleb S.
Hopkins & Pierce
Hopkins, Richard Henry
Howe & Hopkins
Mann, Thomas W.
Newcomb, John
Pierce, Benjamin
Pierce, Cross & Farr
Pierce, Frederick Benjamin
Pierce, Frederick Benjamin, & Co.
Richardson & Huggins
Snow, John

Chichester
Merrill, James O.

Claremont
Barker, Andrew H.
Claremont Cutlery Company
Claremont File Works
Dexter, David
Dexter, Stephen
Durant, L. A., & Co.
Gilmore, Hiram
Gilmore, Leonard
Graves & Eaton
Graves, Bela
Heywood, Simeon
Howard Brush Company
Howard, J. B.
Howard, W. B.
Nutt, Henry
Nutt, Henry, & Co.
Papps, Charles H.
Parmelee, Henry
Philbrook, Alfred S.
Pillsbury, Oliver M.
Randall, Lewis W.
Richardson, Samuel
Smith, Collins & Co.
Smith, Collins & Kempton
Smith, S. C.
Stowell, G. H.
Sullivan Machine Company
Tyler, Benjamin and John
Union Toy Turning Works

Clarksville
Richards, Romance

Colebrook
Graham & Gilkey

Concord (See also Penacook)
Burgum, John
Chandler, Abiel
Chandler, Mary Burgin
Chandler, Timothy
Clough, C. H.
Colby, John V.
Cole, A. J.
Concord File Works
Continental Construction Company
Fellows, Jonathan
Fury, James
Gordon, Edward F.
Haley Manufacturing Company
Hall, Frank P.
Harrison, Henry G.
Hobbs, Gordon & Co.
Holt Brothers
Houston, Harry
Hutchins, Levi
Kimball, John
Martin, C. H., & Co.
Morrill, George Peverly
Nutting & Hayden
Nutting, Luther M., & Co.
Radford, Cass M.
Sargent, Philip
Smith, John
Spiller, Joseph D.
Thompson, H.
Virgin, Simeon
Vogler, J. S., & Co.
Wilson, George W.
Woodbury, Levi
Woodman Brothers

Conway
Clifford, George H.
Pratt, Captain (Solomon?)
Thompson, A. S.
Whitaker, Luther

Cornish
Coburn, Stillman
Eggleston, William
Luther, Jabez
Sawyer, David

Croydon
Ferry, Joel
Morrill & Wilson
Morrill, O. F.
Stockwell Brothers

Danville
George, Currier

Deerfield
Emerson, E. V.
Robinson, Thomas Stewart
Robinson, Thomas Stewart, & Co.

Deering
Goodall, Frank P.

Derry
Noyes, W. O.
Underhill, Hazen R.
Underhill, Hazen R., & Co.
Wilson, Leonard

Dorchester
Noyes, Walter B.

Dover
Durgin, Daniel
Flagg, Joshua Getchell
Flagg, Joshua Getchell, & Son
Fletcher, Tristram H.
Hobbs, George W.
Hobbs, George W., & Co.
Hurd, William
Laskey, L. B., & Co.
Quint, George
Star Stamp Company
Tash, Edwin S., & Co.
Warner, Jethro W.
Weeks, George
Whitehouse, George Leighton
Wiggin & Stevens

Dublin
Bemis & Symonds
Piper, Rufus

Dunbarton
Chamberlain, I. A.
French, G. B.
Hammond, John McCurdy
Jameson, John
Marshall, Ansel
Swan, Benjamin

Durham
Joy, James

Effingham
Drake, J. L.

Enfield
Eaton, E. & E.
Eaton, Edward
Eaton, Edward, Jr.
Garland, J. H.
Richardson, Alpha
Sargent, L. N.
Stearns, Leonard

Epping
Burley, Thomas
Thompson, Levi

Epsom
Tripp, William

Exeter
Burlingame, William
Clifford, Ebenezer
Exeter Machine Works
Gilman, Benjamin Clark
Jones, Daniel
Moses, William P.
Proctor, Amos
Wiswell, Andrew

Farmington
Duntley, Joseph H.
Hall, Andrew J.
Hayes, Israel
Morgan & Marston
Straw, Alonzo
Whitehouse, George Leighton

Fitzwilliam
Taft, Herbert O.

Francestown
Bixby, Daniel
Starrett, Charles Hammond

Franconia
New Hampshire Iron Factory Co.

Franklin
Aiken Brad Awl and Saw Set
  Manufacturing Company
Aiken, Francis Herrick
Aiken, Harriet A. Colby
Aiken, Herrick
Aiken, Jonas Bradley
Aiken, Walter Scott
Barrett, Edward H.
Bickford, Solomon E.
Burleigh, Harry Walter
Flanders, Frederick
Griffin, George Washington, & Co.
Griffin, George Washington,
  Company
Prescott Company
Prescott, Charles B.
Proctor, James

Freedom
Foss, Ivory
Fowler, Cyrus

Fremont
Woodman, B. F.

Gilford
Blaisdell, John
Chase, James
Gilman, Josiah
Gilman, Winthrop
Leavitt, Dudley
Sanborn, Israel

Gilmanton
Marsh, Gilman

Gilsum
Bingham, Charles W.
Campbell, William
Hemenway, Luther
Loveland, Isaac
Smith, David M.

Goffstown
Carr, James
Dimond, Ephraim
Dimond, Israel
Dunlap, John
Hoyt, Thomas Rowell
Hoyt, Thomas Rowell, Jr.
Moore, Orrin
Moore, Orrin, & Sons
Shed, Nathan
Wells

Goshen
Stacy, Byron

Grafton
Lang & Hoyt
Lang, Gilman L.

Greenville
Kimball, Isaac
Newell, Ezra

Groton
Haselton, Rufus B.
Haselton, Rufus B., & Son
Kidder, Daniel

Hampstead
Globe Tool Works
Johnson, William
Jones, J.
Nichols, Daniel
Nichols, Hiram

Hampton
Young, E. P.

Hampton Falls
Healey, W. W.
Pike, Benjamin

Hancock
Lakin, Taylor D.

Hanover
Baldwin, Jedediah
Dame, Richard
Smalley, J. F.

Harrisville
Farwell, C. & H.

Haverhill
Noyes, Person
Noyes, Timothy
Palmer, Lorenzo D.
Pierce Brothers
Pierce, R.
Pierce, R. & C. G.
Pike & Pike
Pike Manufacturing Company
Pike, Alonzo Franklin
Pike, Alonzo Franklin, Manufacturing
  Company
Pike, Isaac

Haverhill-Woodsville
Johnson & Smith
Smith, Charles B.
Wyman & Winslow

Hebron
Hardy, David P.
Hardy, E. D.

Henniker
Abbott, William
Chandler, William
Dunlap, Samuel
Hale, Franklin W.

Hill
New England Novelty Works
Smith
Wadleigh, Warren
Woodward, Frank Ross

Hillsborough
Foss, Obed
Foss, William G.
Mack, Andrew
Wilson, Thomas

Hinsdale
Hinsdale Machine and Tool Company
Holman & Merriman
Hopkins, Richard Henry
Jennings & Griffin Manufacturing Company
Merrill & Wilder
Merrill, John B.
Merrill, P., & Co.
Merrill, Pardon-Haynes
Merrill, Pliny
Owen & Amidon
Owen, David A.
Priest & Wellington
Tolman, Cyrus S.
Tolman, J. C.
Wilder & Hopkins
Wilder & Thompson
Wilder, George Sheldon

Holderness
Tomkinson, J. & R.

Hollis
Farley, Benjamin
French, Nathaniel
Manning, George W.
Pierce, Levi

Hopkinton
Adams, Ezekiel
Long, Isaac
Morse, Joshua

Hopkinton-Contoocook
Berry, Oliver P.
Berry, Oliver P., Company
Haselton, Hermon R.
Haselton, Rufus B.

Hudson
Heald, Addison
Moore & Co.
Moore, John W.
Sargent, Dana
Turner, John
Walton, Samuel, [& Son]
Warren, Cyrus
Warren, George Henry
Warren, George Henry & William
Warren, William
Willoughby, Edwin
Woods, Charles

Jaffrey
Danforth, Jacob
Dean, Hiram
Hathorn, Ebenezer
Lawrence, Artemas
Phelps, Peter
Saunders, John
Stone, John
Webster, Wilbur
Wheeler, John F.

Keene
Allen, Francis E.
Bartlett, Sylvanus
Briggs, E.
Briggs, Nathaniel
Brooks, Henry O.
Brooks, William H.
Davis, Aaron
Ellis, Austin A.
Gerould, Richardson & Skinner
Humphrey Machine Company
Humphrey, John, & Co.
Keene Manufacturing Company
Newcomb & Wilder
Newcomb, Everett
Page, George
Reed, Joseph Mason
Rugg, Elias
Whitcomb & Cross
Whitcomb, Alanson S.
Wilder, Azel
Wilder, Azel, & Co.
Wilder, Peter
Wilson, Joseph

Kensington
Clifford, Ebenezer
Fellows, Jeremiah

Laconia
American Twist Drill Company
Baldwin, Nathan H.
Champlin, John R.
Dearth, Lester A.
Fonda, Isaac
Smith, Barnard H.
Thomas, W. S.
Tucker, Daniel
Wight, George H.
Woodman & Weare

Laconia-Lakeport
Buxton, F.
Crosby, George
House, Charles D.
Wadleigh, Warren

Lancaster
Adams, Harvey
Bachelder, James
Ellis & Olcott
Ellis Brothers
Hall, James H.
Lancaster File Works
Moody & Cave
Moody & Co.
Moody & Ellis
Moody, Carr (Cave?) & Ellis
South Lancaster Lumber Company

Landaff
Noyes, Simon C.
York, V. P.

Langdon
Wheeler, Robert H.

Lebanon
Alden & Kellog
Amsden, Downing
Durant, Edward J.
Emerson & Cummings
Emerson & Kimball
Emerson Edge Tool Company
Emerson, A. V.
Emerson, A. V. & M. W.
Kelly, E. L.
Kendrick & Davis
Kendrick & Davis Company
Lebanon Machine Works
Marston & Stearns
Marston Patent Scythe Company
Marston, David W.
Mascoma Edge Tool Company
Merrill & Dowse
Merrill, Benjamin F.
Perkins, Messer, Colby & Co.

Phillips, Messer, Colby [& Co.]
Purmort, Martin V. [B.]
Simons, Arad
Slayton, Stephen D.
Stearns & Emerson
Stearns & Sons
Stearns Manufacturing Company
Stearns, George W. & Milo Leonard

Lincoln

Sargent, L. B.

Lisbon

Blodgett, Edwin
Dodge, Charles
Dodge, Corydon
Hillard, George W.
Noyes, Simon C.

Littleton

Alexander, Wesley
Applebee, Charles Henry
Dow, James
Ely, Farr & Co.
Greenleaf, Florence M.
Greenleaf, William Gardner
Hartshorn & Co.
Kilburn, Edward
Littleton Hone Stone Company
Littleton Scythe Stone Company
Merrill, George H.
Merrill, Lewis Lovejoy
New Hampshire Scythe Company
Palmer, Freeman
Redington, Henry Cornelius, & Co.
Sanborn & Weeks
Sanborn, David Page
Sanborn, David Page & Francis Davidson
Sanborn, Francis Davidson
Thompson, William D.
Wheeler, W. A.
Witherell, James H., & Co.

Londonderry

Mack, John

Lyman

Smith, Julius
Smith, Perley

Lyme

Dimick, Daniel B.
Palmer, G.
Porter, J. H.
Royal, H. E.

Manchester

Adams, Charles A.
Amoskeag Ax Company
Amoskeag Manufacturing Company Machine Shop
Bailey, William
Baker, C. S.
Baldwin, James, & Co.
Barker, Andrew H.
Blodgett Edge Tool Manufacturing Company
Brown & Stokes
Brown, Peter S.
Burpee, Hamilton & Co.
Carpenter & Co.
Daniels, Albert H.
Dennis, George G.
Dickerman
Dudley, Thomas D., & Co.
Fantom, George
Fantom, George, & Co.
Farnham, J. H.
Farnham, J. H. & W. J.
Felton, S. A., & Co.
Felton, S. A., & Son
Felton, S. A., & Son Company
Forsaith, Hiram
Forsaith, Samuel Caldwell
Forsaith, Samuel Caldwell, & Co.
Forsaith, Samuel Caldwell, Machine Company
Granite File Works
Haines & Wallace
Houghton, Joseph
Hutchinson, Charles H.
Josselyn & Marston
Josselyn, Lewis H., & Co.
Lawson, John H.
Leighton & Son
Leighton, Charles O.
Leighton, William W.
Leighton, William W., & Co.
Libby, Marvin W.
Lowell, A. H.
Manchester Axe Company
Manchester File Works
Manchester Locomotive Works
McCulloch, Eppie J.
Newton, Henry E.
Newton, Henry E., & Co.
Noyes, W. B.
Paige, A. H.
Piper & Reynolds
Piper, Benjamin H.
Piper, Benjamin H., & Co.
Piper, Benjamin H., Company
Reynolds, George
Reynolds, Henry C.
Robie & Newton
Robie, William F.
Sargent, Dana
Sargent, John
Sargent, John G.
Shelters, Leonard
Small, David
Smith, Aaron W.
Star Stamp Company
Stokes, Benjamin S.
Stokes, Septimus C.
Underhill & Leighton
Underhill, Flagg Temple
Underhill, Hazen R.
Underhill, Jesse Johnson
West, Robert L.
Wilder, William
Wilson, Henry G.

Manchester-Goffe's Falls

Thayer, Elihu

Marlborough

Buss, Charles
Fuller, Levi
Thurston, Franklin R.
Wilson, Joseph

Marlow

Edward[s], Reuben J.
Goodnow, L. F.
Huntley, Oli & Eli
Rogers, F. J.
Whittemore, Winslow

Mason

Richardson, E. B.
Richardson, William, & Co.
Whitney

Meredith

American Twist Drill Company
Brown, John
Waukewan Manufacturing Company

Merrimack

Shed, Nathan

Middleton

Brown, Oscar E.

Milford

Emerson & Ware
Heald, Addison
Heald, Addison, & Son
Heald, Daniel Milton
Kimball, Caleb Jewett
Leavitt, Eben J.
Leland & Co.
O'Dell, Francis

Smith, Charles H. V.
Tarbell, Wendell Phillips

Milton
Duntley, Joseph H.
Worster, Isaac
Worster, Isaac & George

Monroe
Belknap, Amos
Blodgett, George W.

Mont Vernon
Upton, Alvan

Moultonborough
Bunker, Nathaniel

Nashua
Alcott & Co.
Alexander & Purinton
American Shearer Manufacturing Company
Atwood, Amos G.
Atwood, James
Atwood, Stephen
Baldwin, Josephus
Ball, Benjamin G.
Blanchard's, Porter, Sons Company
Boynton, L. D.
Boynton, L. D., & Co.
Brown, George
Carpenter, O. C.
Cotton, Nathaniel
Davis, George W., & Co.
Dustin, Jonathan
Eayrs & Co.
Fairbanks, Leonard O.
Fitzgerald, Rufus
Flather & Co.
Flather, Mark
Gage, John H.
Gage, Warner & Whitney
Goodwin, Joseph
Grover, John B., & Co.
Hall, James Horace
Hastings, William N., & Son
Heald, Addison, & Co.
Hinton, John
Ingalls, Eleazer F.
Kendall, P. A.
Kenny, George
Kimball, L.
Mack, Andrew
March, Isaac
McCord, Edward
Miller, Henry J., & Co.
Nashua File Company

Nashua File Works
Nashua Hand Rock Drill Company
Nashua Manufacturing Company Machine Shop
Nashua Rasp Company
Otterson, Jotham Dutton
Papps, Charles H., & Co.
Plaisted & Balser
Porter, Roger W.
Price, Edwin
Priest, Joseph K.
Ridge & Co.
Ridge & Grover
Ridge, Edwin, & Co.
Ridge, John
Rollins, George Augustine, & Co.
Sanders, F. E., Tool Company
Sargent, Dana
Sargents & Cross
Saunders, A. H.
Shattuck & Wells
Smith, Ballard
Smith, Benjamin
Sprague, M. F.
Towns, Carleton J.
Underhill Edge Tool Company
Underhill, George Washington
Underhill, George Washington, & Co.
Underhill, Rufus K.
Warner & Whitney
Warren & Heald
Warren, Cyrus
Warren, George Henry
Warren, William
Weaver, William
Weston, Charles H.
White, Edwin B., [& Co.]
Whiting & Miller
Whitney, George H.
Williams, Charles

Nelson
Atwood, O. P.
Welch & Newcomb

New Boston
Neville, George D.

New Durham
Coburn, Franklin Watson
Coburn, Franklin Watson, & Co.
Coburn, Franklin Watson, & Son
Decatur, N. J.
Fletcher, George W.
Fletcher, George W., & Co.
Fletcher, James H.
Fletcher, Tristram H.
Hayes Brothers
Mussey, Frank

Muzzey, Henry F.
Rice Manufacturing Company
Rice, Edward E.
Roberts, Thomas
Tyler, Merrill A.

New Hampton
Hannaford, Taylor P.
Magoon, Stephen S.

New Ipswich
Bellows, Charles Cotesworth
Gibson, Francis Newton
Hartwell, Ephraim
Hildreth, John Caldwell
Orsmbee & Farwell
Putnam, John
Wilder, Josiah Prescott

New London
Colby & Seaman
New London Scythe Company
Phillips, Messer & Colby
Phillips, Messer, Colby & Co.
Wheeler, Edgar L.

Newfields
Fifield, George E.
Kennard, John
Swamscot Machine Company
United States Tool Company

Newsfields-Rockingham
Joy, Adin Phillips
Joy, Samuel Sumner

Newmarket
Newmarket Machine Company

Newport
Alexander, Elkanah M.
Alexander, George E.
Alexander, Perkins & Co.
Brown, Hial
Chapin, David B.
Chapin, David B., & Co.
Church, Samuel
Dexter, David
Dexter, Stephen
Dodge, Leander F.
Dodge, Leander F., & Co.
Dunton, William
Haven, B. T.
Haven, James
Keith, Ruel
Kimball, S. S.
Larned & Sibley
Larned, Sylvanus

The Toolmakers

Long & Alexander
Long & Beck
Long, Leander
Parmelee, John
Sibley & Dunton
Sibley Scythe Company
Sibley, Ezra Taft
Stowell, Sylvester
Tompkins, G.
Union Wood Turning Company
Wilmarth, George E.
Wilmarth, Jonathan M.
Woodbury, Isaac & Jacob

Northfield
Winslow, Benjamin A.

Northumberland
Poole, Jonathan

Northwood
Brown, J. D.
Hurd, A. A.

Nottingham
Tuttle, A. D.

Orford
Weld, Elbridge G.
Weld, Francis

Ossipee
Smart, L. T.

Pelham
Fox, Josiah F.

Pembroke
Fisher, C. V.
Fisher, Hiram M.
Wilson, Joseph

Penacook
Adams & Rowell
Eaton, Ephraim
Fisher, Hiram M.
Fisher, Hiram M., & Sons
Fisherville Saw Company
Gage, Hiram
Gage, Hubbard & Co.
Gage, Porter & Co.
Leavitt & McDaniel
Locke & Marden
Porter & Rolfe

Peterborough
Childs, Amzi

Day, Robert
Wheeler, C. A.
White, Samuel G.
Wilder, Charles

Piermont
Cleveland Stone Company
Dodge, Charles
Dodge, Corydon
Dodge, Corydon, & Son
Dodge, George
Evans & Emerson
Evans & Libby
Evans & Risley
Gannett, William H.
Palmer, Lorenzo D.
Risley, Lewis E.

Pittsfield
George, William F.
Joy, James

Plainfield
Hildreth, Solomon, & Son
Read, Silas
Spaulding, E. R.
Spaulding, I. W.
Spaulding, Sam

Plainfield-Meriden
Cole & Trench
French, Frank L.
Stearns, Leonard

Plaistow
Frost, H. N.

Plymouth
Forbes, Nathan
Merrill, Jacob
Sargent, L. B.
Tomkinson, J. & R.

Portsmouth
Bartlett & Young
Bazin, Richard C.
Beck, Samuel
Bowles, Thomas Salter
Briard, Elisha
Briard, Samuel
Cotter, Richard
Critchley & Whalley
Critchley, John
Fernald, William [D.]
Foss, Thomas
Green, John
Ham, Ephraim
Hart, William

Hill, John
Hill, John (II)
Hopkins, William
Jackson, Daniel
Jackson, Elisha
Johnson, Thomas B.
Leighton, George H.
Leighton, John
Leighton, Littleton M.
Leighton, Luke M.
Leighton, Mark
Leighton, Paul
Leighton, Samuel
Leighton, Samuel, & Son
Leighton, William, Jr.
Leighton, William F.
Leighton, William M.
Marshall & Trickey
Marshall, Nathaniel
Marshall, Obediah
Martin & Fernald
Martin, B. Franklin
Martin, William
Martin, William M.
Martin, William R.
Melcher, Daniel
Noble, Moses
Odiorne, Thomas
Odiorne, Thomas Henry
Pitman, Nathaniel
Portsmouth Machine Company
Raitt, James W.
Riggs, A. L.
Shackford, John
Shackford, John (II)
Shackford, Samuel
Shillaber, Joseph
Trafton Brothers
Trafton, Alfred S., & Son
Trafton, George A.
Trafton, W. P.
Trundy, John
Walker, Richard
Walker, Stephen H.
Weeks, Benjamin
Whidden, Michael
Williams, William
Wilson, Andrew, & Co.
Woods, Dodge & Co.
Yeaton, Benjamin
Yeaton, William

Raymond
Gannon, George

Richmond
Aldrich, Nathan
Bourn, Reuben
Buffum, James

Garnsey, Cyrus
Garnsey, William
Harris, Luke
Hewes
Holbrook, Enos
Swan, Robert
Thayer, Nelson

Rindge

Allen, Colburn & Co.
Allen, Oratio P., & Son
Russell, Levi
Sawtell, Aaron Servetus
Whiting, Seth

Rochester

Duntley, Joseph H.
Fessenden, James M.
Pearl, Ellsworth
Smith, Elias F.
Wadleigh & Smith
Wadleigh, Warren

Roxbury

Newcomb, Gideon
Newcomb, John

Rumney

Emerton, Frank W. [& Co.]
Emerton, Joseph
Hardy Brothers
Hardy, Baxter P.
Loveland, Lewis [H.]
Nutting, Harris O.
Nutting, T. P.
Nutting, T. P. & H. O.

Salisbury

Couch, John
Couch, Samuel
Dunlap, Samuel
Prince, George Stanley
Webster, Stephen C.

Sanbornton

Calley, Thomas
Smith, Barnard H.
Wadleigh, Warren

Sandown

George, Currier
Hoit, Josiah

Sandwich

Dearborn & Skinner
Dearborn, Warren
Page & Carville

Page, Joel [R.]
Wilmarth, George

Seabrook

Perkins, Joseph

Shelburne

Hall, J. H.

Somersworth

Brooks, Lebbeus
Eureka Wrench Company
Great Falls Saw Set Company
Kinsman, Prescott B.
Lougee, John
Merrill, Josiah
Rust, William Orne
Tebbets & Co.

South Hampton

Eaton, Albert

Stoddard

Beckwith, Alfred
Davis, Fred A.
Robb, Samuel

Strafford

Pease, Daniel
Pease, Daniel, & Son

Stratford

Byron, George W.

Stratham

Merrill, Phinehas

Sugar Hill

Blodgett, Taylor & Wells

Sullivan

Hemenway, Luther
Osgood, H. Melville

Sunapee

Alexander & Perkins
Cummings & Young
Dodge, Simeon S.
Long & Alexander
Long & Sleeper
Savory, A. G., & Co.
Sleeper, Benjamin R.
Sleeper, Benjamin R., & Co.
Smith, John B.

Sutton

Gee, Asa
Jackson, Aura
Parker, George A.
Sargent, Jacob T.

Swanzey

Rand, John A.
Richardson, Wyman
Whitcomb & Cross
Wilson, Stillman

Swanzey-Westport

Bartlett, Sylvanus

Temple

Kimball, Isaac

Thornton

Constantine, S. W.
Moss, F.
Robie, Hiram

Tilton

Tilton & Smith
Wadleigh, Warren

Troy

Aldrich, Moses
Barnard, William
Jackson, Daniel
Sibley, Amos

Tuftonboro

Canney, Wesley J.

Wakefield

Reynolds, J.

Walpole

Ball, Thomas C.
Bond, W. A. & C. B.
Brandell, John
Cobb, Isaac
Huntington, Gurdon
White, George

Warner

Akin, Samuel
Barnett, Ezra

Washington

Ball, W. H.
Butterfield, John L.
Greenleaf, William P.
Laws, Ebenezer
Manley, Josiah

The Toolmakers

Weare

Chase & Drew
Chase, Amos
Chase, Charles F.
Chase, David G.
Chase, E.
Chase, John Winslow
Currier & Chase
Currier, Moses F.
Currier, Moses F. & Daniel G.
Flanders Hardware Company
Flanders, William Wallace
Fox, John M.
Hanson, Daniel
Hanson, James
Perkins, Wheeler, & Brother
Smith & Chase
Thurston, Peleg B.

Webster

Adams, Ezekiel
Harrison, John
Trussell, Moses

Wentworth

Davis, Eben
Fellows, Samuel
Flemaux, Joseph

Westmoreland

Farr & Bryant
Farr, E. A., & Co.

Whitefield

Dexter, L. R.

Wilmot

New London Scythe Company

Wilton

Holt, Henry A.

Winchester

Adamascobite Company
Estes, E. B., & Son
Holmes, William

Wolfeboro

Berry, Oliver P., Company
Coleman, Eben
Doe, Charles O.
Gerry, Eben G.
Piper, A. M.

Woodstock

Chase, Aaron

List of Toolmakers by Product

Augers and bits, braces and stocks

Atherton & Goodrich
Chase, John Winslow
Currier & Chase
Currier Brothers
Currier, Moses F.
Currier, Moses F. & Daniel G.
Fitzgerald, Rufus
Gerrish, Stephen
Goodrich, George
Graves, Caleb S.
Holmes, William
Hopkins & Pierce
Hopkins, Richard Henry
Jennings & Griffin Manufacturing Company
Kilburn, Edward
New England Novelty Works
New Hampshire Iron Factory Company
Newcomb & Wilder
Newcomb, Everett
Newcomb, Gideon
Newcomb, John
Page, George
Pierce, Benjamin
Pierce, Cross & Farr
Pierce, Frederick Benjamin
Richardson & Huggins
Smith, Aaron W.
Smith, Julius
Smith, Perley
Wilder, Azel
Wilder, Azel, & Co.
Wilson, Joseph
Woodward, Frank Ross

Awls

Aiken Brad Awl and Saw Set Manufacturing Company
Aiken, Francis Herrick
Aiken, Harriet A. Colby
Aiken, Herrick
Hemenway, Luther
Lincoln, Josiah S.
Sanders, F. E., Tool Company

Blacksmith's tools

Eaton, Ephraim
Jones, Nathan
Nutting & Hayden
Tyler, Benjamin and John
Wilder, William

Blocks

Bazin, Richard C.
Beck, Samuel
Briard, Elisha
Briard, Samuel
Fernald, William [D.]
Green, John
Ham, Ephraim
Hill, John
Hopkins, William
Jackson, Daniel
Jackson, Elisha
Leighton, George H.
Leighton, John
Leighton, Littleton M.
Leighton, Luke M.
Leighton, Mark
Leighton, Paul
Leighton, Samuel
Leighton, Samuel, & Son
Leighton, William, Jr.
Leighton, William F.
Leighton, William M.
Marshall, Nathaniel
Marshall, Obediah
Martin & Fernald
Martin, B. Franklin
Martin, William
Martin, William M.
Martin, William R.
Melcher, Daniel
Noble, Moses
Odiorne, Thomas
Odiorne, Thomas Henry
Pitman, Nathaniel
Shackford, John
Shackford, John (II)
Shackford, Samuel
Walker, Stephen H.
Weeks, Benjamin
Williams, William
Yeaton, Benjamin
Yeaton, William

Brushes

Abbott, John R.
Carpenter & Co.
Carpenter, O. C.
Dickerman
Felton, S. A., & Co.
Felton, S. A., & Son
Felton, S. A., & Son Company
Goodwin, Joseph
Haley Manufacturing Company

Howard Brush Company
Hurd, William
Josselyn & Marston
Josselyn, Lewis H., & Co.
Laskey, L. B., & Co.
Martin, C. H., & Co.
Miller, Henry J., & Co.
Newton, Henry E.
Newton, Henry E., & Co.
Phelps, Peter
Rice Manufacturing Company
Rice, Edward E.
Robie & Newton
Robie, William F.
Vogler, J. S., & Co.
West, Robert L.
Whiting & Miller
Whiting, Seth
Wilson, Henry G.

Carpenter's and woodworker's tools—general

Boynton, L. D.
Boynton, L. D., & Co.
Jennings & Griffin Manufacturing Company
Lebanon Machine Works
Morse, Joshua
Owen, David A.
Pierce, Levi
Towns, Carleton J.

Carriagemaker's tools

Houston, Harry
Sargent, Philip

Clamps

Fonda, Isaac
Tarbell, Wendell Phillips

Clippers

American Shearer Manufacturing Company
Priest, Joseph K.

Cooper's tools

Farley, Benjamin
Hardy, Ephraim L.
Heald, Addison, & Son
Heald, Daniel Milton
Manning, George W.
Morse, Joshua

Pierce, Levi
Simonds, C.
Underhill Edge Tool Company
Whitney

Crowbars

Alexander, Wesley
New Hampshire Iron Factory Company

Drafting tools

Sprague, M. F.

Drills, reamers, and drill chucks

Aiken, Francis Herrick
American Twist Drill Company
New Hampshire Iron Factory Company
Page, George
White, Edwin B., [& Co.]

Edge tools—general

Adams, Harvey
Amoskeag Ax Company
Bailey, William
Baldwin, Samuel
Baldwin, Samuel, & Co.
Bartlett & Young
Blaisdell, John
Blodgett Edge Tool Manufacturing Company
Blodgett, Edwin
Blodgett, George W.
Blodgett, Taylor & Wells
Brooks, George A.
Brooks, Henry O.
Brooks, William H.
Brown, J. D.
Brown, John
Brown, John Sleeper
Brown, Nathaniel
Brown, Oscar E.
Byron, George W.
Canney, Wesley J.
Chapin, David B.
Chapin, David B., & Co.
Chase & Drew
Chase, Aaron
Cheever, William
Clifford, Marshall
Coburn, Franklin Watson
Coburn, Stillman
Cole, I. H.
Coleman, Eben

Cotter, Richard
Couch, John
Couch, Samuel
Currier, Moses F.
Davis, Aaron
Dimond, Ephraim
Dimond, Israel
Drake, J. L.
Duntley, Joseph H.
Eaton, Albert
Eaton, E. & E.
Eaton, Edward
Emerson Edge Tool Company
Emerson, A. V.
Emerson, A. V. & M. W.
Emerson, E. V.
Emerson, Timothy
Emerton, Frank W. [& Co.]
Flanders Hardware Company
Fletcher, James H.
Foss, Ivory
Fowler, Cyrus
Fox, Josiah F.
Gee, Asa
George, Currier
George, William F.
Gerry, Eben G.
Gilmore, Hiram
Gilmore, Leonard
Hall, J. H.
Hall, James H.
Hardy, David P.
Hardy, Ephraim L.
Heald, Paul
Hillard, George W.
Hobart, George W. L.
Hoit, Josiah
Hurd, A. A.
Ingalls, Eleazer F.
Jones, J.
Kidder, Daniel
Kimball, Caleb Jewett
Kimball, Caleb Jewett, & Son
Kimball, Isaac
Leighton & Lufkin
Leighton, Charles O.
Leighton, William W.
Leighton, William W., & Co.
Lovejoy & Webster
Lovejoy, Abbott
Mack, Andrew
Marshall & Trickey
Merrill & Wilder
Merrill, Lewis Lovejoy
Merrill, Pliny
Milliken, Adams
Morgan & Marston
Moss, F.
Muzzey, Henry F.
Neville, George D.

The Toolmakers

New Hampshire Iron Factory Company
Newell, Ezra
Pease, Daniel
Pease, Daniel, & Son
Pierce, Frederick Benjamin
Pike, Benjamin
Pillsbury, John D.
Poole, Jonathan
Porter, J. H.
Pratt, Captain (Solomon?)
Proctor, James
Raitt, James W.
Reynolds, J.
Rice, Hamlet L.
Richards, Romance
Riggs, A. L.
Roberts, Thomas
Robie, Hiram
Robinson, Daniel B.
Sanborn, David Page
Shillaber, Joseph
Slayton, Stephen D.
Smith
Smith & Chase
Smith, Ballard
Smith, Benjamin
Stowell, Sylvester
Thayer, Elihu
Thayer, Nelson
Thompson, H.
Thompson, William D.
Thurston, Franklin R.
Trafton Brothers
Trafton, Alfred S., & Son
Trafton, George A.
Tucker, Daniel
Underhill & Brown
Underhill & Leighton
Underhill Edge Tool Company
Underhill, Brown & Leighton
Underhill, Flagg Temple
Underhill, George Washington
Underhill, George Washington, & Co.
Underhill, Hazen R.
Underhill, Jay Temple
Underhill, Jesse Johnson
Underhill, Josiah
Underhill, Rufus K.
Underhill, Samuel Graham
United States Tool Company
Upton, Alvan
Weare, Jonathan
Whitaker, Luther
Wilson, Stillman
Woodbury, Isaac & Jacob
Wright, William
York, V. P.
Young, Acanthus
Young, E. P.

Edge tools—agricultural

Aldrich, Moses
Alexander, Wesley
Antrim Shovel Company
Baldwin & White
Ball, Thomas C.
Barnard, William
Barnett, Ezra
Brown & Russell
Calley, Thomas
Church, Samuel
Colby & Seaman
Dexter, David
Dexter, Stephen
Dunton, William
Ely, Farr & Co.
Emerson & Cummings
Emerson & Kimball
Emerton, Joseph
Farr, Ora
French, P.
Garland, J. H.
Graham & Gilkey
Greenleaf, William P.
Hartshorn & Co.
Hartwell, Ephraim
Hewes
Holbrook, Enos
Jackson, Aura
Joy, James
Keith, Ruel
Larned & Sibley
Larned, Sylvanus
Mann, Thomas W.
March, Isaac
Marston Patent Scythe Company
Marston, David W.
Mascoma Edge Tool Company
Merrill, John B.
Merrill, Pardon-Haynes
Messer, William H.
New Hampshire Scythe Company
New London Scythe Company
Noyes, W. O.
Ormsbee & Farwell
Parmelee, John
Perkins, Messer, Colby & Co.
Phillips, Messer & Colby
Phillips, Messer, Colby & Co.
Purmort, Martin V. [B.]
Putnam, John
Redington, Henry Cornelius, & Co.
Richardson, Wyman
Robbins & Flint
Robinson, Thomas Stewart
Robinson, Thomas Stewart, & Co.
Sargent, Jacob T.
Sibley & Dunton
Sibley Scythe Company
Sibley, Amos
Sibley, Ezra Taft
Snow, John
Swan, Benjamin
Tilton & Smith
Treadwell & Co.
Tyler, Benjamin and John
Weld, Elbridge G.
Weld, Francis
Wheeler, Edgar L.
White & Eaton
White, Jonathan
Wilson, Joseph
Witherell, James H., & Co.
Worster, Isaac
Worster, Isaac & George

Edge tools—axes, adzes, etc.

Adams & Rowell
Adams, Ezekiel
Ball, W. H.
Burpee, Hamilton & Co.
Chandler, William
Clifford, George H.
Constantine, S. W.
Danforth, Jacob
Dimick, Daniel B.
Evans, William B.
Fellows, Jonathan
Frost, H. N.
Harrison, John
Jackson, Daniel
Jameson, John
Lang & Hoyt
Lang, Gilman L.
Lawrence, Artemas
Leighton & Son
Manchester Axe Company
New Hampshire Scythe Company
New London Scythe Company
Proctor, Amos
Reynolds, George
Reynolds, Henry C.
Saunders, John
Smalley, J. F.
Smith, Barnard H.
Starrett, Charles Hammond
Stone, John
Thompson, Levi
Trussell, Moses
Underhill, Hazen R., & Co.
Weeks, George
Wilson, Leonard
Witherell, James H., & Co.

Instruments of Change

Edge tools—chisels

Jennings & Griffin Manufacturing Company
Merrill, P., & Co.
Page, George
Wilder & Hopkins
Wilder & Thompson
Wilder, George Sheldon

Edge tools—knives, shaves, etc.

Baldwin & Whittemore
Belknap, Amos
Brown & Stokes
Claflin, John
Claremont Cutlery Company
Coburn, Franklin Watson, & Co.
Coburn, Franklin Watson, & Son
Coffin, John T.
Coffin, John T., & Son
Coffren, John
Cole, A. J.
Doe, Charles O.
Ferry, Joel
Flagg, Joshua Getchell
Flagg, Joshua Getchell, & Son
Fletcher, George W.
Goodell Company
Hardy, E. D.
Hayes Brothers
Hobbs, George W.
Hobbs, George W., & Co.
House, Charles D.
Jennings & Griffin Manufacturing Company
Johnson, Thomas B.
Kimball, Caleb Jewett, Company
Luther, Jabez
Morrill & Wilson
Morrill, O. F.
Otterson, Jotham Dutton
Smith, Collins & Co.
Smith, Collins & Kempton
Smith, John
Spaulding, I. W.
Walker, Saladin A.
Weston, Charles H.
Whittemore, Amos & George Alfred
Wilder & Hopkins
Wilder & Thompson
Wilder, George Sheldon
Wilson, Joseph
Woodbury, Levi
Woods Cutlery Company
Woods, Dodge & Co.
Woods, Walter D.
Woods, Walter D. & Eben F.

Files and rasps

Alcott & Co.
Claremont File Works
Concord File Works
Decatur, N. J.
Dudley, Thomas D., & Co.
Ellis & Olcott
Ellis Brothers
Fantom, George
Fantom, George, & Co.
Farnham, J. H.
Farnham, J. H. & W. J.
Fessenden, James M.
Granite File Works
Grover, John B., & Co.
Harrison, Henry G.
Lancaster File Works
Lawson, John H.
Manchester File Works
McCord, Edward
Moody & Cave
Moody & Co.
Moody & Ellis
Moody, Carr (Cave?) & Ellis
Moore & Co.
Moore, John W.
Nashua File Company
Nashua File Works
Nashua Rasp Company
Nutt, Henry
Nutt, Henry, & Co.
Papps, Charles H.
Papps, Charles H., & Co.
Price, Edwin
Richardson, Samuel
Ridge & Co.
Ridge & Grover
Ridge, Edwin, & Co.
Ridge, John
Stokes, Benjamin S.
Tomkinson, J. & R.
Turner, John
Walker, Richard
Walton, Samuel, [& Son]
Willoughby, Edwin

Fishing tools

Bell, Joseph
Fitzgerald, Rufus
Houston, James
Prescott Company
Prescott, Charles B.
Sargent, L. N.
Trumbull, Walter S.
Way, Charles A.

Glazier's tools

Haselton, Hermon R.
Haselton, Rufus B., & Son
Lougee, John
New England Novelty Works
Stokes, Septimus C.
Woodward, Frank Ross

Gunsmith's tools

Forbes, Nathan
Holmes, William
Kennedy, James

Hackles

Howe & Hopkins
Wilson, Andrew, & Co.

Hammers

Balch, Dan Shaw
Butterfield, William
Coburn, Franklin Watson
Colby, John V.
Eastman, George S.
Eastman, Phineas
Eaton, Edward, Jr.
Ingalls, Eleazer F.
Jones, Nathan
Kittredge, Jonathan
Merrill, Lewis Lovejoy
Underhill Edge Tool Company
Welch, Daniel
Wilson, Joseph

Handles—general

Atwood, O. P.
Baldwin, James, & Co.
Benton, W. W., & Co.
Berry, Oliver P.
Berry, Oliver P., Company
Brown, Calvin M.
Brown, George
Chase, David G.
Chase, James
Dearborn, Warren
Dunlap, John
Durant, L. A., & Co.
Estes, E. B., & Son
Fisher, C. V.
Fisher, Hiram M.
Fisher, Hiram M., & Sons
Flanders, William Wallace
Fuller, Levi
Hardy Brothers

Hardy, Baxter P.
Hawkins, Floyd F.
Holt Brothers
Holt, C. F.
Howard, J. B.
Hutchinson Brothers
Hutchinson, Arthur
Kemp & Call
Kemp Brothers
Kimball, John
Manley, Josiah
Merrill & Dowse
Merrill, Jacob
Merrill, James O.
Messer Brothers
Messer, Frank D.
Morrill, George Peverly
O'Dell, Francis
Page & Carville
Page, Joel [R.]
Patten, Matthew
Piper & Reynolds
Piper, Benjamin H.
Piper, Benjamin H., & Co.
Piper, Benjamin H., Company
Porter, Roger W.
Priest & Wellington
Quint, George
Randall, Lewis W.
Reed, James M.
Richardson, E. B.
Sanborn, Francis Davidson
Smith, Elias F.
Thurston, Peleg B.
Union Toy Turning Works
Union Wood Turning Company
Virgin, Simeon
Wadleigh & Smith
Whittemore, Winslow
Wilder, Josiah Prescott
Wilmarth, George
Woods, Charles

Handles — agricultural tool

Akin, Samuel
Aldrich, Nathan
Alexander & Perkins
Alexander, Elkanah M.
Alexander, George E.
Alexander, Perkins & Co.
Atwood, D. G.
Barrett, Edward H.
Bemis & Symonds
Bond, W. A. & C. B.
Bourn, Reuben
Brown, Hial
Buffum, James
Burtis, R.

Butterfield, John L.
Childs, Amzi
Crandall, C. H.
Cummings & Young
Currier, H. G.
Davis, Fred A.
Day, Robert
Demerse, Lewis
Dodge, Leander F.
Dodge, Leander F., & Co.
Edward[s], Reuben J.
Foss, Obed
Foss, William G.
Garnsey, Cyrus
Garnsey, William
Goodnow, L. F.
Graves & Eaton
Graves, Bela
Harris, Luke
Haven, B. T.
Haven, James
Heywood, Simeon
Howard, Joseph B.
Howard, W. B.
Johnson & Smith
Kemp, O. R.
Kidder, E. P.
King, Henry
Laws, Ebenezer
Long & Alexander
Long & Beck
Long & Sleeper
Long, Leander
Loveland, Lewis [H.]
Marston & Stearns
Messer, William H.
Nutting, Harris O.
Nutting, T. P.
Nutting, T. P. & H. O.
Osgood, H. Melville
Palmer, G.
Parmelee, Henry
Philbrook, Alfred S.
Robb, Samuel
Royal, H. E.
Savory, A. G., & Co.
Sawyer, David
Sleeper, Benjamin R.
Sleeper, Benjamin R., & Co.
Smith, Charles B.
Stacy, Byron
Stearns & Emerson
Stearns & Sons
Stearns Manufacturing Company
Stearns, George W. & Milo Leonard
Stearns, Leonard
Stockwell Brothers
Swan, Robert
Tompkins, G.
Welch & Newcomb
Wheeler, Robert H.

Wilder, Peter
Wilmarth, George E.
Wilmarth, Jonathan M.
Wilson, Thomas

Handles — awl

Campbell, William
Hemenway, Luther
Smith, David M.

Handles — axe

Atwood, James
Baldwin, Josephus
Bingham, Charles W.
Brown, Peter S.
Bunker, Nathaniel
Clough, C. H.
Damon, S. C.
Eggleston, William
Farr & Bryant
Farr, E. A., & Co.
French, Nathaniel
Hall, Elma E.
Hildreth, Solomon, & Son
Humphrey Machine Company
Kelly, E. L.
Leland & Co.
Loveland, Isaac
Marshall, Ansel
McDaniel, T. D.
Parker, C. S.
Parker, George A.
Perkins, Wheeler, & Brother
Rand, John A.
Spaulding, E. R.
Stowell, G. H.
Wadleigh, Warren
Winslow, Benjamin A.
Wyman & Winslow

Handles — brush

Abbott, J. R., & Co.
Ellis, Austin A.
Farr, Olin Ransom
Farwell, C. & H.
Pierce, Frederick Benjamin
Pierce, Frederick Benjamin, & Co.
Richardson, William, & Co.
Smith, Charles H. V.
Taft, Herbert O.
Whitcomb & Cross
Whitcomb, Alanson S.

Handles — chisel

Leavitt, Eben J.

Handles—knife

Bixby, Daniel
Flanders Hardware Company
Huntley, Oli & Eli
Lakin, Taylor D.
Rogers, F. J.
Thompson, E. G.
Thompson, Luke

Handspikes

Atwood, Stephen
Cotton, Nathaniel
Sargents & Cross
Shattuck & Wells

Ice tools

Fisherville Saw Company
Hardy, Baxter P.
New England Novelty Works
Woodward, Frank Ross

Jacks—lever

Durant, Edward J.
Hutchinson Brothers
Hutchinson, Arthur
Joy, Samuel Sumner
Sullivan Machine Company

Jacks—screw

Gage, Hiram
Holman & Merriman
Holmes, Charles W.
Hutchinson, Charles H.
Lowell, A. H.
Reed, Joseph Mason
Sanborn, Francis Davidson
Sullivan Machine Company
Tolman, Cyrus S.
Tolman, J. C.
Woodman Brothers

Jeweller's tools

Allen, Francis E.
Dustin, Jonathan
Exeter Machine Works
Griffin, George Washington, & Co.
Griffin, George Washington, Company

Leather and shoe tools

Aiken, Herrick
Bachelder, James

Bachelder, Otis Freeman
Bellows, Charles Cotesworth
Brown, Oscar E.
Buxton, F.
Chase, Amos
Chase, Charles F.
Chase, David G.
Chase, E.
Chase, John Winslow
Cobb, Isaac
Coburn, Franklin Watson
Coburn, Franklin Watson, & Co.
Coburn, Franklin Watson, & Son
Crosby, George
Duntley, Joseph H.
Flagg, Joshua Getchell
Flagg, Joshua Getchell, & Son
Fletcher, George W.
Fletcher, George W., & Co.
Fletcher, Tristram H.
Gibson, Francis Newton
Globe Tool Works
Goodell Company
Hall, Andrew J.
Hanson, Daniel
Hanson, James
Hayes Brothers
Hayes, Israel
Hobbs, George W.
Hobbs, George W., & Co.
Houston, John P.
Hoyt, Thomas Rowell
Johnson, William
Kimball, Caleb Jewett, & Son
Ladd, Jeremiah
Lincoln, Josiah S.
Moses, William P.
Nichols, Daniel
Nichols, Hiram
Palmer, Freeman
Pendergast, Isaac S.
Perkins, Joseph
Richardson, Alpha
Tash, Edwin S., & Co.
Tuttle, A. D.
Tyler, Merrill A.
Warner, Jethro W.
Webster, Wilbur
Worster, George

Levels

Atwood, Amos G.
Brooks, Lebbeus
Wilson, George W.

Machinist's tools

American Twist Drill Company
Baldwin, Nathan H.

Burlingame, William
Critchley & Whalley
Critchley, John
Davis, George W., & Co.
Exeter Machine Works
Fifield, George E.
Flather & Co.
Flather, Mark
Forsaith, Hiram
Forsaith, Samuel Caldwell, & Co.
Forsaith, Samuel Caldwell, Machine Company
Gage, John H.
Gage, Warner & Whitney
Haines & Wallace
Hobbs, Gordon & Co.
Humphrey Machine Company
Humphrey, John, & Co.
Kimball, S. S.
Merrill, Benjamin F.
Portsmouth Machine Company
Rollins, George Augustine, & Co.
Sanders, F. E., Tool Company
Saunders, A. H.
Swamscot Machine Company
Thomas, W. S.
Towns, Carleton J.
Warner & Whitney
White, Samuel G.
Whitney, George H.
Wight, George H.
Woodman & Weare
Woodman Brothers

Mallets

Sanborn, Francis Davidson
Sargents & Cross

Mathematical instruments

Abbott, William
Baldwin, Jedediah
Blanchard's, Porter, Sons Company
Bowles, Thomas Salter
Champlin, John R.
Chandler, Abiel
Chandler, Timothy
Gilman, Benjamin Clark
Hart, William
Hasham, Stephen
Hastings, William N., & Son
Huntington, Gurdon
Hutchins, Levi
Kennard, John
Merrill, Phinehas
Radford, Cass M.
Robinson, William K.
Smith, John B.

The Toolmakers

Trundy, John
Wheeler, C. A.
Whidden, Michael
White, George
Whitehouse, George Leighton
Wilder, Charles
Wilson, George W.

Measuring tools

Bowles, Thomas Salter
Chandler, Mary Burgin
Dame, Richard
Dearborn, Warren
Greenleaf, Florence M.
Greenleaf, William Gardner
Hale, Franklin W.
Hart, William
Haselton, Hermon R.
Haselton, Rufus B.
Haselton, Rufus B., & Son
Hoyt, Thomas Rowell, Jr.
Humphrey Machine Company
Humphrey, John, & Co.
Kenny, George
Noyes, Simon C.
Sanborn & Weeks
Sanborn, Francis Davidson
Sanborn, Gustavus B.
Sanborn, Israel
Sargent, L. B.
Shelters, Leonard
Wheeler, W. A.

Medical and dental tools

Dustin, Jonathan

Picks

Alden & Kellog
Amoskeag Ax Company
Brooks, William H.
New England Novelty Works
Underhill Edge Tool Company
Woodward, Frank Ross

Plane irons or plow plates

Bartlett & Young
Fellows, Jeremiah
Jones, Daniel
Kennedy, James
Marsh, Gilman
Moore, Daniel
Underhill, Hazen R.

Planes and moulding tools

Amsden, Downing
Brandell, John
Briggs, E.
Briggs, Nathaniel
Burley, Thomas
Chase, James
Clifford, Ebenezer
Dearborn & Skinner
Dearborn, Warren
Dearth, Lester A.
Dodge, Simeon S.
Dow, James
Dunlap, John
Dunlap, Samuel
Durgin, Daniel
Eayrs & Co.
Fairbanks, Leonard O.
Foss, Thomas
Gage, Warner & Whitney
Hall, James Horace
Heald, Addison
Heald, Addison, & Co.
Heald, Addison, & Son
Heald, Daniel Milton
Hill, John
Holt, Henry A.
Long, Isaac
Magoon, Stephen S.
McCulloch, Eppie J.
Merrill, Jacob
Milton, Joseph
Milton, Matthew Harvey
Morse, Joshua
Patten, Matthew
Piper, A. M.
Piper, Rufus
Rhoades, C. W.
Rugg, Elias
Sanborn & Weeks
Sanborn, David Page
Sanborn, David Page & Francis Davidson
Sargent, Dana
Sargent, Philip
Simons, Arad
Sleeper, John
Tyler, P.
Virgin, Simeon
Warren & Heald
Warren, Cyrus
Warren, George Henry
Warren, George Henry & William
Warren, William
Webster, Stephen C.
Wilder, George Sheldon
Woodman, B. F.

Pruning tools

Cole & Trench
Fox, Josiah F.
Gage, Hubbard & Co.
Goodall, Frank P.
Goodell Company
Mussey, Frank
Porter, Roger W.

Punches

Aiken, Jonas Bradley
Chase, John Winslow
Pearl, Ellsworth
Sanders, F. E., Tool Company

Sandpaper

Wiggin & Stevens
Woods, Walter D.

Saw frames

Batchelder, Thomas
Beckwith, Alfred
Davis, Eben
Fellows, Samuel
Fitts, J. E.
Flemaux, Joseph
Hannaford, Taylor P.
Keene Manufacturing Company
Wheeler, John F.

Saw jointers

Noyes, Walter B.
Prince, George Stanley

Saw sets

Aiken Brad Awl and Saw Set Manufacturing Company
Aiken, Francis Herrick
Aiken, Harriet A. Colby
Aiken, Herrick
Aiken, Walter Scott
Baker, C. S.
Bartlett, Sylvanus
Brooks, Lebbeus
Forsaith, Samuel Caldwell
Forsaith, Samuel Caldwell, & Co.
Forsaith, Samuel Caldwell, Machine Company
Great Falls Saw Set Company
Noyes, W. B.
Robinson, Samuel R.
Rust, William Orne
Smart, L. T.
Spiller, Joseph D.
Tebbets & Co.

Sawhorses

Allen, Colburn & Co.
Allen, Oratio P., & Son
Hutchinson Brothers
Hutchinson, Arthur
Russell, Levi
Sanborn, Francis Davidson
Sawtell, Aaron Servetus
Tripp, William

Saws

Adams, Charles A.
Boynton, L. D.
Boynton, L. D., & Co.
Crosby, Milo H.
Fisherville Saw Company
Gage, Hubbard & Co.
Gage, Porter & Co.
Griffin, George Washington, & Co.
Griffin, George Washington, Company
Hinton, John
Kendall, P. A.
Leavitt & McDaniel
Locke & Marden
Noyes, W. B.
Porter & Rolfe
South Lancaster Lumber Company
Waukewan Manufacturing Company

Scrapers

Leavitt & McDaniel
Robinson, Thomas Stewart
Underhill Edge Tool Company

Screwdrivers

Baldwin, Samuel
Robinson, Thomas Stewart
Sanders, F. E., Tool Company

Sharpening stones

Adamascobite Company
Chamberlain, I. A.
Cleveland Stone Company
Dodge, Charles
Dodge, Corydon
Dodge, Corydon, & Son
Dodge, George
Evans & Emerson
Evans & Libby
Evans & Risley
French, G. B.
Gannett, William H.
Hammond, John McCurdy
Littleton Hone Stone Company
Littleton Scythe Stone Company
Moore, Orrin
Moore, Orrin, & Sons
Noyes, Person
Noyes, Timothy
Palmer, Lorenzo D.
Pierce Brothers
Pierce, R.
Pierce, R. & C. G.
Pike & Pike
Pike Manufacturing Company
Pike, Alonzo Franklin
Pike, Alonzo Franklin, Manufacturing Company
Pike, Isaac
Risley, Lewis E.
Whiting, Stephen, & Co.

Shears, etc.

Daniels, Albert H.
Healey, W. W.

Squares

Bickford, Solomon E.
Burgum, John
Flanders, Frederick
Leavitt & McDaniel
Wiswell, Andrew

Steelyards

Dean, Hiram
Hathorn, Ebenezer

Stencils, stamps, etc.

Barker, Andrew H.
Gannon, George
Gerould, Richardson & Skinner
Hall, Frank P.
Kimball, L.
Merrill, George H.
Paige, A. H.
Pillsbury, Oliver M.
Small, David
Star Stamp Company
Trafton, W. P.

Stone tools

Applebee, Charles Henry
Bartlett & Young
Brooks, William H.
Nashua Hand Rock Drill Company
Nutting & Hayden
Nutting, Luther M.
Nutting, Luther M., & Co.
Plaisted & Balser
Underhill Edge Tool Company
Weaver, William
Woodman Brothers

Tailor's or dressmaker's tools

Chandler, Mary Burgin
Dame, Richard
Wiswell, Andrew

Tool containers

Aiken, Herrick
Emerson & Ware
Reed, Joseph Mason

Trowels

Gage, Hubbard & Co.
Leavitt & McDaniel

Vises

Baldwin, Nathan H.
Ball, Benjamin G.
Buss, Charles
Exeter Machine Works
Holmes, Charles W.
Owen & Amidon
Owen, David A.
Union Wood Turning Company

Watch tools

Allen, Francis E.
Granite File Works
Houghton, Joseph
Kendrick & Davis
Kendrick & Davis Company
Smith, S. C.

Wrenches

Aiken, Francis Herrick
Aiken, Harriet A. Colby
Alexander & Purinton
Burleigh, Harry Walter
Dexter, L. R.
Eureka Wrench Company
French, Frank L.
Goodell Company
Joy, Adin Phillips
Kinsman, Prescott B.
Merrill, Josiah
Sanborn, Gustavus B.
Thompson, A. S.

The Toolmakers

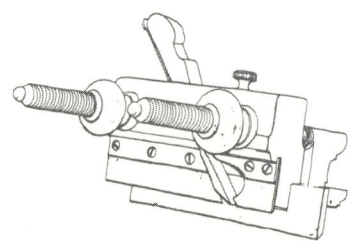

Plates and Illustrations

All illustration is arranged sequentially under the separate headings of Plates, which includes the 91 tools listed in the second section of this volume; Marks, which includes the 58 toolmakers' marks shown in the third section; and Illustration, which includes all general illustration, captioned and uncaptioned, used throughout the catalogue.

Plates

1. Halving Plane by E. Briggs	23
2. Moulding Tool by John Hill	23
3. Sash Plane by Ebenezer Clifford	24
4. Moulding Tool by John Sleeper	24
5. Panel Raising Plane by John Sleeper	24
6. Moulding Tool by Arad Simons	25
7. Panel Raising Plane by Downing Amsden	25
8. Moulding Tool by Joshua Morse, Jr.	25
9.-12. Four Plows by Cyrus Warren	26-28
13. Moulding Tool by Cyrus Warren	29
14. Moulding Tool by Cyrus Warren	29
15. Moving Filletster by Cyrus Warren	30
16. Smoothing Plane by William Warren	30
17. Smoothing Plane by William Warren	31
18. Jointer by George Henry Warren	31
19. Moulding Tool by Addison Heald & Son	32
20. Razee Smoothing Plane by Addison Heald	33
21. Miter Plane by Addison Heald & Son	33
22. Smoothing Plane by Addison Heald	33
23. Moulding Tool by David Page Sanborn	34
24. Moulding Tool by David Page Sanborn	34
25. Plow by David Page Sanborn	35
26. Moulding Tool by David Page Sanborn	35
27. Jointer by Joseph Milton and Matthew Harvey Milton	36
28. Plow by Joseph Milton	36
29. Fixed Plow by Philip Sargent	37
30. Coachmaker's T Rabbet Compass Plane by Philip Sargent	37
31. Plow by Philip Sargent	38
32. Moulding Tool by Philip Sargent	39
33. Razee Jack Plane by Elias Rugg	39
34. Smoothing Plane by Daniel Durgin	39
35.-36. Two Moulding Tools by Dana Sargent	40
37.-38. Two Bench Planes by Eayrs & Company	41
39. Log Calipers by Gustavus B. Sanborn	42
40. Log Calipers by L. B. Sargent	42
41. Log Calipers by William Gardner Greenleaf	42
42. Log Calipers by Florence M. Greenleaf	43
43. Log Calipers by W. A. Wheeler	43
44. Log Calipers by Humphrey Machine Company	43
45. Framing Square by Rufus B. Haselton	44
46. Wantage Rod by Thomas Salter Bowles	45
47. Wantage Rod by Rufus B. Haselton	45
48. Gauging Rod by Thomas Rowell Hoyt	45
49. Lumber Rules by Rufus B. Haselton and/or Hermon R. Haselton	46
50. Dies used by Rufus B. Haselton and Hermon R. Haselton	46
51. Gauge and Dividers patented by George Kenny	47
52. Cooper's Adze probably by Benjamin Smith or Ballard Smith	47
53. Socket Framing Chisel by William W. Leighton	47
54. Slick by Underhill, Brown & Leighton	48
55. Ship Carpenter's Lip Adze by Underhill Edge Tool Company	48
56.-57. Two Hatchets by the Underhill Edge Tool Company	49
58. Broad Axe by Amoskeag Ax Company	49
59. Broad Axe by George D. Neville	49
60. Felling Axe by New London Scythe Company	50
61. Broad Axe by William F. George	50
62. Scythe by Phillips, Messer & Colby	51
63. Bush Scythe by New London Scythe Company	51
64. Scythe by the Sibley Scythe Company	51
65.-66. Two Cooper's Howels and Crozes by Addison Heald & Son	52
67. Cooper's Long Jointer by Addison Heald & Son	53
68. Cooper's Long Jointer by George W. Manning	53
69. Cooper's Leveling Plane by George W. Manning	53
70. Cooper's Downright by Addison Heald and Daniel Milton Heald	54
71. Leather Chamfering Tool by Daniel Nichols	54
72. Leather Chamfering Tool by William Johnson	54
73. Leather Splitting Machine by John Winslow Chase	55
74. Lasting Hammer patented by Jethro W. Warner	55
75. Saw Set by Francis Herrick Aiken	55
76. Saw Set patented posthumously for Lebbeus Brooks	56
77. Saw Set by William Orne Rust	56
78. Cabinetmaker's Bar Clamp by Wendell Phillips Tarbell	57
79. Bush Hammer by Luther M. Nutting and Henry W. Hayden	57
80. Stone Hammer by Luther M. Nutting and Henry W. Hayden	57
81. Tongs by Luther M. Nutting and Henry W. Hayden	58
82. Marking Gauge by David Page Sanborn	58
83. Awls and Tools by Francis Herrick Aiken	59

84. Carpenter's Claw Hammer by Phineas Eastman	59
85. Carpenter's Claw Hammer by William Butterfield	60
86. Axle Gauge by Harry Houston	60
87. Self-Adjusting Carriage Wrench by Harry Walter Burleigh	60
88. Carriage Wrench by Adin Phillips Joy	61
89. Spirit Level by Amos G. Atwood	61
90. Combination Tool by Frank Ross Woodward	61
91. Watchmaker's Staking Tool by Kendrick & Davis Company	62

Marks

Aiken, Francis Herrick	66
Amoskeag Ax Company	66
Amsden, Downing	66
Bowles, Thomas Salter	68
Briggs, E.	68
Briggs, Nathaniel	68
Clifford, Ebenezer	69
Coburn, Franklin Watson	70
Durgin, Daniel	71
Eayrs & Co.	72
Gage, Porter & Co.	74
George, William F.	74
Goodell Company	75
Greenleaf, Florence M.	75
Greenleaf, William Gardner	75
Haselton, Rufus B.	76
Heald, Addison	77
Heald, Addison, & Son	77
Hill, John	77
Hoyt, Thomas Rowell	78
Humphrey Machine Company	78
Humphrey, John, & Co.	78
Johnson, William	79
Kendrick & Davis	79
Manning, George W.	81
Milton, Matthew Harvey and Joseph	82
Morse, Joshua	83
Neville, George D.	83
New London Scythe Company	83
Nichols, Daniel	84
Nutting & Hayden	84
Phillips, Messer & Colby	85
Rugg, Elias	87
Rust, William Orne	87
Sanborn, David Page	88
Sanborn, Gustavus B.	88
Sargent, Dana	88
Sargent, L. B.	88
Sargent, Philip	88
Simons, Arad	89
Sleeper, John	89
Smith, Ballard	90
Tarbell, Wendell Phillips	91
Tuttle, A. D.	91
Underhill & Brown	92
Underhill & Leighton	92
Underhill Edge Tool Company	92
Vulcan Saw Works	92
Warren & Heald	93
Warren, Cyrus	93
Warren, George Henry	93
Warren, William	93
Weeks, George	93
Wheeler, W. A.	94
Woodman, B. F.	95

Illustration

Instruments of Change: the exhibit (frontispiece)	viii
Amoskeag Ax Company: watercolor by Henry Walker Herrick	2
Concord carpenter Benjamin Harrison Couch (1817-88)	3
Mouldings and components of the Tuscan entablature	6
Edge tool advertisement, 1812	8
New Hampshire Iron Foundry stock certificate detail	9
Advertisement for tool handles	10
Quirked mouldings	12
Grecian ovolo mouldings	13
Patent drawing for a drill stock, 1838	15
Patent drawing for a file cutting machine, 1847	16
Patent drawing for a wood bending machine, 1865	17
Blodgett Edge Tool Manufacturing Company (engraving)	17
Cutting files by hand, c. 1872 (engraving)	18
Gage, Warner, and Whitney's Machine Shop, 1865 (engraving)	19
Plow by Cyrus Warren (same as Plate 9)	22
Joshua Morse advertisement, 1819	25
Cyrus Warren advertisement	26
A. Heald & Son advertisement	32
Patent drawing for a bench plane, 1878	33
D. P. Sanborn advertisement	34
G. B. Sanborn advertisement	42
Detail of log caliper calibration	43
Detail of lumber rule calibration	46
Patent drawing for gauge and dividers	47
Broadside advertising axe factory auction, 1868	48
Patent drawing for axe-making machine, 1867	49
Patent drawing for a pronged hoe, 1827	50
Scythe patterns from Phillips, Messer, Colby & Co. flyer c. 1870	51
Patent drawing for a shoe shave, 1858	54
Patent drawing for a shoemaker's tool, 1859	55
Gage, Porter & Co. manufacturing plant (engraving)	56
Patent drawing for a hammer handle, 1839	59
Patent drawing for an auger, 1870	61
Blacksmith's shop, c. 1890	64

Plates and Illustrations

Instruments of Change

has been published in a first edition
of fifteen hundred copies.
Designed by A. L. Morris,
the text was composed in Bem
and printed by Sherwin/Dodge, Printers,
in Littleton, New Hampshire
on Sunray Opaque Vellum.
The cover was printed by Sherwin/Dodge
on King James Cast Coat,
and the book was sewn and bound